The full story of the TOYOTA Gazoo Racing WRC campaign

TOYOTA Yaris WRC

More great books from Veloce:

Rallying:

RAC Rally Action! (Gardiner)

The Daily Mirror 1970 World Cup Rally 40 (Robson)

The Great British Rally – RAC to Rally GB: The Complete Story (Robson & Holmes)

How to Build a Successful Low-Cost Rally Car (Young)

Works Rally Mechanic: BMC/BL Works Rally Department 1955-79 (Moylan)

Toyota:

Toyota Celica & Supra (Long)

Toyota MR2 Coupe & Spyders (Long)

Rally Giants Series:

Audi Quattro (Robson)

Austin Healey 100-6 & 3000 (Robson)

Fiat 131 Abarth (Robson)

Ford Escort Mk1 (Robson)

Ford Escort RS1800 (Robson)

Ford Escort RS Cosworth & World Rally Car (Robson)

Lancia Delta 4WD/Integrale (Robson)

Lancia Stratos (Robson)

Mini Cooper/Mini Cooper S (Robson)

Mitsubishi Lancer Evolution (Long)

Peugeot 205 T16 (Robson)

Saab 96 & V4 (Robson)

Subaru Impreza (Robson)

Toyota Celica GT-Four (Robson)

www.veloce.co.uk

First published in 2025 by Veloce, an imprint of David and Charles Limited.
Tel +44 (0)1305 260068 / e-mail info@veloce.co.uk / web www.veloce.co.uk.

ISBN: 9781787119307
 Readers with ideas for automotive books, or books on other transport or related hobby subjects, are invited to write to the editorial director of Veloce at the above email address. British Library Cataloguing in Publication Data – A catalogue record for this book is available from the British Library.
Design and layout by Veloce. Printed in Malta by Gutenberg Press.

TOYOTA Yaris WRC

The full story of the TOYOTA Gazoo Racing WRC campaign

Peter Lyon & Brian Long

Foreword by Akio Toyoda

Contents

Foreword

by Akio Toyoda

'Modifying a road car to create a race car'. That was Toyota's traditional motorsport approach. My goal was to reverse the process: 'Build a winning race car, and make a road car from there'. That's the way I wanted to make sports cars.

In 2017, Toyota returned to the World Rally Championship with the Yaris WRC. However, this machine was based on the Yaris road car, as this was our conventional way of doing things. We were accumulating several years of experience by competing with the Yaris WRC and, at the same time, developing a 'winning rally car'. That is how the GR Yaris and GR Yaris Rally1 were born.

Coming back to the WRC in 2017 helped us to change our mindset with the aim of 'making ever-better motorsport-bred cars'. In every phase of development of the GR Yaris, our priority was what should we do to win? Everything from the car packaging to the height of the car is designed with victory in mind.

I am truly grateful to TOYOTA GAZOO Racing members who have continued to fight against our rivals in the field of motorsports, while also fighting to change the way we build vehicles. I strongly hope that we can continue to create ever-better motorsport-bred cars.

And finally, I am also very grateful for this book, and to the authors Peter Lyon and Brian Long for compiling the history of our challenge.

Akio Toyoda
Chairman of Toyota
Founder of Gazoo Racing Team

Preface

In this book, we are going to shine a spotlight on Toyota's recent World Rally Championship (WRC) successes via its Gazoo Racing team, examining its roots (including in-depth coverage of the earlier TTE era that first established Toyota's image in rallying), and every event entered along the way.

Both members of the FCCJ in Tokyo at one time, the authors have known each other for decades, but – fittingly – first became pals on the press tour organised for the inaugural Rally Japan, back in 2004.

Peter has long-established links with the Gazoo outfit. In fact, the 5.0-litre V8-powered Lexus IS-F his team drove in the 2010 24-hour Nürburgring race was the very car that Akio Toyoda had driven in the 2008 and 2009 events. Piloted by ex-Indycar racer Hideshi Matsuda, the British driver and editor Owen Mildenhall, and Kazunori Yamauchi (creator and the father of the *Gran Turismo* game), Toyoda was pleased that Peter and his cohorts placed fourth in Class in the car he used to race.

Brian, meanwhile, has written several books on Toyota and Lexus over the years, and proposed this title as the first of several joint-projects the pair are mulling over. His son Louis (Peter's godson) helped with technical challenges relating to picture downloads, before Yuko Nakanishi at head office came to their aid. Her unstinting help has ensured that this book is as visually stunning as it is informative ...

The authors also need to thank the 'father of the Prius' Takeshi Uchiyamada for his work behind the scenes. And, of course, Akio Toyoda for providing us with a Foreword to mark Gazoo's fourth consecutive WRC title.

The Toyota Story

The monumental rise of the Toyota empire is a story to behold. Indeed, several books have been written on the company's business methods, many of which have since been adopted as the industry standard outside Japan. The creation of the Lexus marque is another shining example of the firm's success, and the relatively recent launch of the Gazoo brand has already provided Toyota with a sporting image to envy.

Toyota's roots date back to the establishment of the Toyoda Automatic Loom Works Ltd in 1926, a few miles to the south-east of Nagoya. Sakichi Toyoda, who founded the company, quickly started improving the weaving machines in his factory, and made a small fortune on the patent rights he'd filed. As a motoring enthusiast, this money was duly put towards allowing his son, Kiichiro, to set up an automotive department.

A small engine was produced in 1930, followed two years later by a series of prototype vehicles badged as Atsuta models. Unfortunately, the high cost of these luxury machines made them unsuitable for the market as it stood at that time, and ultimately a decision was made to take the best features of the contemporary Fords and Chevrolets, and merge them into a reasonably priced saloon capable of being mass-produced. The end result was the Toyoda Model AA of 1936 vintage, and the foundation of the Toyota Motor Co Ltd in August 1937 – the 'ta' character replacing the 'da' only to make the name easier to pronounce, as well as providing a lucky number of strokes when it was written in Japanese katakana script.

By the tail end of 1938, production at the recently-acquired Koromo factory site was hovering around 2000 vehicles per month, including cars, trucks and buses. In a bid to become more self-sufficient, a machine tool company was established, along with a steel maker and firms dealing with body pressings; Nippondenso would also join the fray in time. Given all the expansion, it's not surprising that the Koromo area was later renamed Toyota City.

After the Second World War, Toyota found itself in a difficult position, with General MacArthur and his men limiting output to the point where Kiichiro stood down to make way for some fresh ideas. Fortunately, in his role as Managing Director (later named as President and then Chairman), Kiichiro's cousin, Eiji Toyoda, took it upon himself to visit America to learn as much as possible about

◀ *Advertising for the immensely popular Celica, linking the past (via the Model AA), present, and future, seen here in the shape of the EX7.*

The Roots of Rallying

Rallying has been around almost since the birth of the automobile itself, although formats moved quickly, duly evolving into the sport we love today soon after the Second World War. Eventually, in 1953, the European Rally Championship (ERC) was established, its title being a reflection of the sport's popularity in this part of the world, for at this time it was hardly known as a fully-fledged motorsport discipline outside European and Scandinavian borders. It was the drivers that stole the limelight in the ERC, although makers were able to get some good publicity along the way, in much the same way as the bike supplier for a Tour de France winner.

From 1970 to 1972, the International Championship for Manufacturers (ICM) gave makers a chance to shine in rallies quite different to those that made up the ERC. This series was quickly forgotten, however, when the FIA changed the format to the World Rally Championship (WRC) in the following year. It's rather a shame, as the ICM produced some excellent racing, with Porsche claiming the title in 1970, Renault-Alpine in 1971, and Lancia the 1972 edition. Interestingly, the drivers named as European Rally Champions in those particular years drove vehicles of different marques to the ICM winners, so the marketing angle was also evolving in the media, with sponsors slowly but surely starting to plaster the more competitive cars with advertising material.

modern car production. This was put to good use furnishing Allied military orders related to the Korean War, and before long, the business was back on a firm footing.

The first Toyota Crown was launched in 1955, with exports to the US beginning in the second half of 1957. Rapid growth, thanks to the success of vehicles like the Corona, led to the opening of another factory at Motomachi, and from then on, a string of legendary nameplates joined the range, with the Corolla and Starlet at one end of the scale, and the exotic 2000GT at the other. Cars like the 2000GT may seem a little out of place with the mainstream lines, but one also has to remember that Toyota was already a force to be reckoned with in domestic motorsport, with the Toyota 7 (winner of numerous races, including the 1968 Suzuka 1000km classic) being a perfect example of the versatility of the company's engineering team.

With regard to sales, the practical and fuel-efficient Corolla was undoubtedly the car of the 1970s, with almost seven million finding new homes during the decade, many of them Stateside thanks to favourable exchange rates. It helped Toyota move up from being the world's fifth largest manufacturer (in terms of sales) in 1969 to the number three spot in 1972. Its tough dependability made it a good rally car, too, until the Celica started taking its place in this hallowed arena.

Like the second generation Corolla, the TA22 Celica (first announced in September 1970) inherited twin-cam engines to augment the run-of-the-mill lumps, making them ideally suited to competition duty. Long-distance rallies had been a favourite discipline for Japanese manufacturers for years, with Toyota entering a team of Crowns on the Round Australia Rally in 1957, for instance (Nissan would use the Mobilgas Trial event to promote the Datsun name in the following year), while the efforts of Nissan and Mitsubishi on the Safari Rally would result in no less than nine outright victories in the period from 1970 to 1982, helping to put Japanese cars on the map; Toyota's domination in this most challenging of events would begin soon after …

The Early TTE Years

The formation of a works-assisted Toyota rally team coincided with the launch of the World Rally Championship, due to kick off with the 1973 Monte Carlo Rally. This was no coincidence, of course, and Ove Andersson's timely proposal of raising awareness of the Toyota brand through a sustained motorsport programme was something that held great appeal for the company hierarchy back in Japan.

The Swedish rally driver, Ove Andersson, had won four major events in 1971: the Monte Carlo Rally, the San Remo Rally, the Austrian Alpine Rally, and the Acropolis Rally. His efforts helped secure the ICM title for Renault-Alpine that year, and by a convincing margin; the little blue cars ultimately scored twice the amount of points garnered by runner-up Saab.

However, 1972 was a quiet year for the French equipe, prompting Andersson to approach Toyota to prepare a car for him to use in international rallying. It proved a fortuitous move, for Toyota had already shown its potential in the Monte Carlo Rally, with works-prepared Corona 1900GSS models making quite an impact while they were running, and in Japan, the desire to promote the new Celica with a top class driver was very tempting. Thus, a deal was struck, and the Swede was duly entered in the 1972 RAC Rally in a works Celica. He finished the event in a creditable ninth overall, claiming Class honours with almost 12 minutes in hand.

While Andersson was still being called up for Renault-Alpine duty (he was second in the 1973 Monte Carlo Rally driving a Group 4 A110, for instance, and still only in his mid-30s), his association with the Japanese brand would quickly blossom into something that brought a great deal of prestige and glory to both parties.

1972 RAC Rally (Andersson).

Starting off small, acting largely on the requests of Toyota's European importers at that time as much as the factory (makers were able to pick and choose rounds to suit their PR requirements and/or their chances of winning back then), Ove Andersson initially handled Toyota's rally campaign – with the help of his co-driver friend, Arne Hertz, and four mechanics – from his house in Uppsala, a few miles north of Stockholm.

Four Group 2 entries would be instigated through Andersson for 1973, used to enhance the Celica's sporting image at this stage in the proceedings: The Acropolis Rally and the RAC Rally would be full works efforts, with semi-works entries pencilled in for the TAP Rally and the Austrian Alpine event. Ove Andersson would drive the Celica 1600GT on all four occasions, and would also compete in a number of track events over the year, including the Spa 24-hour classic.

Incidentally, while the manufacturers were taking advantage of the new World Championship crown, drivers that sought a measure of personal glory were left to compete for the European Rally Championship title until the World Championship for Drivers was introduced in 1979, running as an internal component of the WRC proper.

1973

The 1973 season was a very special one for rallying enthusiasts, being the first year of the World Rally Championship. The WRC is one of the few motorsport disciplines to last so long in a recognisable format, with Formula One being the other of note – most of the other championships came and went, or were changed so much that their modern image is quite different to when the series in question was conceived. Granted, we have defining periods, with the Group B rally era standing out as a good example, but the basic principal of covering a series of stages (mainly on a mixture of tarmac, gravel and snow) as fast as possible, and being sure to cross the finish line, has remained a constant from 1973 until the present day.

Back then, when the likes of the Group B monsters were still unthinkable, there were four main homologation classes in rallying. Homologation is the type approval process

1973 Austrian Alpine Rally (Andersson).

a vehicle is required to go through in order to compete, with allowances for certain modifications and numbers built: Group 1 (Series-Production Touring Cars, largely standard and with a minimum of 5000 built per year), Group 2 (Special Touring Cars, which were uprated G1 machines, with 1000 units needed per annum), Group 3 (Series-Production Grand Touring Cars, with a 1000 lower limit) and Group 4 (Special Grand Touring Cars, with G2-style modifications applied to the more exotic G3 vehicles, and a minimum of 500 units), with engine displacements adding further divisions within each category. Group 4 was considered the jewel in the crown, of course, allowing makers to fight for overall victory with a touch of glamour, although Group 2 would spawn some exceptional rally cars, too, such as the Ford Escort RS1600, Saab 96 and Opel Ascona. As it happens, these Group definitions had remained unchanged since the start of the ICM series, although the ERC had its own take on these things, but fell into line with the FIA classes in due course.

Ove Andersson teamed up with Jean Todt in Portugal, but their ex-RAC Rally 135bhp Celica crashed out of the event, forcing the Swede to continue his WRC campaign with another vehicle for the rest of the season. Engine maladies sidelined him in Greece, leaving a privateer in a Corolla as the top Toyota finisher, but Austria was much kinder to Andersson. At one point, due to the disqualification of the winner, he was declared seventh overall, but, some months later, Achim Warmbold was awarded the victor's spoils after all, meaning an eighth place finish, and fourth in Group 2. Then, in early November, came a remarkable result – an outright win for the TE27 Corolla of Walter Boyce and Doug Woods in the Press-on-Regardless Rally. Granted, the American event was hardly in the same league as the European rounds in terms of competitiveness, but the sweet-handling Corolla had won by a comfortable margin, and no-one was in a position to question that.

Two weeks later, Andersson teamed up with a local co-driver to tackle the RAC Rally, finishing the British event in 12th, some 24 minutes down on the winning Escort RS1600 of Timo Mäkinen. Sadly, the second car of Leif Asterhag failed to finish, but at least Toyota's commitment stayed firm. Meanwhile, the G4 Renault-Alpines dominated the Tour de Corse to ultimately clinch the WRC title with ease.

1973 WRC season standings

1st	Renault-Alpine	147 points
2nd	Fiat	84 points
3rd	Ford	76 points
10th	Toyota	25 points

1974 & 1975

No-one could have foreseen the oil crisis that began in the autumn of 1973 and continued through to the following spring. Its fallout would have a huge effect long after this, of course, and funding for the rally programme was reduced to a fraction of 1973 levels for the next two seasons, not only at Toyota, but elsewhere, too. It even brought about the cancellation of 'the Monte' and the Swedish Rally, as well as some lesser events, meaning a season reduced to just eight rounds for 1974.

While Renault-Alpine struggled to fend off the Italian challengers in 1974, Ford stayed in touch with the leaderboard thanks to the Escort RS1600, while Toyota fielded the Corolla quite a lot in that year following its success in America in the previous season. With its economy car image and arguably better handling than the larger-bodied Celica, it was right for the time, although the latter model would be the weapon of choice in the ensuing years.

Fiat filled the podium with the Abarth 124 in Portugal, but Ove Andersson and Arne Hertz took fourth and G2 honours with a Japanese-registered Corolla Levin; Björn Waldegård's Celica dropped

1974 Rideau Lakes Rally (Boyce).

out with electrical trouble. There wasn't much to write home about, until Walter Boyce claimed third in a Celica in the Rideau Lakes event, which made up for a disappointing outing in the Press-on-Regardless.

Toyota pulled out the stops for the RAC Rally, where the importer was as strong as the UK's rally culture: Waldegård was fourth overall in his Corolla, while Andersson was forced to retire with a broken stub axle. At least Toyota fans could take heart in the fact that Waldegård was less than two minutes down on the G4 Lancia Stratos that finished in third, although the Escort was seemingly made for the British forests. As a footnote, Pat Moss-Carlsson won the Ladies Prize in Waldegård's TAP Rally car, which had been given a two-litre engine for the event.

1974 WRC season standings

1st	Lancia	94 points
2nd	Fiat	69 points
3rd	Ford	52 points
4th	Toyota	32 points

In his role as MD, despite early concerns that a motorsport programme might bring adverse publicity during the oil crisis, Dr Shoichiro Toyoda (Kiichiro's son) took another look at the situation in the latter half of 1974, and decided to deepen the ties between Toyota and Ove Andersson, leading to the establishment of Toyota Team Europe (or TTE) in February 1975. Headquartered on the outskirts of Brussels in Belgium, Andersson now found himself heading a much bigger operation, with the promise of a decent budget, and two G2 Corollas and two G2 Celicas at his disposal, although the smaller Corollas would be used for most of the year.

With everything up in the air following the move, the 1975 campaign didn't start until the Acropolis for TTE. Both Corollas dropped out, but at least Warmbold's early pace was encouraging, and Andersson was able to guide a G2 TE27 to third a few weeks later in Portugal. Then, thanks to a last minute entry, came the breakthrough the team needed, with Hannu Mikkola and Atso Aho claiming an overall victory with a Corolla in their home event, the 1000 Lakes Rally. The Celica 2000GT's debut, which came on the RAC Rally, was best forgotten, with both cars sidelined, and the Corollas only managing to make up the numbers. As it happens, the two-litre Celicas would be rolled out for service as more powerful Group 4 machines for 1976.

1975 TAP Rally, Portugal (Waldegård).

1975 WRC season standings

1st	Lancia	96 points
2nd	Fiat	61 points
3rd	Renault-Alpine	60 points
7th	Toyota	32 points

1976

The WRC continued with ten rounds for 1976 – actually all ten rallies were the same as those listed in 1975, with the only change being the Rally of Portugal moving from the summer to its now familiar spring slot on the calendar.

As far as the Toyota's were concerned, TTE fielded the Celica 2000GT coupé and TE27 Corolla in Group 4 guise for 1976. This was caused by a change in the homologation rules, with 1975's G2 machines having to run as G4 models for 1976 and 1977, before four-valve per cylinder head transplants were ruled out completely on vehicles that usually had two. For the time being, at least, engineers were still allowed to adopt a far greater level of tuning and modification – breathed on by AC Schnitzer, Toyota's two-litre four-pot twin-cam engine was given a 16v head conversion, for instance, and was now kicking out as much as 245bhp (although 200 was considered the norm on most events).

Regardless of what was being put down through the back wheels, the potential was there for all to see after Ove Andersson and Arne Hertz took their Celica to second overall in Portugal, just three minutes down on Sandro Munari's Lancia

1976 Rally of Portugal (Andersson)

Stratos, and over 40 minutes clear of the third-placed Opel. Debuts don't get much better than that, and it made up for Hannu Mikkola's Corolla crashing out. However, a broken halfshaft put Andersson's Celica on the sidelines in Greece, and Mikkola's Corolla had injector problems.

By the time the 1000 Lakes Rally came around, TTE was using new Belgian-registered Celicas with fresh paintwork. Hannu Mikkola came third in his home event, while Leif Asterhag was tenth in an older Japanese-registered Corolla. Missing the next two rounds, TTE entered two Celica 2000GTs for the RAC Rally, although both suffered mechanical maladies that put them out of the running. Ironically, while Andersson nursed the aging 1000 Lakes Corolla around the forests of Britain to give Toyota a fifth place, the Celica would be TTE's undisputed weapon of choice in the years that followed.

1976 WRC season standings

1st	Lancia	112 points
2nd	Opel	57 points
3rd	Ford	47 points
6th	Toyota	35 points

Ove Andersson.

1977

Sporting fresh paintwork, with red heavy flanks below a white upper body, the Celica 2000GT was the main model fielded by Toyota Team Europe on behalf of the works for 1977. After all, the Corolla Levin had been taken out of production some years earlier back in Japan, and creating

1977 Arctic Rally, Finland (Mikkola).

publicity for current vehicles is ultimately what world class rallying is all about – conjuring up an image for motorsport enthusiasts to go into a showroom and buy the machine wielded by their heroes. On saying that, a Belgian-registered TE27 finished in the latest livery was entered in Sweden, Finland and Britain in a last hurrah.

Internal politics played a part in Fiat taking the place of Lancia as the favoured marque from Turin, with the Abarth-tuned Fiat 131 carrying the hopes of Italian enthusiasts. It was ironic that Sandro Munari did so well in the Stratos, winning 'the Monte' in a season extended to 11 rounds and going much farther afield, with Morocco giving way to new rallies in Canada and New Zealand.

TTE's season kicked off in Sweden, but seventh place with a Celica 2000GT (a Group 2 model) was the best the three-car team could muster. Things improved in the warmer climes of Portugal, with Ove Andersson's G4 machine claiming a well-earned third overall, while Hannu Mikkola's sister car was going well until its wheel studs sheared.

Both works Celicas retired in Greece, and it was much the same story in Finland, as a German pairing (the only 2000GT entered on this event) popped a flywheel. At least Hannu Mikkola driving the smaller-engined Corolla took fourth overall to keep the Toyota flag flying.

An all-out effort was duly staged for the RAC Rally, with three G4 Celica coupés and the sole G4 Corolla rolled out for service again. TTE's effort was rewarded with a magnificent second overall for Hannu Mikkola and Arne Hertz (finishing just over two minutes down on the winning Escort RS1800, but well ahead of the gaggle of Escorts behind); another Celica came 14th, while the third 2000GT and the Corolla were amongst the 115 crews that failed to make the finish.

Despite the limited number of events campaigned (at least compared to Fiat and Ford, with huge budgets at their disposal), Toyota finished the season in third place, which was its best result so far. The Japanese company had beaten Opel, who had the likes of Walter Röhrl on their books, Lancia, Datsun (Nissan's export brand), Porsche and Saab. Unfortunately, the second generation Celica had been introduced in Japan in August 1977, both in coupé and Liftback form, meaning the days of the current car were numbered, just as it was coming good ...

1977 WRC season standings

1st	Fiat	136 points
2nd	Ford	132 points
3rd	Toyota	68 points

1978

The contemporary rules for Group 4 homologation, outlined in the 1976 edition of the International Sporting Code's Appendix J, called for a minimum of 400 cars to be built over 24 months. This allowed for some quite specialised machines to be fielded, although the powers that be were far stricter on issuing certification.

Existing Toyotas with the 16v head were banned for 1978, meaning a return to Group 2 for the first generation Celica 2000GTs. The initial batch of RA40 second generation four-cylinder 8v twin-cam Celica 2000GT coupés were also put in G2, as it happens, although a 16v G4 car was on the cards, and would eventually put in an appearance in 1979.

Meanwhile, 1978 was to prove dismaying. With Jean-Luc Thérier (a legend in the days of the Renault-Alpine A110) and Leif Asterhag joining Ove Andersson, one had every right to expect more. However, Andersson's fourth in Portugal (first in G2) was the best result amongst multiple retirements.

In the background, an RA40 model had been taken to Greece for testing on the Acropolis Rally immediately after its homologation had been granted. This was in readiness for its debut on the 1000 Lakes Rally, where the 180bhp model placed a creditable sixth (first in Class) thanks to Tapio Rainio; the sister car came home in tenth, while a third TTE entry (a first generation two-litre coupé) was ninth.

A few weeks later, Toyota Canada entered a second generation car for Taisto Heinonen, the hall of famer managing to secure fourth overall.

Lining up for the 1978 1000 Lakes Rally.

His Group 2 win also gave Toyota more points in the new scoring system, which was weighted slightly to level up the playing field for those running in the lower categories.

The next big event was the RAC Rally in Britain, where TTE must have been encouraged by the Finnish and Canadian results. However, Thérier had a halfshaft break early on, and Asterhag crashed out, leaving Andersson and his band of merry men empty-handed. It was the Ford Escort that shone again in the UK forests, but Fiat had a devastating machine in the boxy Abarth 131.

1978 WRC season standings

1st	Fiat	134 points
2nd	Ford	100 points
3rd	Opel	100 points
6th	Toyota	50 points

1979

The FIA had introduced the 'Cup for Drivers' in 1977, but the winner needed to compete in ERC and other events, so it was not directly related to the WRC. However, 1979 saw the introduction of a fully-fledged World Championship for Drivers, with WRC events only counting towards the title. As such, the glory endowed on manufacturers since 1973 could now be enjoyed by those piloting the cars as well. As it happens, the first World Champion was Björn Waldegård, who had driven for Andersson's team in 1974 and would return to the Toyota camp in due course, with Hannu Mikkola (another ex-Toyota exponent) coming second.

As for the makers' title chase, in addition to Toyota Canada's efforts (ultimately resulting in a fifth for Taisto Heinonen), Toyota Team Europe expanded its campaign by taking in the Bandama Rally in Africa's Ivory Coast. This was an interesting move, for while the Safari Rally was well-known, attracting huge fields of experienced crews, the Bandama was relatively new, and had only been added to the WRC calendar in the previous year. Over the next few seasons, it would attract some very strong entries, and provide some excellent racing.

The second generation Celica was used exclusively for 1979, although the Group 2 machines of Thérier and Asterhag both retired in Sweden. Thérier dropped out in Portugal, too, with

1979 Bandama Rally (Thérier).

engine trouble ending his rally, but Ove Andersson and Henry Liddon took a magnificent third place there, claiming Class honours along the way. Sadly, there were more DNFs on the Acropolis caused by mechanical maladies, although a seventh for Tapio Rainio in Finland went some way towards restoring TTE honour.

While another oil crisis was hurting motorists and motorsport in the background, TTE's hopes of success were given a welcome boost when the RA40 acquired a 16v head in November 1979, meaning the Group 2 cars were now placed in Group 4. Although this was a more competitive category, the conversion (applied to all TTE Celicas from this date onwards, except the rarely-used RA40-type Liftback models) took power output up to 230bhp, while maximum torque was quoted at 180lbft.

The 16v RA40 coupés used on the RAC Rally were the first to carry German number plates, incidentally, for the TTE operation had just moved to new premises in Cologne. Despite Thérier, Asterhag and Rainio doing the driving, an 11th place was the best they could muster between them, with the clutch giving way on one car and the injection pump on another.

TTE then took two 2000GT Liftback models to Africa. No-one was able to keep up with the Mercedes-Benz team that year, although Ove Andersson could be satisfied that his fifth-placed Celica was the first non-SLC home, easily beating off a strong challenge from Peugeot and Datsun. Given the speed on this event, the decision to use the 8v engine was an odd one, but a gamble that had obviously paid off.

1979 WRC season standings

1st	Ford	122 points
2nd	Datsun	108 points
3rd	Fiat	92 points
5th	Toyota	58 points

1980

With the WRC format now basically settled into something we would recognise today, with lots of familiar events and championship titles both for makers and drivers up for grabs, things stayed much the same for 1980 and 1981, as a big change was waiting in the wings – a change that would launch a legendary era of rallying that few of us will ever forget.

Achim Warmbold, who was German champion in 1980, decided to enter the Monte Carlo Rally in his Fisher HiFi-sponsored Celica 2000GT coupé, but he was destined to crash out of the event very early on.

Turning its back on Sweden for a change, the TTE equipe was pinning its hopes on a good result in Portugal, putting Andersson in one G4 RA40 two-litre Celica coupé, and Thérier in another. This may sound strange, given the Swede's management role, but one has to remember that he was still an A-graded driver (the equivalent of

1980 Acropolis Rally, Greece (Andersson).

a super licence in the rallying world), while the other regulars on the team (Thérier and Asterhag) were Priority B pilots. Anyway, Andersson finished sixth overall, winning two special stages along the way – quite an achievement given the strong competition. Thérier had a halfshaft fail halfway through the event, ending his chances.

The same pair were out again in Greece, this time armed with the latest Celica coupés (updated RA45 models, readily distinguished by their new rectangular headlights), backed up by Asterhag in a third sister car. Sadly, only Andersson survived the first day, eventually finishing the Acropolis in sixth overall. Hannu Mikkola and Tapio Rainio were signed up for the 1000 Lakes Rally, and although Mikkola was very fast, a broken driveshaft put an end to his challenge, while Rainio had to settle for seventh.

Björn Waldegård was called in by Toyota GB to drive Andersson's ex-Acropolis Rally car on the RAC, the G4 2000GT coupé being joined by Leif Asterhag in an old Liftback model sponsored by ABBA, the famous pop group. Both Celicas retired, with only the Ivory Coast Rally left on the WRC calendar.

Backing was secured for three cars via Premoto Toyota, with Ove Andersson joined by Per Eklund and the Lebanese driver, Samir Assef. Assef finished the event in fourth, in touch with the Peugeot just ahead of it, while Eklund was a comfortable seventh; Andersson, having started as the number one seed, had his engine's flywheel give way on the third day. At least the Celicas were at last starting to show some potential in RA45 guise ...

1980 WRC season standings

1st	Fiat	120 points
2nd	Datsun	93 points
3rd	Ford	90 points
7th	Toyota	32 points

1981

As noted in the last section, with plans for a major revamp of the WRC arena afoot, there wasn't much in the way of changes for 1981, although, in hindsight, the entrance of the 4WD Audi Quattro would be significant. The biggest thing of note in the Toyota camp was the arrival of Björn Waldegård as a full-time TTE pilot, with

Per Eklund named as the number two driver; Ove Andersson decided it was time for him to hang up his helmet and concentrate on management.

With a wonderful selection of machinery in the first two rallies of the year, the TTE men knew they had their work cut out in their season opener in Portugal. Waldegård showed his class, though, claiming third in an RA45 coupé, while Eklund had an accident halfway through the event; Achim Warmbold ran out of fuel on one of the earlier stages, ending the third TTE car's charge there and then.

Having moved to a different time slot, Andersson decided it was time to challenge the fast tarmac of the Tour de Corse at last. Waldegård's differential gave way, but Eklund came a respectable sixth against some very fast cars fielded by increasingly professional equipes.

Both 235bhp G4 cars retired on the first day in Greece, but at least Waldegård was able to stay in touch with the frontrunners on the 1000 Lakes Rally (Tapio Rainio was unable to make use of his local knowledge in the second works Celica, having crashed out). Next, Waldegård and Eklund joined Samir Assef for a three-car attack on the Ivory Coast Rally. Waldegård's engine expired but, despite having been upside down at one point, Eklund was a fine second, and Assef a decent seventh after several heavy accidents.

▲ *1981 Ivory Coast Rally (Eklund).*

▲ *Björn Waldegård.*

Another three-car entry was made for the RAC Rally, with the Swedish regulars joined by British driver Terry Kaby on this occasion. Eklund was sixth in his Celica with Kaby close behind in eighth, while Waldegård was forced into retirement early on by some rear suspension damage. With a third generation Celica having been launched in Japan in July 1981 and new rules about to kick in, outings for the RA45-type Celica were very limited indeed after this.

1981 WRC season standings

1st	Talbot	117 points
2nd	Datsun	106 points
3rd	Ford	90 points
8th	Toyota	54 points

The Group B Monsters

The FIA's latest homologation regulations had been hammered out with manufacturers over the autumn of 1980, and came into effect for the start of the 1982 season. Things would never be the same again, with the Group B era providing a level of speed and spectacle that just had to be seen to be believed ...

The arrival of the Group N, A and B categories would tighten up homologation rules, with Group N and A for showroom touring cars (with a minimum of 5000 units a year), and Group B for special Grand Touring models, built in more limited quantities (200 produced within in a year), with an 'Evolution' provision for 20 specials based on these – these were the monsters alluded to. Engine capacity breaks continued, with allowances for NA units against those with forced induction helping to level the playing field. For now, cars homologated in Groups 1 to 4 were still able to compete alongside the new groups, although G1 was automatically classed as Group N or A (A being international level rallies), while G2, G3 and G4 machines went into the Group B box.

1982 RAC Rally, UK (Eklund).

1982

The first rally of the year for TTE was the Port Wine Rally, with Björn Waldegård and Per Eklund campaigning second generation Celica coupés. Waldegård was fast, but forced to drop out with differential trouble. Eklund was second in the end, though, finishing close behind the winning Audi of Michèle Mouton.

The third generation (RA63) Celica coupé made its WRC debut in New Zealand, midway through the season. Powered by a two-litre 16v four pumping out 240bhp, it scored a remarkable one-two finish in the hands of Waldegård and Eklund. It was TTE's first WRC victory – the first of many as it happens.

Next up was the Ivory Coast event, with Ove Andersson unable to resist entering a third car for himself. He dropped out quickly (as did Samir Assef in a locally-registered RA45 model), but the other TTE men were second and third, in touch with Walter Röhrl's Opel up front and comfortably ahead of the works Renault in fourth. Sadly, the second African round of the year only counted towards the driver standings.

This was to be a short, bridging season for the TTE outfit, ending with a seventh and ninth for the Toyota GB-entered Group 4 Celicas in the RAC Rally. A more powerful Group B car loosely based on the turbocharged Celica 1800GT-T model was already waiting in the wings, though, enabling Toyota to build on its reputation as a force to be reckoned with in the rallying arena.

1982 WRC season standings

1st	Audi	116 points
2nd	Opel	104 points
3rd	Nissan	57 points
5th	Toyota	41 points

1983

The Celica Twin-Cam Turbo (or TCT) was an ideal base car for the fast and furious world of Group B, with 20 cars shipped to Cologne to be built into 'Evolution' models; homologation was eventually granted on the first day of July 1983. While there was no 4WD, the rear-wheel drive chassis proved it was able to handle the 320bhp developed by the bored-out 2090cc fuel-injected four (making it a three-litre Class machine after allowing for turbocharging) with a surprising level of ease.

◀ 1983 1000 Lakes Rally, Finland (Kankkunen).

▼ Juha Kankkunen.

TTE decided to forget the first half of the season, and wait until the TCT was ready to race. Given the coupé's homologation date and a lack of enthusiasm for travelling all the way to Argentina, the car's WRC debut therefore came on the 1000 Lakes Rally in Finland. Juha Kankkunen had signed up as a third driver by this time, and it was he who provided the team with the best result – a sixth place on his home event. Waldegård was 12th, but he had been on the pace on quite a few stages, so all was not lost.

Three cars were rolled out for Ivory Coast duty, and although Kankkunen was forced to drop out with a niggling electrical fault, Waldegård claimed Toyota's third WRC win after fending off Hannu Mikkola's Audi, while Eklund was third by a huge margin. For the record, Samir Assef took his older RA45 Celica to a clear fourth, giving the company another reason to bask in Bandama glory.

Sadly, TTE was unable to keep up the momentum, and the RAC Rally was full of disappointment. Rising star Kankkunen was the top finisher in seventh, while the two Swedes were forced to drop out; again Waldegård had been fast, but an accident on the notoriously tough Grizedale stage put a sudden end to his rally.

When looking at the points standings, one should remember that Audi, Lancia and Opel all mounted a very serious assault on the championship, with no expense spared on logistics to allow teams to compete all over the globe. Rallying had certainly become big business, although this era of generous support from the makers is exactly what the sport needed – no longer was it playing second fiddle to the various forms of track racing ...

1983 WRC season standings

1st	Lancia	118 points
2nd	Audi	116 points
3rd	Opel	87 points
6th	Toyota	24 points

1984

With 30 more horses under the bonnet and a lot more torque on hand, the 1020kg (2244lb) Celica Twin-Cam Turbo coupé was entered in five of the ten WRC rounds that counted towards the maker's title (the other two were reserved for drivers), guided in the main by the same three drivers as 1983.

Portugal saw both cars fall by the wayside on the third day – one had steering problems, and the other a broken propshaft. However, Björn Waldegård gave Toyota a Safari win on its first attempt (something done only once before), with the TCT model becoming the first ever turbocharged car to win the African classic. The fact that Eklund had an accident early on and guest driver, Sandro Munari, had had to drop out on the final day, did little to overshadow this remarkable achievement.

Toyota Team Europe's next outing was the Sanyo Rally of New Zealand, with Waldegård fifth and Kankkunen crashing out. Their fates were reversed in Finland, as it was Kankkunen who shone on home territory, although both drivers were destined to retire in Britain three months later. Indeed, it was the third car of Eklund that was the top finisher on the RAC – the Swede clinching third place after beating Michèle Mouton's Audi Quattro by a few seconds. Interestingly, although the Ingolstadt machine was still a huge threat, along with the Lancia 037 Rally, it was the Peugeot 205 T16 that dominated the second half of the season ...

1984 WRC season standings

1st	Audi	120 points
2nd	Lancia	108 points
3rd	Peugeot	74 points
4th	Toyota	62 points

▲▼ *1984 Safari Rally (Waldegård).*

While the Group B monsters and the glamour of the World Rally Championship naturally stole the limelight, one should also note the increasing importance of the AE86 16v Corolla in Group A rallying, helping Toyota secure the manufacturers' title in the highly-competitive British Championship, for instance. The six-cylinder Celica Supra would make an impact in the following year.

1985 Ivory Coast Rally (Kankkunen).

1985

The calendar looked familiar, the Celicas looked familiar, and the faces of Waldegård and Kankkunen were familiar in the TTE camp (Eklund would have a few WRC outings driving an Audi, but most of his season was spent securing the Group A drivers' title in the British Open Championship). Toyota Team Europe entered five rounds again, but dropped the Rallye de Portugal in favour of a return to the Ivory Coast.

While a locally-entered car crashed out early on, Juha Kankkunen and Fred Gallagher claimed a fine victory on the Safari Rally in April, followed home by Björn Waldegård and Hans Thorszelius (last year's winners) to give Toyota a memorable one-two victory.

Sadly, both cars retired in New Zealand, and Kankkunen joined the many non-finishers on the 1000 Lakes. At least Waldegård was seventh in Finland, adding a few more points to Toyota's tally.

Back in Africa, the Group B Celicas were untouchable on the Rallye Côte d'Ivoire, with Kankkunen winning and Waldegård second, both cars recording the same amount of penalties, with well over an hour in hand on the third-placed Nissan 240RS. The Celica TCT gained the nickname of 'The African King' and it's easy to see why given the dominance of the model in the Safari and Ivory Coast events.

1985 RAC Rally (Kankkunen).

The RAC Rally wasn't as kind to the Toyota men, with Waldegård having an accident, and Kankkunen only managing to get fifth place. Notwithstanding, fifth was still a good result given the competition and, his skill behind the wheel duly spotted, the young Flying Finn was rewarded with a seat on the Peugeot team for 1986 – a move that would enable him to be crowned World Champion straight away.

1985 WRC season standings

1st	Peugeot	142 points
2nd	Audi	126 points
3rd	Lancia	70 points
5th	Toyota	44 points

1986

There were supposed to be 11 rounds counting towards the maker's title (America was brought back into the WRC fold via the Olympus Rally to give 13 rounds in total for 1986), but the San Remo event was marred by politics, and the results were duly wiped from the record books. Not that it mattered much to Toyota fans, for in the days before the FIA made teams compete in every round of the WRC, TTE was happy to enter only the rounds that its masters considered it could win or held significant dealer interest.

Now a touch heavier but developing around 380bhp, the Celica TCT coupé was entered in just three rallies for 1986, with the non-championship, high-profile Hong Kong-Beijing Rally also being featured on the TTE calendar. As it happens, there was nothing to write home about on the latter event (it was the same story in 1987), and although a great deal of time and money was wasted on the proposed ten-off Group S car (Group S was being lined up to replace Group B in 1988), there was still plenty to celebrate in Cologne and back at Toyota head office during the year.

First, Björn Waldegård reigned supreme in Kenya, winning and showing the way home for teammate Lars-Erik Torph, who finished second; Erwin Weber was eight minutes away from claiming third, but had to settle for fourth in the end. Amazingly, Waldegård had led the Safari from the fifth stage all the way through to SS71 – the finish in Nairobi.

Waldegård then won the Ivory Coast Rally, with Torph second and Weber third – the latter pair even using the same cars as they had on the Safari. Even though Weber nearly had to drop out with suspension trouble, a fourth car driven by Robin Ulyate would have made sure that Toyota pilots filled the podium anyway. It was a convincing display by 'The African King' and folks making up the TTE equipe.

Choosing to stay away from the forests of Britain and try the US round instead (Toyota even sponsored the event), Waldegård and Torph were joined by Steve Millen in a third Celica TCT coupé. Millen crashed out at the start of the second day, but Torph was fourth, and Waldegård fifth. What a shame neither the Ivory Coast or Olympus Rally rounds counted toward the manufacturers' title, otherwise Toyota's points tally would have looked much healthier.

1986 WRC season standings

1st	Peugeot	137 points
2nd	Lancia	122 points
3rd	Volkswagen	65 points
6th	Toyota	20 points

Although the African Championship had been around for longer, it was the Middle East Championship (inaugurated in 1984) that provided Toyota with an arena in which it could truly shine. Although a Porsche driver claimed the title in 1984 and 1985, Mohammed Ben Sulayem won it for the next six years on the trot, piloting a Toyota Celica on each occasion. For several seasons, he was able to make use of the Twin-Cam Turbo model, for its days were already numbered in the WRC.

▼ *1986 Safari Rally, Kenya (Waldegård).*

The Group A Era

Sadly, the Group B cars were just too fast. A series of fatal accidents in 1986 gave the FIA no option but to rethink the WRC format in a hurry, with the obvious answer being to ban Group B machines, forget any thoughts of introducing Group S, and make Group A the main category in the championship.

One of the advantages of being a works-supported team is the level of communication it has with the factory – being kept in the loop by the product planning and engineering departments. While few could have foreseen the sudden demise of Group B rallying, considering its popularity with fans and sponsors alike, at least the shift to a Group A-based World Rally Championship could be orderly and worthwhile, given TTE's links with Toyota head office in Japan.

1987

While some makers kept using their Group B creations in self-governing events like the Paris-Dakar Raid and Pikes Peak hillclimb, as well as national championships (where their use was still allowed by the FIA), the end of the Group B category in the WRC proper naturally meant adopting a new machine for TTE's rally programme. However, the rather abrupt ban meant that the perfect car for the job wasn't ready for the 1987 season. Instead of rushing, though, Toyota declared it would expand its rallying activities in 1988, and decided to field the latest Supra as a stopgap until its new warrior could be prepared and tested, hopefully allowing it to be competitive straight out of the box.

Introduced at the start of 1986, the rear-wheel drive MA70-type Supra was powered by a selection of straight-six engines, with a 260bhp normally-aspirated three-litre lump initially chosen for WRC duty. Just three events were entered, though, and even then only two would count towards the manufacturers' championship.

First up was the Safari Rally, with Björn Waldegård, Lars-Erik Torph and Robin Ulyate guiding the elegant coupés. Waldegård was forced to drop out with engine trouble, but Torph was a clear third (finishing behind two works Audis), and Ulyate was sixth. Two of the same cars were then shipped to the States, allowing Waldegård to take sixth in an event dominated by the Lancias; Torph retired.

Before heading to the Ivory Coast, Björn Waldegård won the non-championship Hong

▼ *A Supra tackling the 1987 Safari Rally.*

Mohammed Ben Sulayem (the current FIA boss) with the ex-works Celica TCT he used to win the Middle East Championship.

Kŏng-Beijing Rally in a turbocharged Supra. With 30bhp more on tap, the turbocharged car finished a full 30 minutes ahead of the second-placed Nissan 200SX. The third NA machine used on the Safari was joined by two new 290bhp models, but after Henry Liddon (a key man behind the scenes at TTE) and his assistant Nigel Harris died in a plane crash, Ove Andersson withdrew the team from the Bandama immediately after SS12.

1987 WRC season standings

1st	Lancia	140 points
2nd	Audi	82 points
3rd	Renault	71 points
7th	Toyota	22 points

1988

Introduced in August 1985, the fourth generation Celica moved across to a front-wheel drive platform, with a two-litre 16v four in the top models. Just over a year later, in October 1986, the turbocharged ST165 GT-Four variant was announced for the liftback bodyshell, with the 185bhp on tap being put down through four wheels rather than two.

During the early years of the fourth generation car, more effort was put into releasing different bodies and new grades than a rally programme, but after Toyota Motor Sales started importing a facelifted version of the GT-Four into America for the 1988 MY (named the All-Trac Turbo in the States), it was obvious that it was only a matter of time before the model was seen in the World Rally Championship.

The first event of the year for TTE was the Safari Rally, campaigned with Supra Turbos. They finished fourth, fifth and seventh, driven respectively by Kenneth Eriksson, Juha Kankkunen (tempted back to the Toyota camp) and Björn Waldegård. It was an all-star line-up that would serve TTE well as it got to grips with the undoubted complexity of the new Celica, tuned to give 265bhp.

Homologation was granted for the Celica GT-Four on the first day of May 1988, with the car making its WRC debut within a week on the fast roads of Corsica. A sixth for Eriksson was tempered by a retirement for Kankkunen, and indeed, the Finn dropped out of the next four events he was entered in, too. That said,

Kankkunen was blisteringly fast, but despite his best efforts, and those of Waldegård as well, Toyota fans had to wait until the San Remo Rally in October to be offered any glimmer of hope, when Eriksson finished sixth.

The last round of the season was the RAC Rally in Britain. Toyota GB sponsored a four-car assault on the snow-laden forests, but sadly Kenneth Eriksson and Jimmy McRae dropped out early (both with engine maladies) and Juha Kankkunen had an accident close to the end, having led the field for much of the rally. At least Björn Waldegård put the ST165 on the podium for the first time with a fine third place. Would 1989 be Toyota's year?

1988 WRC season standings

1st	Lancia	140 points
2nd	Ford	79 points
3rd	Audi	71 points
5th.	Toyota	46 points

While this was the last year for the works Audi Sport team, rally fans had plenty to keep them interested, including a newly-formed Asia-Pacific Championship (APRC), that would become increasingly important as the years passed, duly attracting top drivers and top teams in a bid to garner publicity in the region. Indeed, it was a golden era for motorsport in general, with Group C racing reaching a pinnacle, F1 still interesting, and the likes of the Paris-Dakar Raid providing a true spectacle.

1989

As well as witnessing the launch of the company's Lexus marque, the 1989 season marked Toyota's first serious attempt at gaining the WRC title, with the company represented by the TTE outfit in virtually all of the 13 rallies instead of just a handful. Three 265bhp Celica GT-Fours were present in many of the events, calling for some new blood behind the wheel, as Toyota stalwart Björn Waldegård only had a few outings: Juha Kankkunen acted as the number one driver, while Carlos Sainz made an exciting new addition to the team. Other TTE-related pilots during the year included Kenneth Eriksson, Leif Asterhag and David Llewellin, with Ian Duncan and Billy Rautenbach being called up for Safari duty, and mention should also be made of Patrick Snyers, who provided some colour in his Bastos-sponsored machine.

The new Celica making its debut in Corsica, 1988.

1989 Monte Carlo Rally (Kankkunen).

The season kicked off in Sweden, and although it was only for drivers' points, it provided some useful feedback on a car that was fast but temperamental. Sporting a different livery to the official TTE entries, the Toyota Team Sweden Celicas held up well, with Eriksson ultimately finishing on the podium.

Toyota returned to Monte Carlo for the first time in a long while, and although the works Lancia Deltas dominated the event, Kankkunen's fifth and a sixth for Snyers gave something worthwhile to take back to the TTE offices in Cologne. Portugal was less kind, however, with all three cars retiring.

The Supra Turbos were out again for the Safari Rally, with Waldegård guiding the best of the three Toyotas home to fourth overall. This would be the last WRC appearance for the six-cylinder machines, though, and TTE's sole African excursion of the year (like the NZ round, the Bandama counted towards the drivers' championship only, so Toyota stayed away).

The Tour de Corse saw Kankkunen finish third, right on the pace, but Sainz and Snyers were both forced to drop out with mechanical maladies. No-one finished in Greece, and the Argentina round was snubbed. This break in the calendar allowed TTE to regroup a little, and the GT-Fours were remarkable on the 1000 Lakes Rally, taking 29 of the 43 stages. Sadly, Sainz was delayed when he landed on his roof on day two, dropping him back to third; Eriksson was fourth, and Kankkunen a non-finisher after an electrical fire.

Things were definitely looking up, though, and TTE's perseverance was finally rewarded with a one-two victory in Australia, and more good results on the San Remo. Pentti Airikkala ruined the perfect end to the season, winning the RAC in style in a rather staid-looking Mitsubishi, followed home by three TTE Celicas (only the Toyota GB-entered car of Llewellin failed to finish, although the Welshman had already been crowned British champion, and would be again in 1990).

Incidentally, Kankkunen's third in Britain allowed him to finish third overall in the drivers' championship; Erikkson was sixth, and Sainz eighth. Notwithstanding, the Finn had already lost patience with TTE, and signed for Lancia just before winning the Rally Australia.

1989 WRC season standings

1st	Lancia	140 points
2nd	Toyota	101 points
3rd	Mazda	67 points

1990

While a fifth generation Celica (the ST185-type) had been announced in the autumn of 1989, TTE continued to field the ST165 model, which was just starting to come good. The loss of Kankkunen meant that Carlos Sainz moved up to the number one spot, ably backed up by Armin Schwarz and Mikael Ericsson for the majority of the season – one which saw Toyota enter 11 of the 12 rallies on the calendar, even though the New Zealand round was reserved for drivers to score points.

Despite an appeal on the use of a suspect turbocharger (brought to FISA's attention by Ove Andersson, as it happens), Didier Auriol was declared the winner of 'the Monte' for Lancia, with Sainz less than a minute behind in second. The other two cars finished in the top seven, and both were quick if one looks at each stage position.

Although both cars retired in Portugal, Björn Waldegård won the Safari in a guest appearance, leading home his teammates that ultimately finished in third and fourth. This would be Toyota's only African adventure for 1990, as the Bandama Rally was largely left to a swarm of Corolla-wielding privateers.

In Corsica, Schwarz was forced out with transmission trouble, although Sainz was second to Auriol, again with only seconds separating the two. Sainz then won in Greece after a tight battle with Kankkunen, and then made it a double in New Zealand. Miki Biasion ruled supreme in Argentina, the Lancia pilot having eight minutes on Sainz in second, but the Spaniard got his revenge in Finland, handily beating off a Mitsubishi challenge; Ericsson, who had won the event last year, had an accident on the third day, putting him out of the rally.

Down Under, Sainz was second to Kankkunen, with Ericsson suffering transmission trouble, and San Remo proved a tough sortie, with

▼ *1990 Acropolis Rally, Greece (Sainz).*

Carlos Sainz.

lots of crumpled metal going back to Cologne. Accompanied by his regular co-driver, Luis Moya, Sainz hung on to take third, though, and the points scored here would have a special significance.

After winning the season finale in Britain, Carlos Sainz was duly crowned World Champion, with a commanding lead over the Lancia men, although when the latter's points were combined, it was the Italian maker that was ultimately able to win the manufacturers' title, with Toyota a close second. Sainz also claimed the APRC silverware, by the way, as did Toyota ...

1990 WRC season standings

1st	Lancia	137 points
2nd	Toyota	131 points
3rd	Mitsubishi	56 points

1991

The driver line-up was pretty similar for 1991, with Marc Duez adding another dimension to the WRC circus with his Group A Toyota FINA Team machine. On the subject of the cars, the ST165 GT-Four was still the weapon of choice for TTE (endowed with more power now that the early reliability issues had been addressed), although the homologation of the ST185 equivalent in Group N was a sure sign that its days were numbered.

With Sweden back and Spain newly added to the calendar, the season consisted of 14 rallies, although the latter pair joined the New Zealand and Ivory Coast events as those counting towards the drivers' championship only.

The season started well, with Sainz winning the prestigious Monte Carlo Rally, and Schwarz right on the pace in fourth; Duez was 11th, pipped out of a top ten spot by a Ford Sierra Cosworth 4x4 driver – the Sierra trying to capture the spirit of the legendary Escorts of the past.

Mats Jonsson was second in Sweden in a Toyota Team Sweden car, but TTE was back in action in Portugal, claiming another win thanks to Sainz. Schwarz actually took four stages, but an accident ended his rally before the first day came to an end.

With Sainz's engine giving way, the Safari Rally fell to Juha Kankkuken and Lancia, but Mikael Ericsson wasn't far behind in second in his GT-Four, and Björn Waldegård was a clear fourth. This would be Waldegård's last outing for Toyota, as it happens, and he would hang up his helmet once and for all soon after.

Sainz won yet again in Corsica, with tarmac specialist Duez coming fourth, and keeping up with Schwarz until the latter had an accident. The Spaniard let the Acropolis slip away by a minute, but the Greek event showed just how closely the Lancias and Toyotas were matched, with Schwarz and Ericsson putting in some good times to claim fifth and sixth.

Sainz kept his title hopes alive with a win in New Zealand, while Ross Meekings took Group N honours in his ST165 GT-Four – the first time that Toyota was able to win both Classes in a major rally. An eight-second gap allowed Sainz to be the star of the show again in Argentina, with more TTE cars in sixth and seventh. However, the 1000 Lakes Rally proved more difficult for the Celica runners, with Sainz losing a lot of time after a heavy accident. He still finished fourth, but Kankkunen was the man hogging the top spot of the podium.

Sainz also had an eventful time Down Under, retiring in the end, and leaving Schwarz to uphold Toyota honour with a fine third place. The Lancias dominated in the San Remo, but Kankkunen retired after losing a wheel, meaning that although only sixth, Sainz stayed ahead in the driver standings, and Schwarz added a few more points to Toyota's tally with an eighth.

The big guns stayed away from the Ivory Coast

1991 Catalunya Rally (Schwarz). (Courtesy CC/Ramon Espiña Fernandez)

Rally, opting for the Catalunya Rally instead. Sadly, Sainz was left on the roadside with electrical problems, and the win clocked up by Schwarz gave Toyota nothing more than good publicity and a slight reduction in the points garnered by Kankkunen.

Everything hinged on the RAC Rally, but Sainz was out of luck – his engine played up, handing Kankkunen the spoils and the World Championship title. Notwithstanding, Sainz was third and Duez eighth, in a rally that witnessed Subaru joining the club of top contenders.

1991 WRC season standings

1st	Lancia	137 points
2nd	Toyota	128 points
3rd	Mitsubishi	62 points

1992

The ST185 version of the two-litre turbocharged 4WD Celica was homologated on the first day of 1992. The blanket use of smaller turbo restrictors for 1992 did little in capping power output, for the newcomer was still endowed with over 300bhp, against 235 for the Group N machine. Carlos Sainz and Armin Schwarz were named as the main drivers, joined by the highly-experienced Markku Alén on most events.

The calendar looked much the same as 1991, so things kicked off with 'the Monte' and the long-awaited debut of the TTE ST185. The new model was on the pace from the start, with Sainz and Schwarz winning nine stages between them, and the Spaniard ultimately finishing in second, sandwiched between two Lancias.

Mats Jonsson won his home event in a Toyota Team Sweden ST165 model, and Sainz and Alén were third and fourth in the rather different climes of Portugal. Then, in just its third rally, the ST185 won the Safari in the hands of Carlos Sainz, with Mikael Ericsson guesting in fourth, and Markku Alén just behind him; older machines came home in sixth and seventh.

The TTE guys managed to keep up with the Lancias and Fords in Corsica, claiming fourth and fifth along the way, but the Acropolis was a disaster, with all three team cars crashing out. Sainz then won in New Zealand to keep his title hopes alive, with a second in Argentina also helping his cause.

Alén was third in his home event, unable to stop the Martini-sponsored Lancias, and it was the same story for Sainz in Australia. Staying away from the San Remo and Bandama meant that the Catalunya Rally was next, and here Sainz was in fine form, putting a smile on the faces of his countrymen as he held the winner's trophy aloft; Schwarz was fifth, with three Lancias ahead of him and another three behind him.

Like last year, everything hinged on the

▲ 1992 Acropolis Rally, Greece (Alén).

▼ Markku Alén.

Lombard RAC Rally in Britain. Fortunately, Carlos Sainz was able to hold off Ari Vatanen's Subaru to claim the win and the World Championship title, with Markku Alén a solid fourth. In the maker's fight, Lancia had strength in numbers, and managed to keep up its remarkable unbeaten record in the Group A era.

1992 WRC season standings

1st	Lancia	140 points
2nd	Toyota	116 points
3rd	Ford	94 points

1993

The FIA introduced a number of changes for 1993, including a new F2 category (contested by NA front-wheel drive machines) to encourage more entries, and dropping the homologation limit from 5000 units for Group A to 2500 per annum. The Group A cars were to be run on lower octane fuel, and made significantly heavier as well. As far as the Celicas were concerned, Pirelli tyres were replaced by Michelin rubber for 1993, and the 4WD system was updated, too.

Although the Bandama Rally was gone, now all 13 of the remaining rounds counted towards both championships – the one for manufacturers and the one for drivers – with the best eight scores making up the final totals. The TTE outfit pinned its hopes on ex-Martini Racing men Didier Auriol and Juha Kankkunen in the main, the return of the latter happening after Carlos Sainz went in the opposite direction and moved to Lancia.

Auriol had a taxing Monte, although the Frenchman ultimately came through to fend off the Ford challenge and claim victory by a few seconds. Kankkunen couldn't match his pace, but still finished fifth, just ahead of Schwarz, now driving a Lancer Evolution for Mitsubishi Ralliart.

Mats Jonsson won in Sweden again, this time in a ST185 model, with Kankkunen close behind, although TTE stayed away from Portugal to concentrate on sending four cars to Africa for the Safari Rally. It proved to be a good call, as the

Toyota's team ready for the 1993 Safari Rally.

works Toyotas filled the first four places, with Kankkunen leading them home.

Ford showed its potential with the new Escort RS Cosworth in Corsica, but Celicas were second and third, making up for the disappointment the team was about to experience in Greece. At least the long trip to Argentina was rewarded with a win for Kankkunen and a third place for Auriol, although differential problems in New Zealand meant they both finished in the top five rather than the top three.

Hannu Mikkola was called up as a guest for the 1000 Lakes, and came seventh, backing up his teammates who stood first and third on the podium. Kankkunen, having done the business on his home event, won the next rally, too, in Australia, although Auriol retired with engine trouble on this occasion.

San Remo was snubbed, but a second and third in Spain sealed the two WRC titles up for grabs for the TTE outfit. As if to confirm his position at the top of the table, Juha Kankkunen duly won the RAC Rally, claiming his fourth drivers' championship (including two with Lancia and the other with Peugeot) in style; Auriol finished the season in a creditable third place, but his time would soon come.

Although Toyota had helped drivers take the crown (namely Carlos Sainz in 1990 and 1992), this was actually the first ever World Rally Championship title for a Japanese manufacturer, with Ove Andersson stating: "This was just a dream 20 years ago." Indeed. But having made history, neither Toyota nor Andersson's Cologne-based equipe representing it were going to rest on their laurels ...

1993 WRC season standings

1st	Toyota	157 points
2nd	Ford	145 points
3rd	Subaru	110 points

1994

The Kankkunen and Auriol double act continued for 1994, with the ST185 rally car gaining a little more power and improved traction. The championship was fought over ten rounds, with three extra events thrown in for F2 runners.

The season started in an uncertain manner, for Auriol crashed when leading, and Kankkunen's car was also bruised and battered. He'd done enough to hold onto second place, though, despite some stiff competition from the Ford, Mitsubishi and

Subaru camps. There was no doubt TTE meant business in Portugal, for while one car crashed out, the team's regular drivers duly scored a convincing one-two victory.

Ian Duncan proved his reputation as a Safari specialist, taking the silverware for TTE in Kenya, with Auriol coming third, making up for the other two works machines dropping out.

Didier Auriol.

The momentum was kept up in Corsica, with Didier Auriol winning, Andrea Aghini third, and Juha Kankkunen fourth. The Greek excursion was not so kind, though, with Kankkunen's third being the best Toyota. Auriol got his revenge for not finishing the Acropolis with a win in Argentina, and with three cars in the top seven in New Zealand, Toyota's prospects were looking good. This observation was strengthened in Finland, despite Kankkunen having a tough time of it.

An interesting 1000 Lakes entry was the Group N car of Tomas Jansson – the new Celica. Having been introduced as a road car at the end of 1993, the sixth generation Celica (ST205) was homologated as a Group A machine in May 1994, and ran for the first time in that guise in the non-championship Rally Australia. Despite its F2 status, the fact that it was part of the APRC meant that it was well supported, and Kankkunen's second place was not something to be sniffed at.

In Italy, Auriol took the Rallye Sanremo with an ST185 model, while Kankkunen was seventh in the new car, just over four minutes behind. The same arrangements were made for the RAC Rally, as it happens, but this time it was the Finn that finished ahead, recording a fine second place to Auriol's sixth. It was perhaps fitting that this was the case, for TTE (by now a subsidiary of Toyota) would use the ST205 almost exclusively from now on.

Anyway, the important thing is that Toyota had done enough to secure its second WRC title, and Didier Auriol (then 36, and six months older than teammate Kankkunen) was crowned top driver.

1994 Safari Rally, Kenya (Kankkunen).

1994 WRC season standings

1st	Toyota	151 points
2nd	Subaru	140 points
3rd	Ford	116 points

1995 & 1996

The 1995 season saw the introduction of yet smaller turbocharger restrictors, and a modified points scoring system for the eight WRC rallies held for Group A machines (five more were classed as F2, or W2L events, with five shared with Group A cars to give a total of ten W2L rounds).

TTE rolled out the ST205 Celica liftback coupé, modifying it through the year to test different systems. Armin Schwarz rejoined the team, augmenting the championship-winning skills of Didier Auriol and Juha Kankkunen.

Oddly, Auriol and Schwarz struggled on 'the Monte' leaving Kankkunen to keep Toyota in with a chance. His third place was certainly useful, but the Subarus and Fords were fast, and Mitsubishi had a new warrior in the LanEvo II. It was this latter vehicle that scored a one-two in Sweden, although works Celicas filled the next three places. Next was the turn of the Impreza to spoil the party in Portugal, although Kankkunen was only 12 seconds behind the winner, while Schwarz and Auriol came home in fourth and fifth.

Next was the only works-supported outing for the ST185 for 1995 – the non-championship Safari Rally. Yoshio Fujimoto won the event (the first and so far only Japanese driver to do so), with Ian Duncan third, but sadly no points were to be gained, just pride and some nice publicity. More good PR came when Auriol won in Corsica, and only Colin McRae's Subaru managed to beat the three TTE cars in New Zealand.

Things were less convincing in Australia, but still Toyota led the championship, and Kankkunen was on course for another title, too. Unfortunately, he crashed in Spain, as did Schwarz, but the exclusion of Auriol was the biggest news of the event. Scrutineers had found a problem with the turbocharger restrictor set-up on the TTE cars, leading to a very harsh penalty. Naturally, Ove Andersson – on the verge of a third title in a row – was furious, and engineering supremo Dieter Bulling resigned before the FIA World Council hearing.

Ultimately, as well as drivers being stripped of their points (thankfully at least Fujimoto's W2L result in Africa was allowed to stand), TTE was excluded from the 1995 World Rally Championship, and were not allowed to compete for 12 months, in effect ruling out almost all of the 1996 season. Indeed, the official works team would not be seen in the WRC arena until the second-half of 1997, when it returned with an all-new machine based on the Corolla.

1995 WRC season standings

1st	Subaru	350 points
2nd	Mitsubishi	307 points
3rd	Ford	223 points

With TTE banned, the Celicas ran under the Toyota Castrol Team and HF Grifone banners for 1996, but Toyota couldn't score points, only drivers (the same was ultimately true of 1997 due to the way the championship system was set up). No WRC wins were recorded all year, although the W2L category provided a happy hunting ground for the Toyota drivers: The win for Armin Schwarz on the RAC Rally was particularly satisfying.

1995 Monte Carlo Rally (Auriol).

Age of the Corolla WRC

Toyota returns to the WRC scene with a new machine built specifically to comply with the latest World Rally Car (or WRCar) regulations – an evolution of the rules that almost all of the top teams would embrace.

The 1997 season started much like the 1996 one, with the Toyota Castrol Team and HF Grifone outfits acting as a focal point for a myriad of ST205 Celica entries. There were a few notable results (like Ian Duncan's third on the Safari and Freddy Loix coming second in Portugal), but despite having kept some good drivers onboard, no wins were recorded, as rivals moved forward and Toyota found itself unable to. However, the return of the official works team (albeit with cars carrying Toyota Castrol Team livery rather than TTE colouring, in a nod to the outfit that kept the brand in the spotlight during some trying times), marked by the debut of the Corolla WRC, would bring the Japanese maker back in from the wilderness.

1997

The WRCar regulations were due to take effect from the 1997 season, allowing makers to bypass the established homologation system by creating and registering a turbocharged 4WD car loosely based on a more mundane mass-production vehicle. This brought about a series of specialised two-litre machines, officially classed as Group A (A8 to be precise), meaning that cars already homologated in this category could still compete. As it happens, Mitsubishi decided to continue with its established 'LanEvo' models until 2001, although Ford, Subaru and Toyota went down the WRCar route.

Ove Andersson was in his element, and although his rivals at Ford and Subaru had the jump on him with their 300bhp models, both in terms of build numbers and real-world testing, he was confident that the Corolla WRC would allow him to regain the world championship title for Toyota. Based on the bug-eyed European export version of the E110 Corolla (introduced in Japan with more conservative styling in 1995), the homologation papers for the TTE-prepared four-cylinder hatchback came through on the first day of August 1997.

Being far from Cologne, ST205s were used in New Zealand, but the Corolla WRC duly made its debut a few weeks later in Finland, where the logistics were easier to handle. While two Celicas finished ahead of the newcomer, Didier Auriol guided one Corolla to eighth place despite a series of niggling problems, and Marcus Grönholm even led the rally at one point in the sister car, although a lack of fuel pressure ultimately put him out on the last day.

Both 300bhp Corollas were sidelined with electrical problems in Indonesia, but a fifth and eighth on the San Remo confirmed that progress was being made. Indeed, Freddy Loix clocked up no less than six stage wins – more than anyone else apart from Colin McRae, who went on to win the Italian event. Auriol had a nice run in Australia, claiming a podium position, and while he crashed out on the RAC, Grönholm picked up the pieces with a solid fifth place.

Sadly, registered manufacturers (or more accurately, the equipes designated by them) had to enter every round by this time, meaning Toyota was unable to record any points. Subaru

1997 Rally Finland (Grönholm).

was declared the 1997 champion (its third title on the trot), with Ford second and Mitsubishi third; there was no fourth team able to qualify.

1998

While the new FIA rules demanded a huge budget that most makers – at least those without a reputation in rallying to uphold – found hard to justify, Peugeot announced its intention to return to the WRC scene via a limited campaign, with Citroën also destined to join the fray alongside the likes of Renault, SEAT and Hyundai.

Ove Andersson managed to tempt Carlos Sainz back into the TTE fold, with his confidence in the Spaniard immediately rewarded with a win on the Monte Carlo Rally – the first event of a 13-round season. Sainz was backed up by Didier Auriol for 1998, although Corollas were starting to filter through to other teams by now as well.

As already noted, Sainz won 'the Monte' after 'LanEvo' man Tommi Mäkinen dropped out, although Auriol struggled to overcome lost time from a bent steering rack. However, Mäkinen got his revenge in Sweden, leaving Sainz to pick up second; Marcus Grönholm kept up the 'Flying Finn' tradition with a fifth in a HF Grifone Celica ST205, with Auriol sixth and a third works Corolla crashing out.

Auriol was the top finisher on the Safari (a clear fourth), as Sainz fell by the wayside with suspension trouble. Portugal saw a good selection of Corolla WRCs, with two works cars, Grönholm in a new HF Grifone-owned vehicle, Freddy Loix in a Belgian machine, and Thomas Radström in a Swedish one. As it happens, it was Loix that shared the podium with Sainz, as the other three Corollas all retired. Across the border in Spain, Auriol clocked up his first win of 1998, with Loix second, and Sainz seventh, keeping his title hopes alive.

Corsica was a Subaru and Peugeot affair, but Sainz was second in Argentina, finishing a few seconds down on Mäkinen; Auriol's engine popped. Colin McRae (Subaru) won in Greece, but Auriol was second, and two more 1972cc turbocharged Corollas followed the third-placed Ford home. Then, in New Zealand, Toyota scored a convincing one-two victory, although Mäkinen won his home event, pushing the Corollas down to second, fourth, sixth and seventh.

San Remo was tough, with Sainz fourth, and Andrea Aghini being the only other top ten finisher in a HF Grifone car. At least Australia proved kinder, with Sainz and Auriol on the podium, providing a real showdown for the final round in Britain. For most of the RAC Rally, it looked as if Carlos Sainz would be crowned champion, but his failure to reach the line on the final stage handed the title to Mitsubishi's Tommi Mäkinen by just two points. Toyota had to settle for second as well, although HF Grifone

▲▼ *1998 Monte Carlo Rally (Sainz), with a UK advert proclaiming the victory.*

won the FIA Teams' Cup with ease as a form of mild consolation ...

1998 WRC season standings

1st	Mitsubishi	91 points
2nd	Toyota	85 points
3rd	Subaru	65 points

1999

There were no major changes on the Japanese teams contesting the 14 rounds of 1999, although Ford had its new Focus RS WRC, and many were watching to see how the Peugeot 206 WRC fared. Sainz and Auriol were the main Toyota pilots once more, augmented by a whole host of guest drivers, including ex-F1 star Martin Brundle on one occasion, who cut his teeth racing Celicas in his younger days. Sadly, even with Arne Hertz in the passenger seat, it didn't stop him crashing out of his home event – the famous and notoriously difficult RAC Rally.

Meanwhile, Sainz had an accident at the beginning on the Monte Carlo Rally, leaving Auriol to uphold Toyota honour with a decent third place. Mäkinen won again in Sweden, with Sainz and Auriol split by a Ford, although both managed to get on the podium in Kenya (Colin McRae scoring a win for Ford, with the results then mirrored in Portugal, albeit with Sainz and Auriol swapping places). Amazingly, a Formula 2 Kit Car (the Citroën Xsara) won the next two rounds, duly bringing about rule changes for 2000, but Auriol stayed on the pace in Spain and Sainz in Corsica.

Subaru reigned supreme in Argentina, leaving Toyota to pick up third and fifth (Mäkinen was fourth), and the Acropolis went Subaru's way, too: At least Sainz was second, making up for Auriol's DNF due to suspension failure. The works Toyotas were fourth and sixth in New Zealand, with Sainz third in Finland after Auriol dropped out. Next, the circus travelled to China for the first time, with Auriol claiming the silverware, and Sainz standing on the third step of the podium, looking a bit shorter than Richard Burns of Subaru.

Back to the traditional calendar, and the San Remo classic saw Mitsubishi and Peugeot men finishing just ahead of Auriol, with Aghini a fine fifth in the HF Grifone car; Sainz crashed out early on, but made up for the mistake by taking second place Down Under. Even though both works cars dropped out of November's RAC Rally with suspension maladies, Toyota still managed to pip Subaru to the post in the manufacturer's title chase (despite the blue machines claiming a one-two win in Britain), with Auriol ultimately finishing third at the end of the season, and Sainz fifth, some 18 points down on the winner.

1999 WRC season standings

1st	Toyota	109 points
2nd	Subaru	105 points
3rd	Mitsubishi	83 points

While Tommi Mäkinen walked away with the driver's title again (his 62 points allowing him to bag a third World Rally Championship with a fair safety margin), Toyota declared that it had achieved enough in the rallying arena, and was now ready to challenge another motorsport discipline – Formula One. The official works team would not be seen in the WRC again for almost two decades ...

1999 Swedish Rally (Auriol).

The Gazoo Story

While Toyota has become a household name, along with that of the brand's luxury Lexus division, Gazoo and the product range it has spawned is still fairly unknown outside motorsport circles. Here, Peter Lyon takes us through Gazoo's evolution, with a few personal memories thrown in for good measure.

Toyota's Gazoo Racing (TGR), the brand's in-house motorsport and performance division, has competed in everything from the Le Mans 24-hour Race, to the World Endurance Championship, the World Rally Championship, NASCAR, the Dakar Rally, the World Rally-Raid Championship, and Japan's Super GT Series.

On the performance car side of the equation, Gazoo is involved in the creation of vehicles in no less than three categories. Wearing a 'GR' prefix, GR Series models are specially developed bespoke sports cars like the GR86, GR Supra, GR Yaris and GR Corolla. In contrast, GR Sports models are mildly customised versions of big sellers such as the RAV4, Land Cruiser, Hilux and Corolla Sport, and GRMN models – which stands for 'Gazoo Racing tuned by Meister of Nürburgring' – are top-of-the-line limited production conversions of existing models.

With its high profile race victories in the 24-hours of Le Mans and WRC, and award-winning sports cars like the GR Yaris, the Gazoo brand has made a meteoric rise to international fame and recognition in a surprisingly short time.

But Gazoo Racing actually had humble beginnings. Founded as a passion project in 2007 by motorsport enthusiast and then-EVP Akio Toyoda and chief test driver and sports car visionary Hiromu Naruse, Gazoo started life as an amateur racing project – known then simply as Team Gazoo – building and racing Toyota Altezza sedans in events at the legendary Nürburgring racetrack in Germany.

It took two years for the team to be properly recognised by Toyota as a fully-fledged racing team, as company bosses just rated the team at the 'same level as a bunch of enthusiasts.' So it was in 2009, when Toyoda ascended to CEO of Toyota, that he was able to announce 'Toyota Gazoo Racing' and start competing under that name, although he decided to give himself a nickname – Morizo – to maintain brand neutrality. After all, his last name was Toyoda and difficult to disguise.

I myself had the pleasure to meet, interact and even train with the Gazoo team in 2009, when I caught up with a group of company test drivers and racers at the Nürburgring Nordschleife track in Germany as we practiced for our 2010 entry in the gruelling Nürburgring 24-hour Race.

Before venturing to the track itself, my team members completed over 100 virtual practice laps of the Nürburgring on the popular *Gran Turismo* driving simulator, giving us intimate knowledge of the circuit's complex layout and braking points. Unleashed onto the real-world track soon after, we were required to train in a Toyota Supra A80 and V8-powered Lexus IS-F sedan that Gazoo team drivers were also using. In late 2009, my team and I were required to compete in at least two short four-hour sprint races at the track as a prerequisite to competing in the 2010 24-hour classic.

Toyoda, who I saw many times at the track, surprised many industry pundits when he donned a racing suit and helmet in those early Gazoo years and got behind the wheel of the Supra, Lexus IS-F and V10-powered LFA supercar in the Nürburgring 24-hours, competing at speeds of up to 180mph (almost 300km/h).

As heir to the Toyota CEO position, Toyoda never did anything at the track without the advice and mentorship of his racing guru and lifelong friend, Hiromu Naruse. The talented test driver had first visited the legendary German track in 1970 to race a Celica and had fallen in love with its complexity and challenges. He once told me that "Japanese circuits only reveal one-tenth of a car's performance, but the Nürburgring uncovers 100 percent of a car's capabilities. And then some. That's why we need to test and develop our sports cars here."

During one pit stop in a four-hour sprint race, Toyoda told me that, in his first few races, he felt frustration because every car that sped past him during the race seemed to be yelling that "Toyota could never make a machine like this." He added that it was here, at the so-called 'Green Hell', that a big part of his motivation to build more competitive cars was born.

Over the succeeding years, Toyoda proved to be a hands-on President by not only competing in several Nürburgring 24-hour races himself, but also taking on test-driving duties to evaluate the all-new GR Yaris rally machine that was being groomed for WRC competition from 2017. And that is the main subject of this book ...

Cars from part of the Gazoo racing programme for 2017.

The Changing Face of Rallying

A lot had happened in the world of rallying in the years between 1999 and Toyota's WRC comeback almost two decades later. Things like stricter rules on testing, a reduction in recce runs, fewer mechanics, introducing limits on tyre numbers, and enforcing the use of engines and chassis parts for two rallies, which not only kept costs in check (an important point given the further expansion of the calendar) but also helped create more reliable components.

The WRCar rules changed for 2011, again with budgets in mind, but they would change once more as Toyota rejoined the rally scene, so there's no need to detail them here. Meanwhile, a successful revival of the short-lived Power Stage (basically a specific SS on the final day, largely for the benefit of television) enabled drivers to score additional points, initially with the top three home getting a bonus, and duly extended to the top five for 2017; it was held over a minimum of six miles (10km). There were also several changes made on the rejoining of rallies, with harsh time penalties for missing stages, but at least crews could continue on most events (organisers were able to control this rule), unless it was the final day, and the ability to pick up valuable Power Stage points was left intact even if the main points allocations had slipped out of reach.

For 2013, the FIA reduced the minimum number of events necessary to qualify for the World Championship to just seven rounds (out of 13 at the time), with only one needing to be specified outside Europe (the minimum requirement was duly dropped completely in 2016 to attract more entries, although most of the leading teams continued to enter virtually every race in order to accumulate as many points as possible). However, WRC teams were obliged to nominate at least one driver for a minimum of ten rounds. At the same time, the championship Classes became defined as WRC (the main, top category), WRC2 (formally Super 2000, somewhere between Group A and Group N), and WRC3 (for production cars); Junior WRC was basically an evolution of the lesser Super 1600 category, launched in 2001.

The Yaris base car

The Yaris name has been around since 1999, basically replacing the Starlet and Tercel-badged models in the Toyota line-up. As such, it was a compact FF machine, and most popular in hatchback form (the home market called this XP10 variant the Vitz, although some places used the Echo nameplate instead). The sporty RS grade showed the way forward, and was continued in the second generation XP90 series of 2005 vintage.

The third generation (XP130), first introduced for the 2011 season, looked much sharper than its predecessors, and continued to be built in Japan until the end of 2019 (French production for Europe ran into the middle of 2020). By this time, the model had already received two facelifts, with the original 2017 WRC machine featuring the later-style nose and taillight graphics. The rally car was based on the two-door hatchback shell, which was often referred to as a three-door configuration.

The 2017 Season

The 2017 season was contested over 13 rounds, which was one less than the previous year, although on saying that, the main event left out of the calendar – Rally China – had been cancelled anyway in 2016 due to heavy flooding. With a maximum Special Stage distance of 312 miles (500km) imposed per event (and at least 25 percent of the total distance to made up of Special Stages, including a single Power Stage), the WRC schedule therefore looked like this, at least as far as the Gazoo team was concerned (the Junior World Rally Championship, supporting the WRC and featuring younger drivers and Ford Fiesta R2s only, was held over just six rounds).

2017 Season Rounds

Rally	Date	Surface
Monte Carlo Rally	19-22 January	Tarmac
Rally Sweden	9-12 February	Snow
Rally Mexico	9-12 March	Gravel
Tour de Corse	7-9 April	Tarmac
Rally Argentina	27-30 April	Gravel
Rally de Portugal	18-21 May	Gravel
Rally Italia Sardegna	8-11 June	Gravel
Rally Poland	29 June-2 July	Gravel
Rally Finland	27-30 July	Gravel
Rallye Deutschland	17-20 August	Tarmac
Rally Catalunya	6-8 October	Mixed
Wales Rally GB	26-29 October	Gravel
Rally Australia	17-19 November	Gravel

FIA rule changes and season prospects

The 2017 season basically marked a new era in the sport of rallying, with Akio Toyoda being the first to sign up for what was basically an attempt at recreating the reign of the amazing Group B machines. The new cars would continue to run with a 1.6-litre four with forced induction, but the turbo restrictor size went up from 33mm (1.3in) diameter to 36mm (1.4in), allowing power to increase from around 310bhp to roughly 380bhp. Keeping the boost in check made sure that the torque output remained similar to 2016 levels. A six-speed transmission was specified with paddle shifts, with 4WD achieved via passive diffs front and rear, and the revival of an active centre-differential – something not seen since 2010 – to increase grip.

In addition to an increase in the car's maximum width (up 55mm/2.2in to 1875mm/73.8in), designers were allowed a lot more freedom with regard to the aerodynamics package, such as a new front splitter, rear diffuser, wider wheelarches with myriad cooling ducts, and a massive rear wing that sat higher than before. These changes combined to enhance downforce and make the cars look very aggressive. As well as

The new Toyota pictured with its rivals for 2017.

being more powerful, the 2017 machines were also lighter, with the minimum weight reduced by 25kg (55lb) to 1175kg (2585lb).

Only manufacturer outfits were allowed to run the latest ultra-quick cars, restricting their use to top-drawer pilots as a consequence (ultimately, in the name of safety), although there was no longer a requirement to nominate the number one driver in a WRC team. A manufacturer was now able to enter a third vehicle, but only the best two finishers would be eligible to score championship points (Power Stage points continued to be awarded to drivers and co-drivers only).

Incidentally, the scoring system for rallies cut short was revised, meaning that full points were awarded for events that were almost completed; half points for 50 to 75 percent complete; one-third points for 25 to 50 percent complete, and no points for events cancelled a quarter of the way through. The full points available were 25 for a win, 18 for second, 15 for third, and then 12, ten, eight, six, four and two, down to a single point for tenth; extended Power Stage bonuses were now five points for first, down to one for fifth.

With old rivals like Mitsubishi, Subaru and Peugeot no longer in the picture, and Volkswagen

An early prototype photographed at TMG in Cologne with an illustrious predecessor.

▼ *The engine used in the Yaris WRC.*

pulling out of rallying after a brief but impressive career (claiming the World Championship title in each of the four years the German brand had entered in the WRC arena, from 2013 to 2016), Toyota found itself up against Ford (using the Fiesta WRC), Citroën (C3 WRC) and Hyundai (with the i20 Coupe WRC) in the makers' title chase; the older Ford Fiesta RS WRC and Citroën DS3 WRC were still able to make an impression in the hands of pilots that failed to get works-nominated drives. With new cars for all of the teams, it was futile to predict what was going to happen – the only clear advantage was Ford having the services of Sébastien Ogier, who had dominated the leaderboard since the 'official' retirement of Sébastien Loeb...

The Gazoo team cars and their drivers

The 1.6-litre Yaris WRC had a four-cylinder (83.8mm x 72.5mm bore and stroke) turbocharged engine with direct fuel-injection, tuned to give over 380bhp and no less than 313lbft of torque. Power was transmitted through a six-speed sequential gearbox, and four-wheel drive, with

▲▼ *Testing in progress during 2016.*

Akio Toyoda (Team Founder, left) with Tommi Mäkinen.

two mechanical differentials either side of an active centre diff with various torque split options; Michelin tyres were employed, as per virtually all of the top runners in 2017.

Tipping the scales at 1190kg (2618lb) and coming with a liquid-cooled braking system specific to tarmac and gravel events, once Toyota Motorsport GmbH (TMG) had done the initial groundwork, serious testing of the Yaris WRC began in April 2016 under the watchful gaze of Tom Fowler – the man who was named as Chief Engineer. Fowler went on record saying that the new cars only just made it to Monte Carlo, but then making a vehicle from scratch is never an easy task.

As it happens, Fowler came from the Tommi Mäkinen Racing outfit, as Tommi Mäkinen (the four-time world rally champion) had been appointed Team Principal by the team's founding father Akio Toyoda back in the early part of July 2015, six months after Toyota first announced its return to rallying. Setting up his headquarters for the Gazoo Racing WRC challenge in Puuppola in the south of Finland, Mäkinen quickly put together a team of experienced engineers and designers,

The car for the 2017 season. It is shown here equipped with tarmac rally wheels, which, like the gravel rims, were supplied by the OZ Racing concern.

◀◀ *Jari-Matti Latvala.*

◀ *Juho Hänninen.*

and brought the necessary knowhow into the equation, in much the same way as Ove Andersson had done decades before in the 1970s.

The driver line-up for 2017 included three Finns: Jari-Matti Latvala, Juho Hänninen, and Esapekka Lappi. Their co-drivers were, respectively, Miikka Anttila, Kaj Lindström, and Janne Ferm.

Coming from a rallying family, Latvala was born in 1985, and started his WRC career at a very early age; indeed, he was just 17 when he entered the 2002 Rally GB. He impressed straight away, and after Marcus Grönholm retired, he was given the number two car in the works Ford team in 2008. He climbed to second in the World Championship in 2010, and stayed with Ford until he received an offer from Volkswagen to join its new team for 2013. In the four years of the VW programme, he was runner-up twice and third once in the drivers' table.

Juho Hänninen was born in 1981, and made his WRC debut in 2006 driving a Group N Mitsubishi. MMSP gave him a Lancer WRC05 to drive on a number of occasions in the following year, but time was running out for what was left of the pukka Ralliart operation, and the Finn eventually found a winning team in Skoda, claiming victory in several SWRC events and earning a works drive as a result. 2013 was quiet, as he signed up to develop the new Hyundai, which he duly drove in 2014. After another quiet spell, Hänninen became a Toyota team member, but would ultimately spend just one year in the works driver's seat; 2018 would be spent mainly in a testing role for Gazoo.

We will take a look at the then reigning WRC2 champion Esapekka Lappi's career in the next chapter, although it should be mentioned that Lappi was heavily involved in the early testing of the Yaris ...

ROUND 01

Monte Carlo Rally

19-22 January

While alternative starting points – a quaint feature of the classic Montes of yore – had been dropped for the elite drivers many years earlier (back in the mid-1990s in fact), as always, the Monte Carlo Rally was centred on the sinuous

Rd 01 #10 Latvala.

black top roads overlooking Monaco. Initially scheduled to include 17 stages over 239 miles (383km), for 2017, most of the action was based in and around Gap to the north of the principality.

As it happens, the first special stage (SS1) was cancelled, as was SS16, thus reducing the overall stage distance, although the rally was still over 220 miles (352km) in the end, making the Monte one of the most demanding of all of the events on the WRC calendar. Factor in the unpredictable winter weather, along with what amounts to almost three times the SS distance to cover on the road in order to get to each stage (the so-called liaison distance), and it quickly becomes clear why the Monte Carlo Rally is often considered the ultimate test of a machine and the person driving it.

Toyota entered two cars for the Monte – one for Latvala (#10), and the other for Hänninen (#11). The shakedown went smoothly enough (especially considering that studded tyres were deliberately avoided in order to preserve them for the actual rally), with no major changes found necessary.

The rally proper set off from the front of the famous casino in the centre of Monte Carlo, and went straight into the darkness of the mountains, where light snow and icy roads awaited the 73 starters. Hänninen finished the day in third, having softer tyres more suited to the conditions than his teammate, but a coming together with a roadside tree damaged his suspension on SS5 on the second; Latvala ended the day in fourth, trailing a Hyundai and two Fords.

Fortunately, Hänninen's car suffered only light damage, and the Finn was able to restart the rally on the third day, albeit a long way down the field. A puncture dented his charge, and Latvala suffered electrical maladies, but a heavy knock at the rear-end for the top Hyundai allowed the latter to move up to third on the leaderboard nonetheless, as the remaining crews lined up for the four stages reserved for the final day. While the record books will proclaim it as the first win for Ford since 2012, Latvala was superb on Day 4, allowing him to move up to second overall. Hänninen was also fast, earning bonus points on the final Power Stage.

▲ Rd 01 #11 Hänninen. *▼ Rd 01 #10 Latvala.*

Monte Carlo Rally *Overall results, with 54 finishers*

1st	Sébastien Ogier/Julien Ingrassia	Ford Fiesta WRC	4:00:03.6
2nd	Jari-Matti Latvala/Miikka Anttila	Toyota Yaris WRC	4:02:18.6
3rd	Ott Tänak/Martin Järveoja	Ford Fiesta WRC	4:03:01.4
16th	Juho Hänninen/Kaj Lindström	Toyota Yaris WRC	4:32:20.4

ROUND 02

Rally Sweden

9-12 February

At this, the 65th running of Rally Sweden, Toyota bounced back from defeat in the Monte to capture its first rally victory since returning to the WRC after a 17-year absence. Given its mid-February position on the calendar, the entire event was, not surprisingly, heavily snowbound. At the rally base of Torsby, in the south-west of the country, 41 starters (with 14 in the top WRC Class) lined up for stages characterised by slippery surfaces and gentle corners through forest areas.

Having only just finished snow and ice testing in neighbouring Finland, Toyota drivers Jari-Matti Latvala and Juho Hänninen both arrived in Sweden filled with confidence in their Yaris WRC machines. The rally was made up of 18 stages over 208 miles (332km), with some of the early ones in Norway. At the Super Special Stage on Day One in Karlstad, Latvala started cautiously in extremely slippery conditions but still managed to record the fastest time, making this SS the first stage win for Toyota since 2000.

On Day Two, a fresh layer of snow had fallen overnight, giving Latvala a slight advantage as he started from second place. After recording a few top three finishes on a number of stages, he secured his second stage win on SS4. With his pace slightly slower than Hyundai's Thierry Neuville, Latvala finished Day Two in 2nd place, just 28.1 seconds behind. Meanwhile, Hänninen, who had been pushing hard, lost control in SS5 and crashed into a tree, forcing him to retire from the rest of the day's stages.

Thierry Neuville led for much of the rally, but crashed out on the final Super SS of the Day Three, incurring a significant time loss. That left Latvala (the only other man to lead the event) with a clear run home. Holding on to a slender lead over Ford's Ott Tänak, Latvala focused on the fortunate turn of events to record his fourth stage win of the rally after receiving much-needed encouragement from Team Principal Tommi Mäkinen, who had advised him to "forget about the settings, and focus purely on driving fast."

Neuville rejoined the rally, as did Hänninen, but their lost time meant that they had no chance of reaching the podium. At the end of the final day, we saw familiar faces on the podium, with Latvala now leading the championship. For 'Flying Finns' Latvala and Mäkinen, who had both won Rally Sweden three times, this victory was a sign of things to come.

◀ *Rd 02 #10 Latvala.* ▼ *Rd 02 #11 Hänninen.*

Rally Sweden *Overall results, with 32 finishers*

1st	Jari-Matti Latvala/Miikka Anttila	Toyota Yaris WRC	2:36:03.6
2nd	Ott Tänak/Martin Järveoja	Ford Fiesta WRC	2:36:32.8
3rd	Sébastien Ogier/Julien Ingrassia	Ford Fiesta WRC	2:37:03.1
16th	Juho Hänninen/Kaj Lindström	Toyota Yaris WRC	2:59:09.2

Rd 02 #10 Latvala.

ROUND 03

Rally Mexico
9-12 March

In what is thought to be the toughest rally of the WRC due to its high temperatures and high altitudes, Rally Mexico poses unique challenges for all competitors. Based on gravel roads in León in Guanajuato state with altitudes exceeding 2000 metres, oxygen density is around 70% of that at sea level, causing 'breathing' difficulties for people and car engines alike.

Originally scheduled for 20 stages over 231 miles (370km), Rally Mexico's start on Day One was a damp one, with the first two stages then cancelled on Day Two. Luckily for organisers, SS4 and SS5 covered the same ground anyway (47 miles/75km in total). It was an amazing contrast with Sweden, some of the villages seemingly stuck in time.

Adding to Toyota's technical and physical challenges at this altitude, the Yaris WRC is the only car in the WRC field to have not competed here before, therefore denying engineers the opportunity to analyse past data for development purposes. To compensate for these shortcomings, Toyota attempted to conduct tests in thin air conditions in Spanish mountains and high temperature regions of southern Europe, but poor weather conditions prevented these tests.

As a result, on the rally's long gravel stage, which covered some 54km, both Yaris WRCs suffered from engine overheating. With their power-units switched from 'stage mode' to 'road section mode' to avoid engine damage, the reduced performance meant significant time loss. Gazoo engineers, however, collected the data they needed that day to make the necessary adjustments to both soft- and hardware aspects, allowing both Latvala/Anttila and Hänninen/Lindström teams to compete at speed, and with

Rd 03 #10 Latvala.

Rd 03 #11 Hänninen.

Rd 03 #10 Latvala.

no more heat-related or other mechanical issues.

Through some inspired driving, Latvala was able to make up time lost due to problems, eventually finishing in sixth place. Meanwhile, Hänninen, who started in the lead position on Day One and suffered from bad health throughout the rally, finished seventh – his best finish of the season so far.

Having led for most of the event, Kris Meeke in his Citroën C3 WRC, won despite a remarkable detour into the parking lot at one point, while Ford increased its lead in the title chase.

Rally Mexico *Overall results, with 22 finishers*

1st	Kris Meeke/Paul Nagle	Citroën C3 WRC	3:22:04.6
2nd	Sébastien Ogier/Julien Ingrassia	Ford Fiesta WRC	3:22:18.4
3rd	Thierry Neuville/Nicolas Gilsoul	Hyundai i20 Coupe WRC	3:23:04.3
6th	Jari-Matti Latvala/Miikka Anttila	Toyota Yaris WRC	3:26:44.9
7th	Juho Hänninen/Kaj Lindström	Toyota Yaris WRC	3:27:10.8

Rd 03 #11 Hänninen.

Rd 04 #10 Latvala.

ROUND 04

Tour de Corse

7-9 April

An integral part of the WRC series since 1973, the Tour de Corse-Rallye de France is one of the leading tarmac rallies on the WRC calendar, and is almost certainly the most famous tarmac rally in the world.

With 78 crews starting the rally, a shakedown was held on April 6, followed by ten reasonably lengthy stages over three days and 198 miles (317km), with the Power Stage being by far the shortest. The Tour de Corse is a very different discipline to that of Mexico, with the island of Corsica offering nothing but dry and incredibly fast and twisty tarmac surfaces.

Rd 04 #11 Hänninen.

Latvala had won here in 2015 with a different team, but he was not happy with his Yaris' handling, and was therefore only able to record times between fifth and seventh fastest. In SS1, Juho Hänninen misjudged the grip levels at a transition between roads, carried too much speed into the corner and crashed, giving Gazoo disappointing results.

Team Principal Tommi Mäkinen decided to make some sweeping changes to Hänninen's car, which was being repaired after crashing out. Mäkinen's gamble paid off. Although the first SS of the second day was twistier and more difficult than the previous day's, Hänninen managed to set the second fastest time. He then proceeded to set the third fastest time on the following SS. During a special 30 minute service time that allowed mechanics to work on cars, the team chose to implement the same setup changes on Latvala's Yaris, finishing with not one minute to spare.

The modifications worked like a charm as Latvala recorded the second and third fastest times on Day Two's two afternoon SSs, finishing the day in fourth position overall. On the final day, Latvala was unable to maintain the previous day's pace and dropped to fourth in the standings while Hänninen, having survived hitting stonework on a bridge, drove off course with just 5km to go and was forced to retire. As it turned out, Toyota Gazoo Racing WRT was just seconds shy of a podium finish at the Tour de Corse, its first ever full-tarmac rally.

Citroën's Kris Meeke led for much of the early part of the rally, until his engine gave way on SS7, putting him out of the event. This allowed Thierry Neuville to take the win, moving Hyundai ahead of Toyota in the rankings.

Tour de Corse *Overall results, with 58 finishers*

1st	Thierry Neuville/Nicolas Gilsoul	Hyundai i20 Coupe WRC	3:22:53.4
2nd	Sébastien Ogier/Julien Ingrassia	Ford Fiesta WRC	3:23:48.1
3rd	Dani Sordo/Marc Marti	Hyundai i20 Coupe WRC	3:23:49.4
4th	Jari-Matti Latvala/Miikka Anttila	Toyota Yaris WRC	3:24:03.0
DNF	Juho Hänninen/Kaj Lindström	Toyota Yaris WRC	–

ROUND 05

Rally Argentina

27-30 April

On the outskirts of Cordoba, torrential rain had fallen in the lead up to Rally Argentina. But after the traditional Thursday shakedown, the skies cleared and the warmth returned. In front of thousands of rally-adoring fans – the most passionate in South America – the event began on Argentina's notoriously rough, narrow and dusty gravel roads. And if the rains set in, the river crossings can be as spectacular as the Argentinian scenery. For this reason, Rally Argentina is a favourite rally for many WRC drivers.

This event has been around since 1980, and has been on the World Rally Championship calendar virtually every year since. There were only 22 entries, but three cars for each of the four big teams entered. Overall there were 18 stages covering 224 miles (358km), but adding in liaison distances took the event total up to 860 miles (1380km).

After the recce, all drivers were of the opinion that this year's stages were 'extremely severe', and that it would be impossible to avoid sharp stones scattered across the exposed bedrock. On Day Two, the rally lived up to its reputation with most cars returning battle-scarred to the service park, and some were even forced to withdraw.

Luckily the two Toyotas suffered only minor body damage, although Juho Hänninen's car was afflicted with an engine issue caused by relentless road impacts that led to a reduction in power. Team engineers managed to resolve the issue, but Hänninen still lost a substantial amount of time. Tommi Mäkinen commented, "Competing in rallies and facing unexpected problems is a tremendous asset for us. By overcoming each problem, we can acquire great experience and large amounts of data, and we can use this in the next rally."

▲ *Rd 05 #11 Hänninen.* ▼ *Rd 05 #10 Latvala.*

Jari-Matti Latvala, meanwhile, was enjoying a superb start, lying second overall after the morning's session. Then, after overrunning a corner and striking the roadside bank with his

Rd 05 #11 Hänninen.

Rd 05 #10 Latvala.

Yaris WRC, one of his tyres came off its wheel rim, forcing him to drive the last 15km with only three functioning wheels. While he did lose significant time, Latvia still managed to finish in fifth place while Hänninen placed seventh, a good result considering the conditions.

Elfyn Evans in his Ford Fiesta WRC had led the rally for nearly the whole event, but after clipping a bridge on the final stage, Hyundai's Thierry Neuville managed to squeeze in front of the Briton, beating him by just 0.7 seconds, one of the closest finishes in WRC history.

Rally Argentina *Overall results, with 17 finishers*

1st	Thierry Neuville/Nicolas Gilsoul	Hyundai i20 Coupe WRC	3:38:10.6
2nd	Elfyn Evans/Daniel Barritt	Ford Fiesta WRC	3:38:11.3
3rd	Ott Tänak/Martin Järveoja	Ford Fiesta WRC	3:38:40.5
5th	Jari-Matti Latvala/Miikka Anttila	Toyota Yaris WRC	3:39:58.7
7th	Juho Hänninen/Kaj Lindström	Toyota Yaris WRC	3:49:27.5

ROUND 06

Rally de Portugal

18-21 May

Boasting dry and dusty conditions, and several big jumps to entertain the crowd, Rally de Portugal began with 64 starters, including three cars from each of the top teams. The event was run over 19 stages covering 218 miles (349km). Talented Finnish wheelman, team test driver and 2016 WRC2 Champion Esapekka Lappi joined the Toyota Gazoo Racing for Rally de Portugal, making it the first time that Gazoo had entered three Yaris WRCs.

By increasing the number of vehicles entered from two to three, simple arithmetic suggested to Team Principal Tommi Mäkinen and Gazoo Racing bosses that 50 percent more data can be accumulated. Taking things at a steady pace, Lappi drove within his comfort zone for the first day, getting used to the car and posting a modest 11th on the time sheets.

By Day Three, he had grown accustomed to his machine, recording the sixth fastest time in SS12 and the fifth quickest in SS14. However, on SS15, he lost control on loose gravel and the right-rear of his Yaris struck a wall causing significant damage and forcing the Finn to limp back to the service park.

On Day Four, during the penultimate SS18, Lappi recorded his best stage result (a fourth place), and then followed it up with another fourth fastest time in the final Power Stage – the team's best result in Portugal. He finished the event in tenth overall. Impressed with Lappi's driving, Mäkinen said, "He is a diamond in the rough, just like the Yaris WRC."

Meanwhile, in seventh, Juho Hänninen was the highest placed Gazoo driver at Rally de Portugal, having put in some sparkling performances. He did however, lose a minute due to a mechanical issue on SS14, but still managed to complete the event, which he had stated was his main goal in Portugal.

Gazoo's other pilot Jari-Matti Latvala, suffered his first rollover of the season, incurring a significant time loss as a result. However, he did not retire but competed to the end, securing a ninth-place finish. This turned out to be a particularly stressful drive for Latvala as he was plagued by ill health – including back pains, high fever and stomach pains – for the duration of the rally. Having had little sleep, he dug deep and persevered to the finish before finally being hospitalised with dehydration. The two points secured by Latvala in the face of such adversity hold a significance far in excess of their numerical value.

With the lead changing six times during the rally, Sébastien Ogier in his Ford Fiesta WRC took control during Day Three and managed to hold off Hyundai's fast-finishing Thierry Neuville, winning by 15 seconds.

Rd 06
▶ *Top: #12 Lappi.*
▶ *Centre: #10 Latvala.*
▶ *Bottom: #11 Hänninen.*

Rally de Portugal *Overall results, with 41 finishers*

1st	Sébastien Ogier/Julien Ingrassia	Ford Fiesta WRC	3:42:55.7
2nd	Thierry Neuville/Nicolas Gilsoul	Hyundai i20 Coupe WRC	3:43:11.3
3rd	Dani Sordo/Marc Marti	Hyundai i20 Coupe WRC	3:43:57.4
7th	Juho Hänninen/Kaj Lindström	Toyota Yaris WRC	3:46:44.6
9th	Jari-Matti Latvala/Miikka Anttila	Toyota Yaris WRC	3:48:39.3
10th	Esapekka Lappi/Janne Ferm	Toyota Yaris WRC	3:51:09.0

Rd 06 12 Lappi.

ROUND 07

Rally Italia Sardegna

8-11 June

Winding its way around the island of Sardinia in hot, dry gravel conditions, round seven of the WRC was the 14th running of the Rally d'Italia Sardegna. And welcoming 53 starters, once again, three cars were entered from each of the major manufacturers: Toyota, Ford, Hyundai and Citroën.

The proper stages commenced on Day Two, and Jari-Matti Latvala, who came to Italy in third place in the drivers' standings, was the third driver to start. On dry loose gravel, early starters suffered from a lack of grip due to this slippery surface, and invariably incurred significant time deficits. But despite this disadvantage, Latvala ended Day Two just 9.8 seconds off the top in fourth place.

Meanwhile, Juho Hänninen and Esapekka Lappi were among the last of the drivers to start, and they used their advantage to record a series of strong results – Hänninen scoring one and Lappi three fastest times. Hänninen even led the rally for a time, and was in second place until he spun into a wall on the final stage of Day One.

The highlight of the rally was Lappi's drive in SS5. He had lost use of second gear in SS2 and consequently performed poorly in SS3 and SS4.

Rd 07 #11 Hänninen.

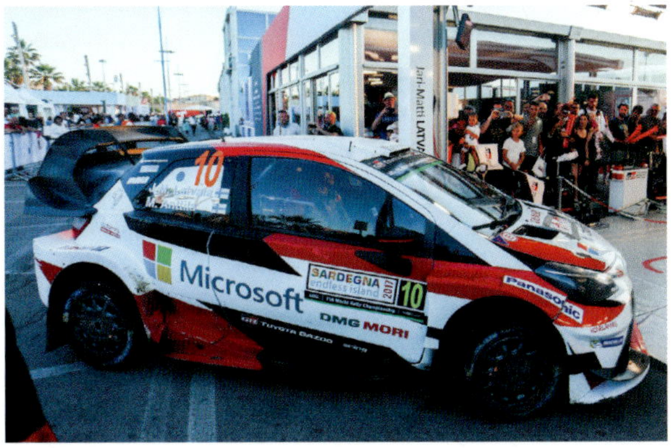

▲ *Rd 07 #10 Latvala.* ▼ *Rd 07 #12 Lappi.* ▲ *Rd 07 #10 Latvala.*

However, in SS5 he recorded his fastest stage time, leading Lappi to joke, "Maybe we only need five gears to win stages!"

From its first event in Mexico, the team had struggled with engine overheating issues in hot climates but gradually came up with countermeasures and good results. After spinning into a wall, Hänninen damaged the front section of his vehicle and cooling fluid spilled out of his car's radiator, but the engine persevered and proved its durability.

With the high temperatures and tough road surface conditions particularly harsh on tyres, many drivers were forced to retire. Despite this, Latvala, Hänninen and Lappi skilfully overcame the challenges and entered the final day in strong positions. Latvala coolly struck the ideal balance between risk and reward, continuing to attack while safeguarding his second place position. Showing driving skills that combined power and youth, Lappi increased his total stage best times to six, winning SS18 and securing a career-high fourth position. Hänninen dropped time as a result of power steering issues, but managed to minimise his losses to finish in sixth.

With five lead changes, Ott Tänak in his Ford Fiesta held on to win the rally by 12 seconds over Toyota's Latvala, with Gazoo capturing an encouraging seven stage victories throughout the event.

Rally Italia Sardegna *Overall results, with 41 finishers*

1st	Ott Tänak/Martin Järveoja	Ford Fiesta WRC	3:25:15.1
2nd	Jari-Matti Latvala/Miikka Anttila	Toyota Yaris WRC	3:25:27.4
3rd	Thierry Neuville/Nicolas Gilsoul	Hyundai i20 Coupe WRC	3:26:22.8
4th	Esapekka Lappi/Janne Ferm	Toyota Yaris WRC	3:27:28.0
6th	Juho Hänninen/Kaj Lindström	Toyota Yaris WRC	3:28:53.6

ROUND 08

Rally Poland
29 June-2 July

Rally Poland is one of the oldest and fastest of the high-speed gravel rallies on the WRC calendar, with the event primarily travelling through grasslands along narrow roads with soft, sand-like surfaces.

Some 47 crews lined up for the Rally Poland in 2017 with drivers competing over 23 stages – although SS6 was cancelled – and covering 195 miles (312km). Occasional heavy rain on the first two days caused havoc for drivers in the slippery conditions with one wheelman saying, "The tyres had zero grip, and I didn't have full control while driving."

As Tommi Mäkinen tells us, Toyota Gazoo Racing excels at high-speed rallies, allowing Jari-Matti Latvala to record successive fastest times in SS3 and SS4 in the early stages of the rally. Latvala's incredible attack was ably supported by the Yaris WRC, which had been optimised for the rally's high speeds.

However, softened by the rain, Poland's roads highlighted new issues for the Gazoo team, as deep ruts began to form along the course. Latvala and Juho Hänninen were dissatisfied with the car's handling in the ruts, and were unable to increase their pace in the way they desired.

As the drivers and engineers worked together for a breakthrough, Latvala finally discovered the right solution and managed to regain speed. In third place and with victory still a distinct possibility, Latvala continued to fight until a minor mechanical issue robbed him of the chance of a podium finish.

Rd 08 #12 Lappi (left) and #11 Hänninen.

Rd 08 #10 Latvala.

Rd 08 #11 Hänninen.

Rd 08 #10 Latvala.

On Day Three, Latvala was forced to stop driving and lost the opportunity to compete with the leaders. Third driver Esapekka Lappi started well but lost a wheel on SS4 forcing him to retire on Day Two, so Latvala's inability to battle for the lead was a severe blow to the Gazoo equipe. However, Hänninen continued to perform doggedly, and so the team was able to gather a large amount of competitive data from the rally. In the end, Hänninen finished in tenth, Latvala in 20th, and Lappi an early retirement.

In an event where the lead changed ten times, Thierry Neuville in his Hyundai won, finishing over 100 seconds ahead of fellow Hyundai teammate and New Zealander Hayden Paddon in his i20. For Toyota, Rally Poland became an event they'd rather forget, with only the bonus points gleaned from the Power Stage to celebrate. The battle for third in the championship was tight after Poland, with Latvala just ahead of Tänak. Toyota was also third, but now a long way behind Ford and Hyundai.

Rally Poland

Overall results, with 40 finishers

1st	Thierry Neuville/Nicolas Gilsoul	Hyundai i20 Coupe WRC	2:40:46.1
2nd	Hayden Paddon/Sebastian Marshall	Hyundai i20 Coupe WRC	2:42:10.0
3rd	Sébastien Ogier/Julien Ingrassia	Ford Fiesta WRC	2:43:06.9
10th	Juho Hänninen/Kaj Lindström	Toyota Yaris WRC	2:45:39.8
20th	Jari-Matti Latvala/Miikka Anttila	Toyota Yaris WRC	3:08:47.1
DNF	Esapekka Lappi/Janne Ferm	Toyota Yaris WRC	—

ROUND 09

Rally Finland

27-30 July

When Toyota's then-president Akio Toyoda visited Finland for the first time in 2014, he was so impressed with the country and its rally courses that he decided to make the country his WRC team's home base and hire four-time WRC drivers' champ Tommi Mäkinen as project leader. That proved to be an inspired move.

Rally Finland is held on gravel roads that wind through forests near Jyväskylä in the central part of the country. Cars and their drivers compete at the absolute limit in a rally that boasts the highest average SS speed in the WRC. Is it any wonder then that the drivers and co-drivers for the three Yaris WRC cars are all Finnish? And might we be surprised that this rally enabled the Yaris to show its full potential while turning out to be Gazoo Racing's best result so far? Not at all.

In dry and sunny conditions, the rally started with 61 entries, but, as expected, the attrition rate was high as the event weaved its way over 25 stages and 196 miles (314km). The famous 'yumps', carried over from the classic 1000 Lakes days, were crowd pleasers, but multiple heavy landings hurt the chances of several favourites.

Meanwhile, in the Toyota camp, Latvala and Lappi were trading fastest times and the lead. Latvala recorded the best time on SS3 – the third stage of the rally – and led the rally standings after SS4. Then Lappi, in only his fourth World Rally event, recorded the fastest times in four consecutive stages, from SS4 to SS7, taking the lead away from Latvala as they entered SS10.

Lappi then repeated his back-to-back top result by posting the four fastest times again in SS9 to SS12, only to see Latvala return the favour by putting down five best times in a row from SS14 to SS18 and snatching the lead away from him. Lappi then posted the quickest time in SS19 to recapture the lead from Latvala, just before the latter suffered

Rd 09 #11 Hänninen.

Rd 09 #12 Lappi.

Rd 09 #10 Latvala.

Rd 09 #12 Lappi.

rare electrical problems that ended his charge to victory. This was Lappi's first WRC win and Toyota's second for the season.

Although not posting any fastest stage times, fellow Finn Juho Hänninen had put in consistently quick times that accumulated enough to allow him to finish on the podium in third place. When Lappi completed the final SS, Mäkinen, Latvala, and Hänninen rushed over and celebrated the victory of their young teammate as if it was their own.

Rally Finland *Overall results, with 42 finishers*

1st	Esapekka Lappi/Janne Ferm	Toyota Yaris WRC	2:29:26.9
2nd	Elfyn Evans/Daniel Barritt	Ford Fiesta WRC	2:30:02.9
3rd	Juho Hänninen/Kaj Lindström	Toyota Yaris WRC	2:30:03.2
21st	Jari-Matti Latvala/Miikka Anttila	Toyota Yaris WRC	2:49:42.7

ROUND 10

Rallye Deutschland

17-20 August

Based in Saarbrücken, Rallye Deutschland features fast tarmac stages that criss-cross vineyards stretching along the Moselle River. With 62 teams entering the event, 21 stages were held over 193 miles (309km), with only one on Day One. In Germany, it was Juho Hänninen's time to shine.

Although the second half of the rally was dry, early rains caused mud from vineyards to spill out onto the course, forcing many drivers to veer off and end up in the scenery. Juho Hänninen was one of them. Luckily, his Yaris WRC only suffered minor damage and he was able to continue without issue, finishing Day Two sixth in the overall standings.

In the gruelling Baumholder Military Training Area SS10 stage, that features huge concrete block barriers called 'hinkelsteins', and concrete roads, Hänninen showed his mettle by posting the fastest time over the rally's longest stage. After that great effort however, a freak impact damaged his dampers causing him to lose significant time, but the Finn still managed to finish Day Three in fifth position overall. He then recorded the best time in SS18 to gain enough points to give him his career-best result at a tarmac rally with an impressive fourth place on the leaderboard.

Jari-Matti Latvala was also satisfied with the state of his Yaris WRC, and at one point he sat in fifth place in the overall standings. However, after initially being delayed with an ignition system

Rd 010
▲ *Left: #11 Hänninen.*
▲ *#10 Latvala.*
◀ *#11 Hänninen.*

▼ *Rd 010*
#12 Lappi.

issue, then suffering a puncture on Day Three, he fell out of contention and finished the rally in seventh place.

Rally Finland winner Esapekka Lappi knew how to hustle along German roads and win in a WRC2 class 'R5' machine. But driving in Germany in a much faster World Rally car for the first time was a challenge for the WRC newbie. He damaged his suspension, was forced to retire on Day Two and then could not achieve the times he wanted on Day Three. After intensive discussion with his engineers, they found a solution that not only enabled Lappi to improve his performance, but gave the Finn a fastest time in SS19. He would finish the rally in 21st.

Despite a strong challenge from Citroën's Andreas Mikkelsen, who posted two fastest stage times, Tänak led for most of the rally and went onto win by over 16 seconds. Meanwhile, the Toyota wheelmen picked up useful Power Stage bonuses.

Rallye Deutschland *Overall results, with 54 finishers*

1st	Ott Tänak/Martin Järveoja	Ford Fiesta WRC	2:57:31.7
2nd	Andreas Mikkelsen/Anders Jaeger	Citroën C3 WRC	2:57:48.1
3rd	Sébastien Ogier/Julien Ingrassia	Ford Fiesta WRC	2:58:02.1
4th	Juho Hänninen/Kaj Lindström	Toyota Yaris WRC	2:59:20.9
7th	Jari-Matti Latvala/Miikka Anttila	Toyota Yaris WRC	3:01:29.9
21st	Esapekka Lappi/Janne Ferm	Toyota Yaris WRC	3:15:36.9

ROUND 11

Rally Catalunya

6-8 October

Commonly known as Rally Catalunya, Rally de España earns classic rally status as one of the few truly 'mixed' rallies left, boasting tarmac surfaces combined with gravel roads. The two surfaces challenge service teams who must utilise their short 75 minutes of working time to swap over the gravel setups used on Day One – including dampers, springs, brakes, gears and tyres – to tarmac settings for Day Two and Three.

Tracing its roots back to 1957, it was first added to the WRC calendar in 1991, and has become a firm favourite with motorsport enthusiasts ever since. With 70 starters, the rally was run over 19 stages covering 195 miles (312km), although the total distance was 811 miles (1298km) if one includes the road sections between them.

Toyota had proven its winning pace and durability on gravel rallies like Rally Finland, but the Yaris' tarmac performance had been spotty at best. In Spain, with unfamiliar gravel conditions on Day One, all three Toyota drivers posted uncompetitive slow times.

After some major modifications, it appeared that Toyota was on the right track when Jari-Matti Latvala recorded the fastest time on SS4. But then on SS5, Lady Luck ran out and the Finn was forced to retire when he hit the car's lower frame severely damaging the lubrication system.

Latvala's short-lived success on tarmac fortunately found its way to Juho Hänninen who recorded back-to-back fastest stage times in SS8 and SS9, finishing in fourth place overall on Day Two, proving that the Yaris WRC could compete with the rally leaders on tarmac.

Lappi had showed in Finland that he performed well in high speed rallies, but the ultra-high speed cornering on Spain's tarmac and the extremely strong tyre grip on offer proved challenging for him, causing him to lower his pace and fall behind in the time slots. On SS9

▲ *Rd 011 #10 Latvala.* ▼ *Rd 011 #12 Lappi.*

▼ ▶ *Rd 011 #11 Hänninen.*

Rd 11 #12 Lappi.

however, he found his rhythm and managed to post the second fastest time before recording the third quickest times in the following two stages, jumping four places from tenth to sixth in the overall standings. Unfortunately, Lappi's luck ran out too when he ran wide on a corner, struck a guard rail in SS15 on Day Three and was forced to retire.

Meanwhile, Hänninen, following on from his fourth place in the previous rally in Germany, completed the Spanish rally on Day Three in fourth place again.

Latvala and Lappi may have both retired but this event was a particularly poor result for Hyundai as well, with not one car finishing inside the top ten. In contrast, it was the end of Kris Meeke's unlucky streak when he captured his first victory of the season in his Citroën C3.

Rally Catalunya *Overall results, with 53 finishers*

1st	Kris Meeke/Paul Nagle	Citroën C3 WRC	3:01:21.1
2nd	Sébastien Ogier/Julien Ingrassia	Ford Fiesta WRC	3:01:49.1
3rd	Ott Tänak/Martin Järveoja	Ford Fiesta WRC	3:01:54.1
4th	Juho Hänninen/Kaj Lindström	Toyota Yaris WRC	3:02:15.2
DNF	Jari-Matti Latvala/Miikka Anttila	Toyota Yaris WRC	—
DNF	Esapekka Lappi/Janne Ferm	Toyota Yaris WRC	—

ROUND 12

Wales Rally GB
26-29 October

Boasting complex topography and vastly differing levels of grip on the Welsh gravel, Wales Rally GB is well known on the rally circuit as an event that can experience four seasons in a single day. When it rains, which it invariably does, the gravel becomes waterlogged, turning fast corners into slow muddy bends. The challenge here for engineers is to optimise car settings for both dry and wet conditions.

Some 75 teams started the rally, covering 21 stages over 190 miles (304km). The shakedown and ceremonial start took place on Day One and was typically damp at times.

The event began in semi-dry conditions, with the surface dry in patches, but, as more cars completed the course, the surface became extremely muddy and grip levels varied wildly even in the course of a single SS. All three Toyota drivers had difficulties adapting to the tricky conditions. With no designated service period during Day Two, drivers had to fend for themselves as conditions changed, with Jari-Matti Latvala finishing the day in fifth position. After the team worked on the cars at the end of Day Two, all three Yaris WRCs handled significantly better the following day.

One unique issue of Rally GB is mud accumulation on the underbody and how it can alter a car's front-rear weight distribution, which in turn impacts the vehicle's handling. Large clumps of mud sticking to the rear underbody can adversely shift weight to the rear end, which would lighten the front and cause the car to understeer. Luckily, drivers and their service teams were able to overcome these issues and push hard.

On Day Three, Latvala upped his pace and rose to fourth overall, just 4.1 seconds behind third place. Latvala eventually finished fifth and Esapekka Lappi ninth. Rally GB was Juho Hänninen's final rally for Toyota Gazoo Racing. After struggling to adapt in the early stages, he rapidly raised his level of performance, recording the fifth fastest time on SS10 and the second fastest on SS11. However, on SS14, a short, tarmac stage, Hänninen mis-timed his braking and crashed into a hay bale, damaging the suspension and body of his Yaris WRC, forcing him to retire.

Completely dominating Rally GB and posting the fastest stage times in no less than nine stages, it turned out to be a fitting win for Elfyn Evans in his Fiesta on home ground. Meanwhile, Evans' teammate Sébastien Ogier sealed the drivers' title – his fifth in a row!

Rd 012 Top to bottom: #12 Lappi; #10 Latvala; #10 Latvala; #11 Hänninen.

Wales Rally GB *Overall results, with 65 finishers*

1st	Elfyn Evans/Daniel Barritt	Ford Fiesta WRC	2:57:00.6
2nd	Thierry Neuville/Nicolas Gilsoul	Hyundai i20 Coupe WRC	2:57:37.9
3rd	Sébastien Ogier/Julien Ingrassia	Ford Fiesta WRC	2:57:45.8
5th	Jari-Matti Latvala/Miikka Anttila	Toyota Yaris WRC	2:57:50.9
9th	Esapekka Lappi/Janne Ferm	Toyota Yaris WRC	2:59:47.1
DNF	Juho Hänninen/Kaj Lindström	Toyota Yaris WRC	—

ROUND 13

Rally Australia
17-19 November

Run in Coffs Harbour, north of Sydney, Rally Australia is about as far away from the team's European base in Finland as you can get. Drivers and team staff first have to get physically used to the drier Australian summer and environment before starting the rally week.

The rally had 33 starters over 21 stages, which was ultimately reduced to 19, wiping 19 miles (31km) off the event that was originally scheduled for 199 miles (318km).

After leaving Juho Hänninen in Europe, Toyota arrived in Australia with just two cars. In describing the road conditions in Australia, Esapekka Lappi said, "The gravel course here is not like any other rallies. It is difficult to describe the type of road that it is."

In Thursday's shakedown, Latvala and Lappi tried out different suspension settings. Latvala started off confidently, but after suffering front-end damage in SS1, it became difficult for him to generate sufficient downforce, leading to poor handling.

The Finn also had problems with his intercom wiring, which interfered with his ability to communicate with co-driver Miikka Anttila. So, in a rare development that drivers dread, Latvala was forced to drive without pace notes. In SS2, he repaired the wiring himself and had his team repair the damaged body later in the day, enabling him to push hard again.

Meanwhile, Lappi experienced a power steering problem in SS2, and was forced to contend with heavy steering without any power assist, but somehow managed to finish all of the morning SSs, albeit having lost a lot of time.

On Day Two, Latvala's team made the right tyre choice allowing him to record the second

Rd 013 #11 Lappi.

Rd 013 #11 Lappi.

Rd 013 #10 Latvala.

best time in SS9 and the best time in SS10. Day Three brought torrential rain that caused 'river-like' flows surging down some downhill sections. Lappi said, "You have no control at all. It's like you are on a boat." In the final SS Power Stage, which has bonus points, he recorded the third fastest time and finished his debut season in sixth place overall.

Starting 20 seconds behind first place on Day Three, Latvala pushed to the max on slippery roads and managed to narrow the difference down to just 9.9 seconds in SS18. In the final Power Stage, and in full attack mode, Latvala was matching the leader's time until his left front wheel clipped a tree, damaging the suspension and forcing him to retire.

Hyundai's Neuville led from SS10 and never looked like losing. He beat Ford's Ott Tänak by 22 seconds to finish second to Ogier in the driver rankings.

Rally Australia *Overall results, with 25 finishers*

1st	Thierry Neuville/Nicolas Gilsoul	Hyundai i20 Coupe WRC	2:35:44.8
2nd	Ott Tänak/Martin Järveoja	Ford Fiesta WRC	2:36:07.3
3rd	Hayden Paddon/Sebastian Marshall	Hyundai i20 Coupe WRC	2:36:43.9
6th	Esapekka Lappi/Janne Ferm	Toyota Yaris WRC	2:39:34.3
DNF	Jari-Matti Latvala/Miikka Anttila	Toyota Yaris WRC	—

2017 SUMMARY

The season reviewed in a way that provides a quick reference from a Toyota/Gazoo perspective, with driver performance, round by round (overall position, followed by the Power Stage position in brackets), and year-end positions within the FIA WRC championship.

	Latvala	Hänninen	Lappi
Rd 01	2nd (–)	16th (3rd)	– (–)
Rd 02	1st (1st)	23rd (9th)	– (–)
Rd 03	6th (4th)	7th (9th)	– (–)
Rd 04	4th (1st)	DNF (–)	– (–)
Rd 05	5th (5th)	7th (8th)	– (–)
Rd 06	9th (7th)	7th (11th)	10th (4th)
Rd 07	2nd (5th)	6th (10th)	4th (1st)
Rd 08	20th (1st)	10th (10th)	DNF (–)
Rd 09	21st (4th)	3rd (5th)	1st (6th)
Rd 10	7th (3rd)	4th (11th)	21st (2nd)
Rd 11	DNF (–)	4th (5th)	DNF (–)
Rd 12	5th (3rd)	DNF (–)	9th (7th)
Rd 13	DNF (–)	– (–)	6th (3rd)

Drivers

1st	Sébastien Ogier	Ford	232
2nd	Thierry Neuville	Hyundai	208
3rd	Ott Tänak	Ford	191
4th	Jari-Matti Latvala	Toyota	136
9th	Juho Hänninen	Toyota	71
11th	Esapekka Lappi	Toyota	62

Co-drivers

1st	Julien Ingrassia	Ford	232
2nd	Nicolas Gilsoul	Hyundai	208
3rd	Martin Järveoja	Ford	191
4th	Miikka Anttila	Toyota	136
8th	Kaj Lindström	Toyota	71
10th	Janne Ferm	Toyota	62

NB: Points totals include Power Stage bonuses for drivers and co-drivers.

Manufacturers

1st	Ford	M-Sport World Rally Team	428
2nd	Hyundai	Hyundai Motorsport	345
3rd	Toyota	Toyota Gazoo Racing WRT	251

The 2018 Season

The 2018 season was again contested over 13 rounds, with Rally Poland being replaced by the Rally of Turkey after several safety concerns failed to be addressed. Otherwise, apart from a little shuffling, things looked much the same as they did in 2017 as far as the main WRC calendar was concerned; the Junior World Rally Championship was run over only five rounds this year.

2018 Season Rounds

	Rally	Dates	Surface
	Monte Carlo Rally	25 -28 January	Tarmac
	Rally Sweden	15-18 February	Snow
	Rally Mexico	8-11 March	Gravel
	Tour de Corse	5-8 April	Tarmac
	Rally Argentina	26-29 April	Gravel
	Rally de Portugal	17-20 May	Gravel
	Rally Italia Sardegna	7-10 June	Gravel
	Rally Finland	26-29 July	Gravel
	Rallye Deutschland	16-19 August	Tarmac
	Rally of Turkey	13-16 September	Gravel
	Wales Rally GB	4-7 October	Gravel
	Rally Catalunya	25-28 October	Mixed
	Rally Australia	15-18 November	Gravel

FIA rule changes and season prospects

There were no major changes to the rules for 2018, with the more sensible placing of manmade obstacles being written in stone and, from the start of April, tighter regulations on clocking-in times for Power Stages to eliminate unfair advantages gleaned from deliberately turning up late in order to tackle better road conditions.

It was the same four teams as those present in 2017 contesting the World Rally Championship proper. Ford increased its support for the M-Sport outfit (as reigning champions, it would have been foolish not to get closer to Malcolm Wilson's team), while Citroën cut back on its rally programme a little, although Sébastien Loeb made his services available for the odd event, in addition to helping improve the C3 WRC over the off-season. All four major teams were now running exclusively on Michelin rubber, incidentally.

The Gazoo team cars and their drivers

The 2018 Toyota Yaris WRC was unveiled at the Autosport International Show in the English Midlands a couple of weeks ahead of the Monte. Given the lack of changes in the regulations, naturally the revisions applied to the new car were refinements of the existing package – evolution rather than revolution …

The main difference, and the easiest to spot, was the new front-end styling aimed at improving aerodynamics and reducing lift. The cooling was enhanced at the same time, which was a welcome upgrade on events staged in warmer climes. Beyond that, one would have been hard pushed to

The WRC warriors for the new season.

tell a 2018 car from its immediate predecessor – even the livery and wheel designs were the same, although the eagle-eyed would have noticed the Microsoft logo replaced by a DMG Mori one on the trailing edge of the huge rear wing.

Team Principal Tommi Mäkinen was on hand in Birmingham, and stated: “After a very pleasing first season, we are excited to build on that in the year ahead. We saw last year that the car was already capable of winning rallies, but the competition also allowed us to discover areas that we could improve. We're going to keep learning this year, too, as part of our mission to make ever-better cars.”

Meanwhile, the driver line-up included Jari-Matti Latvala and Esapekka Lappi, who were retained at the Gazoo equipe from the previous season, with the Finnish pair duly joined by the Estonian wheelman Ott Tänak for 2018.

Latvala continued for yet another season with Miikka Anttila in the seat beside him (Anttila had been navigating for Latvala for a decade by this time), hoping to improve on his fourth place in last year's championship.

Responsible for one of the two Toyota wins in 2017, Esapekka Lappi was also looking to move up the final placings, teaming up with the experienced Janne Ferm again. Lappi was born in southern Finland in 1991, and began his rallying career at the tender age of 20. He was soon signed up by Skoda, and managed to claim the ERC title in 2014. He also won the WRC2 championship

The Toyota Yaris WRC in 2018 guise.

with the Czech maker in 2016, giving Mäkinen the confidence to sign his fellow countryman for the then-new Gazoo Racing WRT outfit.

Partnered by Martin Järveoja since 2017, Ott Tänak actually finished last year's season ahead of Latvala, so in replacing Hänninen (ironically, the man that beat him to the SWRC crown in 2011), he was an important addition to the Gazoo family. Tänak looks incredibly young, but was actually born in 1987, and had started his career competing in his national championships as far back as 2008. He signed a five-year contract with Ford in 2011, but couldn't get into winning ways until 2017, when he won two rallies for the M-Sport team. His time had obviously come, and Mäkinen, having spotted his potential, wanted to nurture his skills and make him an even better driver.

▲ *Ott Tänak.*

◀ *Esapekka Lappi.*

ROUND 01

Monte Carlo Rally
25-28 January

The 86th running of the famous Monte was based in the Hautes-Alpes region of France with the start taking place in the prestigious Casino Square in Monaco. After the shakedown on Wednesday, some 67 crews tackled 17 stages over 243 miles (389km). Citroën had two cars – the other main teams had three each.

The big news for Toyota's Gazoo Racing team was the addition to the driver line-up of Ott Tänak who had replaced Juho Hänninen. Even though SS1 had numerous slippery frozen patches that caused grief for some drivers, Yaris WRC pilot Esapekka Lappi started well by recording the third fastest time on the first special stage.

Rd 01 #9 Lappi.

▲ *Rd 01 #7 Latvala.*

▲▼ *Rd 01 #8 Tänak.*

Meanwhile, Tänak showed his mettle by winning SS3 on Day Two, and rising to fourth in the overall standings. He then placed second or third in the following stages, won SS6, and climbed to second overall.

Day Three presented a literal shopping list of surface conditions – dry, wet, fresh snow, half-melted snow, frozen, and muddy – making it difficult to guarantee that vehicle settings and tire choices were 100 percent correct. But even with the compromises made, the Gazoo drivers pushed hard, capturing good results.

Tänak won SS10 and SS11, while Jari-Matti Latvala, who had risen from fifth to third overall on Day Two, maintained the stable pace of a veteran driver. Lappi temporarily dropped to fifth overall due to a puncture but, thereafter, recovered strongly to finish Day Three fourth in the rankings, with the other Yaris WRC models holding onto second and third place..

With roads honeycombed by snow and icy patches, the final day started in the French mountains to the north of Monaco. Wanting to maintain their positions, Tänak and Latvala drove sparingly and completed all four SSs. Their steady pace allowed Tänak to finish in second place overall while Latvala picked up third, giving the Gazoo team a string podium finish. Sitting in fourth place at the end of Day Three, Lappi however dropped several places after driving off course in the Power Stage, falling to seventh overall, and denying the team of a 2-3-4 finish.

At the rally to watch the team's progress, Gazoo Racing Company's president, Shigeki Tomoyama, was pleased with the double podium but made it clear what the team's aim was in 2018. "Our goal this year is to fight for the title and become champions. For this reason, we must further refine the cars and fight for victory."

Sébastien Ogier in his Ford had led from the start, winning four stages, and finished in first place nearly one minute ahead of Tänak.

Monte Carlo Rally *Overall results, with 47 finishers*

1st	Sébastien Ogier/Julien Ingrassia	Ford Fiesta WRC	4:18:55.5
2nd	Ott Tänak/Martin Järveoja	Toyota Yaris WRC	4:19:53.8
3rd	Jari-Matti Latvala/Miikka Anttila	Toyota Yaris WRC	4:20:47.5
7th	Esapekka Lappi/Janne Ferm	Toyota Yaris WRC	4:23:53.0

ROUND 02

Rally Sweden

15-18 February

For the Gazoo rally team, Rally Sweden holds a special place in the team's heart as it was their first victory after making a memorable 2017 comeback to competition. The Yaris WRC had performed superbly and the drivers, especially Latvala, excelled in the snowy conditions. They were keen to emulate that success but it wasn't to be.

This year, some 66 crews took to the ceremonial start, with Citroën entering a third car. The rally was held over 19 stages covering 196 miles (314km), although that distance rose to 875 miles (1400km) if one includes all road sections.

After the first few cars had driven through SS1, the fresh snow was driven away to reveal a surface of hard-packed ice underneath, allowing the studded tires to grip and achieve their full potential.

Ott Tänak recorded the best time on Day One's Super Special Stage, while Jari-Matti Latvala was second. For the woodland SSs that began on Day Two, the starting order was determined by driver placings in the overall championship standings.

For this reason, Tänak, who finished second at the previous rally in Monte Carlo, would start second, Latvala third, and Esapekka Lappi seventh. On Day Two, Latvala's fears were realized with the majority of stages on Day Two covered with fresh snow. Tänak managed to finish fastest on SS2, but, from SS3 onwards, he lost a lot of time due to the soft snow. Teammate Latvala suffered the same fate.

Ruts caused by competitors in a secondary event called Rally Sweden Historic, hampered the top placed drivers in the early stages of the afternoon. The later starters therefore had an advantage as course conditions improved, leading to insurmountable time gaps being created. For the duration of Rally Sweden, both Latvala and Tänak battled hard but finished in a disappointing seventh and ninth place respectively.

Rd 02 #8 Tänak.

Rd 02 #9 Lappi.

Rd 02 #9 Lappi.

Rd 02 #7 Latvala.

Tänak commented that "If the driving conditions had been the same for everyone, then the Yaris WRC would have won – its performance on snow is that good." A collision with Citroën's Kris Meeke on SS13 who had crashed, did not help his case either.

Making his first appearance in Rally Sweden, Lappi had showed early speed and was second at one time. But when he hit a snow wall in SS6, he lost 30 seconds, dropping him to seventh. He recovered miraculously on the final day to win two stages (including the Power Stage, earning extra bonus points) – a result that placed him in fourth overall at the finish.

With none of the top four drivers having any chance of winning this year's rally due to the conditions, Hyundai's Thierry Neuville quickly took the lead, and held onto it until the end. This result elevated him and his team to number one spot in the championship standings.

Rally Sweden *Overall results, with 58 finishers*

1st	Thierry Neuville/Nicolas Gilsoul	Hyundai i20 Coupe WRC	2:52:13.1
2nd	Craig Breen/Scott Martin	Citroën C3 WRC	2:52:32.9
3rd	Andreas Mikkelsen/Anders Jaeger	Hyundai i20 Coupe WRC	2:52:41.4
4th	Esapekka Lappi/Janne Ferm	Toyota Yaris WRC	2:52:58.9
7th	Jari-Matti Latvala/Miikka Anttila	Toyota Yaris WRC	2:54:18.0
9th	Ott Tänak/Martin Järveoja	Toyota Yaris WRC	2:55:57.5

ROUND 03

Rally Mexico

8-11 March

In hot, dry and dusty conditions, Rally Mexico got underway with 29 starters, covering 22 stages over 215 miles (344km). Having won this rally in 2016, Jari-Matti Latvala was very positive about the team's chances this year, although he did voice concern about the event's 2000m-plus high altitude driving and above-average temperatures.

To address that concern, Gazoo engineers had taken a Yaris WRC back to Japan at the end of 2017 to solve its engine issues in hot, high altitude conditions. The team had experienced significant difficulties in Mexico the previous year, and were hoping for a vast improvement.

Things started out well with Tänak driving superbly, winning the final three stages on Day Two and ending the day in third overall. Latvala and Lappi, on the other hand, struggled. This was Lappi's first appearance at Rally Mexico, while Latvala was significantly handicapped by being third on the start list and having to face slippery gravel conditions. The mechanical issues

Rd 03 #8 Tänak.

Rd 03 #9 Lappi.

reappeared, however, and both drivers were dogged by problems with their engine cooling systems.

Days Two's slow and twisty sections meant lower average speeds, which in turn translated into engine cooling problems. To prevent overheating, the team therefore had to limit engine output, forcing Latvala and Lappi to drive with their engine performance capped.

Only Tänak was able to avoid significant restrictions on engine output, due in part to his different style of driving. Engineers quickly modified the cooling systems allowing Latvala to improve his pace and climb to seventh overall. However, an alternator failure sidelined him that day, while Lappi had gone off course in SS7 forcing him to retire. Only Tänak was able to hold the fort, proving that the Yaris was indeed competitive, rising up to third place just 11 seconds off the lead.

On Day Three, the team's worse-case scenario happened when Tänak was forced to retire due to a turbo malfunction that caused the car to lose power. On the Final Day, Latvala recorded his first stage win of the rally, while Tänak, whose car had been repaired, won the last two stages including the Power Stage. At the finish, Latvala was the leading Gazoo team driver in eighth, Lappi was 11th, and Tänak 14th

Winning five stages on his way to victory, Ford's Sébastien Ogier was supreme, although the legendary Sébastien Loeb showed he still had what it takes via a guest appearance for Citroën. Meanwhile, Toyota's men were lucky to pick up bonuses in the Power Stage.

Rally Mexico *Overall results, with 21 finishers*

1st	Sébastien Ogier/Julien Ingrassia	Ford Fiesta WRC	3:54:08.0
2nd	Dani Sordo/Carlos del Barrio	Hyundai i20 Coupe WRC	3:55:11.6
3rd	Kris Meeke/Paul Nagle	Citroën C3 WRC	3:55:27.2
8th	Jari-Matti Latvala/Miikka Anttila	Toyota Yaris WRC	4:09:45.1
11th	Esapekka Lappi/Janne Ferm	Toyota Yaris WRC	4:25:05.8
14th	Ott Tänak/Martin Järveoja	Toyota Yaris WRC	4:56:50.8

Rd 03 #7 Latvala.

▲ *Rd 04 #8 Tänak.*

▼ *Rd 04 #9 Lappi.*

ROUND 04

Tour de Corse

5-8 April

The Tour de Corse – Rallye de France – welcomed 87 starters in mostly dry and sunny conditions, ready to do battle over 12 stages and 209 miles (334km). All major teams entered three cars except Citroën who only brought two. Boasting more than 65 years of history, this traditional tarmac rally has been held on the island of Corsica since 1956.

As Gazoo team driver in 2017, Juho Hänninen had shown great skill on snow and gravel, as well as tarmac, and so the team used his valuable contributions during testing to optimize the Yaris WRC's performance. Thanks to Hänninen's input, all three Toyota drivers felt confident starting the event.

However, when the rally began, the Yaris WRC found it difficult to replicate that same performance. With SS1 wet in parts, Tänak

Rd 04 #7 Latvala.

Rd 04 #8 Tänak

and Latvala struggled, complaining about the car's behaviour on the wetter sections of road. However, pushing hard, Tänak still managed to finish the stage some 18 seconds adrift of the leader, although he recorded the third fastest time on the 49-kilometer-long SS1. Lappi was 43 seconds and Latvala 46 seconds behind. SS2 was a shorter stage, and Lappi was second fastest, just two seconds off first. Latvala and Tänak also both managed to stay within about seven seconds of the leader.

After adjusting ride height and damping force, Latvala increased his pace while Lappi, also happy with his car's handling, excelled by recording the fastest time of SS4. Latvala placed second, just 1.7 seconds behind. On SS7, all three drivers clocked leading times, Tänak first, Lappi third, and Latvala fourth. Then, in the repeat afternoon stages, Lappi laid down the two fastest times.

In a rare result, Tänak was joint-fastest alongside Lappi on SS10 – the final stage of Day Two – and rose up the overall standings from fourth to second. Latvala, meanwhile, had run the back of his car into a tree on SS8, damaging the car's roll cage, and forcing him to retire from the event. In the 55km-long SS11, Tänak was an impressive winner, finishing 12 seconds ahead of Kris Meeke – a result that secured him second place in the overall standings. Driving superbly, Lappi had equalled Tänak's time at the first split in SS11, but a puncture soon afterwards saw him lose almost two minutes changing a tyre, placing him in sixth overall.

In Corsica, Toyota performed superbly with Lappi winning four stages and Tänak two, and his podium finish was a great result. Sébastien Ogier was again untouchable from start to finish, although Lappi and Loeb kept him on his toes.

Tour de Corse *Overall results, with 71 finishers*

1st	Sébastien Ogier/Julien Ingrassia	Ford Fiesta WRC	3:26:52.7
2nd	Ott Tänak/Martin Järveoja	Toyota Yaris WRC	3:27:28.8
3rd	Thierry Neuville/Nicolas Gilsoul	Hyundai i20 Coupe WRC	3:28:00.2
6th	Esapekka Lappi/Janne Ferm	Toyota Yaris WRC	3:29:26.2
DNF	Jari-Matti Latvala/Miikka Anttila	Toyota Yaris WRC	—

ROUND 05

Rally Argentina
26-29 April

The Rally Argentina has been around since 1980, and been on the World Rally Championship calendar virtually every year since. Its rough, narrow and dusty roads make it a challenge for car and driver alike, and if the rains come, the river crossings are as spectacular as the Argentinian scenery.

In a rally that proved to be a major turnaround for Toyota's fortunes, only 27 cars entered, with three cars for each of the four big teams. The rally was held over 18 stages covering 224 miles (358km), but adding in liaison distances took the event total up to 812 miles (1300km); the typical South American rutted dirt tracks thankfully stayed dry throughout the event.

Having suffered several issues in Argentina in 2017, engineers ensured that ride height and damping force were optimally set to ensure that the Yaris WRCs did not bottom out as they had in the previous year.

In the opening Super Special Stage, Ott Tänak recorded the second fastest time. On SS3, Jari-Matti Latvala, who had been in third position overall after SS2, damaged his front suspension after he struck a rock. This collision damaged the engine's lubrication system, forcing him to abandon the rally. Tänak meanwhile, went on the win this stage as well as SS4.

In the afternoon stages, which were repeats of the morning SSs, Tänak blitzed the field by winning the next three stages from SS6 to SS8. Then, on the following morning, he repeated that brilliant effort by posting the fastest times in SS9 through SS11, giving him six consecutive stage wins and putting him firmly in the lead. He also won SS13 and SS14, giving him ten stage victories altogether and a 46 second lead over second place. The Estonian's victory was his third rally win in total – and his first since joining the Gazoo team.

Competing in his first-ever Rally Argentina, Esapekka Lappi still managed to finish in eighth place even after suffering four punctures. In an explanation from the team as to why Lappi got so many punctures, apparently Lappi mimics Tänak's precision driving, but tends to operate the car differently and take slightly different lines, exposing him to more loose rocks.

While this rally was all about Tänak, who took the lead early on Friday, Lappi did well considering his misfortunes, and Latvala was forced to drop out with lubrication system damage.

Rd 05 #7 Latvala.

Rd 05 #8 Tänak.

Rd 05 #9 Lappi.

Rd 05 #8 Tänak (right) with Järveoja.

Rally Argentina *Overall results, with 19 finishers*

1st	Ott Tänak/Martin Järveoja	Toyota Yaris WRC	3:43:28.9
2nd	Thierry Neuville/Nicolas Gilsoul	Hyundai i20 Coupe WRC	3:44:06.6
3rd	Dani Sordo/Carlos del Barrio	Hyundai i20 Coupe WRC	3:44:44.6
8th	Esapekka Lappi/Janne Ferm	Toyota Yaris WRC	3:48:01.5
DNF	Jari-Matti Latvala/Miikka Anttila	Toyota Yaris WRC	–

ROUND 06

Rally de Portugal

17-20 May

Based in Braga in the north of the country, Rally de Portugal welcomed 87 crews to compete in 20 dusty and rock-strewn stages over 224 miles (358km) in what is regarded as the most 'standard' of the WRC gravel rallies.

Day One saw the teams carry out their shakedowns and compete in a short SS1 only. Ott Tänak won the opening Super Special Stage, which was set on a rallycross circuit, and so secured first place in the start list. However, on SS2 – the opening stage of Day Two – multiple large stones in the cornering line struck the front underside of Tänak's car, damaging his engine and forcing the Estonian to retire. On SS3, Jari-Matti Latvala drove over a large stone on the inside of a corner and

Rd 06 #8 Tänak.

▲ *Rd 06 #9 Lappi.*

▲ *Rd 06 #7 Latvala.*

◀ *Rd 06 #9 Lappi.*

damaged his front-right suspension. Unable to continue, he had to stop his car on the course.

After engineers repaired the damage that night, Latvala was able to rejoin the rally on Day Three, but the time already lost meant that Toyota could no longer push for a podium finish.

Course conditions continued to deteriorate. The more the rally cars sped over the roads, the more the surface conditions worsened. Esapekka Lappi, at the wheel of the No 9 Yaris WRC, was unable to hide his surprise at the unexpectedly rough conditions: "The surface conditions during the afternoon stages were among the worst I have ever experienced. They were worse even than Argentina!"

Lappi struggled during the morning stages of Day Two, and fell to 11th overall, some 26 seconds behind the leader. The Finn had been confident of challenging for a podium position when he started the rally, so this was an unforeseen setback. However, the main reason for Lappi's lacklustre performance was the fact he was unable to generate sufficient tyre grip, and he was therefore unable to attack as much as he would have liked.

The team modified his suspension settings which restored his confidence in the Yaris and helped him to elevate his speed on Day Three. He recorded two top-three SS times and engaged in a hard-fought battle with Ford's Teemu Suninen and Hyundai's Dani Sordo for third place. On Day Four, the final day of the rally, Lappi was even quicker, posting top-three times on each of the day's five SSs. On SS16 and SS20 which was the designated Power Stage, Lappi recorded the fastest times of all, giving him fifth overall.

The rally lead swapped half a dozen times on Day Two before Hyundai's Thierry Neuville took command, winning four stages and putting him in first place in the championship.

Rally de Portugal *Overall results, with 45 finishers*

Pos	Driver/Co-driver	Car	Time
1st	Thierry Neuville/Nicolas Gilsoul	Hyundai i20 Coupe WRC	3:49:46.6
2nd	Elfyn Evans/Daniel Barritt	Ford Fiesta WRC	3:50:26.6
3rd	Teemu Suninen/Mikko Markkula	Ford Fiesta WRC	3:50:33.9
5th	Esapekka Lappi/Janne Ferm	Toyota Yaris WRC	3:50:51.3
24th	Jari-Matti Latvala/Miikka Anttila	Toyota Yaris WRC	4:38:36.9
DNF	Ott Tänak/Martin Järveoja	Toyota Yaris WRC	—

ROUND 07

Rally Italia Sardegna

7-10 June

The second largest island in the Mediterranean Sea, Sardinia played host to the seventh rally of the season – Rally Italia Sardegna. With 45 starters for 2018, and only two Citroëns, the competitors drove over 20 stages covering 196 miles (314km) in wet conditions for the first two days.

Jari-Matti Latvala in the No 7 Yaris WRC, who finished Day Two in third place overall, commented: "As far as I can remember, it hasn't rained at this rally for about 10 years." Involved in several accidents, Latvala had been on a poor run of form over the last few rallies.

Ott Tänak rebounded from his poor finish in Portugal to set the best time of SS4. Going into SS9, the final stage of Day Two, Tänak was in third place overall, when his front end hit the ground hard while landing a jump, damaging the car's cooling system and forcing him to retire. Mechanics repaired his car allowing him to rejoin the rally on Day Three.

In the previous year, Esapekka Lappi had secured fourth overall in his first ever Rally Italia Sardegna in a World Rally Car. On SS2, the first stage of Day Two, he was the victim of a slow puncture, so was unable to drive as fast as he wanted and dropped to tenth overall. Lappi recovered on SS6, recording the second fastest time, and on SS9, he set the second fastest time after teammate Latvala's winning run to improve his position to fourth overall.

By the end of Day Two, both Latvala and Lappi were in a position to challenge the top of the leaderboard having engaged in a fierce battle. On Day Three, Lappi managed to close the gap to Latvala before the latter once again pulled away to hold a six second lead. Latvala then recorded the second fastest time on SS12, followed by a fastest stage time for Lappi on SS13. Even Tänak got back into the action, setting the best time on SS10.

Rd 07 #9 Lappi.

After completing SS16, the final stage of Day Three, Latvala's Yaris WRC suffered an unexpected problem with its alternator, forcing them to retire for the day. This result pushed Lappi into third place overall but, because there were acceptable gaps to second and fourth, the Finn decided to take few risks, giving him his first third (podium finish) of the season. Meanwhile Latvala finished in seventh while Tänak placed ninth.

Sébastien Ogier had led for most of the rally, but thanks to the Ford driver's silly mistake with a time card, Thierry Neuville nudged ahead in the very last stage to consolidate the championship lead.

◀ *Rd 07*
#8 Tänak.

▼ *Rd 07*
(Left) #7
Latvala.
▼ *#9 Lappi.*

Rally Italia Sardegna *Overall results, with 34 finishers*

1st	Thierry Neuville/Nicolas Gilsoul	Hyundai i20 Coupe WRC	3:29:18.7
2nd	Sébastien Ogier/Julien Ingrassia	Ford Fiesta WRC	3:29:19.4
3rd	Esapekka Lappi/Janne Ferm	Toyota Yaris WRC	3:31:15.0
7th.	Jari-Matti Latvala/Miikka Anttila	Toyota Yaris WRC	3:40:40.8
9th	Ott Tänak/Martin Järveoja	Toyota Yaris WRC	3:42:36.9

ROUND 08

Rally Finland

26-29 July

The 67 starters in this year's Rally Finland were greeted by a very different course boasting updates to around 65 percent of the stages. Higher than average summer temperatures and new narrower roads combined to create looser than normal gravel surfaces. The rally was held over 23 stages covering 198 miles (317km), although it was 892 miles (1427km) including transport distance. Dry throughout, the rally turned out to be a shining moment for Toyota, with all Yaris WRC drivers trading fastest stage times.

As the third placed driver in the championship, Ott Tänak started in third and duly showed his dominance in Finland by posting the SS1's fastest time to finish the first day in top spot. On Day Two, when the rally switched to gravel stages, Tänak was again fastest in SS2. On this approximately 20km long Special Stage, the two drivers who started ahead of the Toyota driver were some 15 to 20 seconds slower – revealing just how slippery a surface Tänak had to contend with.

On the following stage, SS3, Jari-Matti Latvala in the No 7 Yaris WRC went quickest. Esapekka Lappi, last year's winner, was delayed due to an issue with his centre differential, but there could be no denying the outstanding performance of the Yaris WRC. From SS4, Citroën's Mads Østberg, showed superb pace to overtake Tänak at the top of the rally standings. In the stages that followed, Tänak and Østberg traded fastest times in a fierce battle for supremacy, with the former winning the day with five stage victories, consolidating his number one spot in the standings.

On Day Three, Tänak outdid his Day Two performance by posting another five consecutive fastest times from SS12 to SS16. Even taking things easier on Day Four, he still managed to win the very last Power Stage (SS23), giving him 12 stage victories.

After crossing the finish line, Tänak parked his Yaris WRC and, together with his co-driver Martin Järveoja, stood atop the roof of the car. The two rally winners were subsequently joined on the Yaris WRC by Team Principal Tommi Mäkinen and Team Chairman Akio Toyoda. Latvala, who picked up four stage wins, finished

Rd 08 #8 Tänak.

▲ *Rd 08 #7 Latvala.* ▼ *Rd 08 #9 Lappi.*

in third overall, missing out on second place by just 3.2 seconds.

Even though Lappi had lost time due to a centre differential issue, he fought back hard, recording three back-to-back wins on Day Three, getting as high as fourth. However, a crash on the first Special Stage of Day Four forced him to retire from the rally, but with Tänak and Latvala both on the podium, it was a superb result for Gazoo.

Rally Finland *Overall results, with 51 finishers*

1st	Ott Tänak/Martin Järveoja	Toyota Yaris WRC	2:35:18.1
2nd	Mads Ostberg/Torstein Eriksen	Citroën C3 WRC	2:35:50.8
3rd	Jari-Matti Latvala/Miikka Anttila	Toyota Yaris WRC	2:35:53.6
DNF	Esapekka Lappi/Janne Ferm	Toyota Yaris WRC	—

ROUND 09

Rallye Deutschland
16-19 August

As the second full tarmac event on the WRC calendar, Rallye Deutschland welcomed 60 starters who competed over 18 stages covering 204 miles (326km). There was the odd shower on Friday when the racing began, otherwise conditions were dry. The German event was another triumph for Tänak who led from start to finish.

In the short, opening SS1, Ott Tänak recorded the fastest time. Then, on the first stage of Day Two, Sébastien Ogier went quickest, forcing Tänak into second place. The Gazoo driver fought back on the 22km-long SS3, finishing five seconds ahead of the Frenchman, so regaining the rally lead. Tänak proceeded to record fastest times in all of Day

▲ *Rd 09 #7 Latvala.*

▶ *Rd 09 #8 Tänak.*

Two's remaining special stages, ending the day in first overall. He won five stages straight giving him an unbeatable lead.

The renowned Panzerplatte stage, which takes place inside the local military training grounds, was one of the highlights on Day Three, with Tänak posting the fastest time in SS9. Tänak entered the final day of the rally with a strong lead and, opting to play it safe, he dropped his pace significantly. On the rally-concluding Power Stage, however, which had bonus championship points riding on it, the Estonian went full pedal but lost out to Ogier by just 0.1 second. The Frenchman fell down the rankings after he suffered a puncture, and a seismic battle ensued between Hyundai's Dani Sordo and Gazoo's Jari-Matti Latvala.

In fifth at the end of Day Two, Latvala pushed hard and secured two SS wins to move into third spot. Aiming to finish second behind Tänak, the Finn started the final day well. But in SS16, he suffered an issue with his hydraulic system; he had to switch from changing gears with paddles to an emergency bypass system which placed an excessive burden on the drive system that eventually broke. He was unable to continue, giving up his podium place.

Lappi, despite suffering on the tricky road surfaces, had continued to drive at a steady place. He scored a best time on SS10 on his way to securing third place, which was his first podium finish since Rally Italia Sardegna, two rounds ago.

Tänak dominated from start to finish, picking up his third victory of the season, and his second in a row following his success in Finland. Thanks to the large number of points amassed by Tänak and Lappi, the Gazoo Team climbed to second in the manufacturers' standings, just 13 points behind Hyundai.

▲ *Rd 09 #9 Lappi.*

▼ *Rd 09 #8 Tänak.*

Rallye Deutschland *Overall results, with 45 finishers*

1st	Ott Tänak/Martin Järveoja	Toyota Yaris WRC	3:03:36.9
2nd	Thierry Neuville/Nicolas Gilsoul	Hyundai i20 Coupe WRC	3:04:16.1
3rd	Esapekka Lappi/Janne Ferm	Toyota Yaris WRC	3:04:37.8
DNF	Jari-Matti Latvala/Miikka Anttila	Toyota Yaris WRC	—

ROUND 10

Rally of Turkey
13-16 September

Rally Turkey rejoined the WRC calendar for the first time in eight years. Centred around Marmaris in the south-west of the country, and known as a rally run in high temperatures, 45 teams entered the event, including three cars for each of the four big World Rally Car teams. The rally was held over 17 stages covering 195 miles (312km), with a shakedown and brief SS1 only on the Thursday. Overnight rain soon dried up to give dusty conditions for almost all of the event.

Having won the last two rallies on the trot, Toyota was looking for its third straight victory. To alleviate the over-heating issues drivers were having with cooling systems, the Gazoo team enlisted the help of Denso Corporation, which fitted the cars with newly designed, high-performance radiators.

The appalling road conditions meant that the team had to significantly lift the Yaris' ride height, which meant decreased levels of tyre grip. The first gravel road stages took place on Day Two, but the team's drivers were unable to achieve the time records they wanted. Jari-Matti Latvala was 16.3 seconds off the top in fourth place; Ott Tänak was 31.9 seconds behind in fifth, while Esapekka Lappi was some 36.8 seconds back in seventh.

On Day Three, Tänak and Latvala turned their fortunes around thanks to engineers coming up with the ideal ride height settings for optimum traction. As a result, Tänak secured two, and Latvala one, stage wins on Day Three. With the leading drivers falling out of contention, Tänak rose to first in the overall rally standings, with Latvala 13.1 seconds behind in second place. Lappi, however, drove out of bounds on SS10 due to inaccurate corner information in his pace notes. His car slid down a slope damaging the vehicle and forcing him to retire.

With Tänak hanging onto an almost unbeatable lead, while having a strong chance of winning the driver's championship, and Latvala safe in second, it was decided that the two drivers should not take risks. Tänak and Latvala managed to safeguard their positions on Day Four, so giving

◀ *Rd 10 #9 Lappi.*

▼ *Rd 10 #7 Latvala.*

▲ ▶ *Rd 10 #8 Tänak.*

the team its first one-two finish since its return to the WRC in 2017. This win saw Tänak rise to second in the championship standings, and Latvala to fifth, while the Gazoo team was now on top of the manufacturers' championship.

The team's brilliant performance could be attributed to the new high-performance radiators, the ideal ride height settings giving maximum tyre grip and the ability of Tänak and Latvala to survive this rally of attrition with safe, inspired steering.

Rally of Turkey *Overall results, with 31 finishers*

1st	Ott Tänak/Martin Järveoja	Toyota Yaris WRC	3:59:24.5
2nd	Jari-Matti Latvala/Miikka Anttila	Toyota Yaris WRC	3:59:46.8
3rd	Hayden Paddon/Sebastian Marshall	Hyundai i20 Coupe WRC	4:01:10.8
DNF	Esapekka Lappi/Janne Ferm	Toyota Yaris WRC	—

ROUND 11

Wales Rally GB
4-7 October

For as far back as anyone still alive can remember (the inaugural rally took place in 1932 after all), this UK-based event was always known as the RAC Rally, in reverence of the Royal Automobile Club behind it. This was the 74th running of the event, famous for its gruelling forest stages, although a few tarmac roads are always thrown into the equation. The weather, of course, is another factor to add in, for the British climate can be rather hostile in the winter months.

The Wales Rally Great Britain, as it's called now, saw 57 starters, with only two Citroën C3s joining the fray. Based in Deeside in the far north of Wales, the event involved 23 stages over 199 miles (318km), with a further 677 miles (1084km) of liaison distance to add in. Unusually, the Power Stage was held early on the final day rather than being the last SS, as per tradition.

The Gazoo team started strongly, thanks to the pre-rally data on wet weather traction that Ott Tänak and Jari-Matti Latvala were able to generate by driving on muddy surfaces. On Day One, Esapekka Lappi secured the best time on the short SS, with Latvala finishing second. On Day Two, Tänak took victory in all three of the morning SSs.

In the afternoon, Tänak recorded fastest times on a further two stages and ended the day in first overall, holding a lead of 28.8 seconds over second place. He could almost taste his third straight win. Latvala also recorded stage wins as he ended the day in third place, just 2.5 seconds behind second. Lappi struggled early on, but he eventually improved his pace and finished fourth overall behind Latvala.

On Day Three, Tänak extended his lead over

▲ *Rd 11 #8 Tänak.*

▲ *Rd 11 #9 Lappi.*

second to as much as 48 seconds at one point. But on SS16, he hit the ground hard after landing a jump, damaged his car's under guard and radiator and was forced to retire for the day. Meanwhile, Latvala and Lappi both drove superbly, each rising one place in the rankings to second and third respectively.

On Day Four, Latvala and Ford's Sébastien Ogier were locked in a titanic battle for the top spot. Latvala won SS20 and the Power Stage to seize the lead by a small margin. But Ogier was a formidable opponent, and after winning the last three SSs of the day, beat Latvala by just 10 seconds to capture victory in Wales. Latvala had to be content with second with Lappi finishing a strong third.

◀ *Rd 11 #7 Latvala.*

Wales Rally GB *Overall results, with 48 finishers*

1st	Sébastien Ogier/Julien Ingrassia	Ford Fiesta WRC	3:06:12.5
2nd	Jari-Matti Latvala/Miikka Anttila	Toyota Yaris WRC	3:06:23.1
3rd	Esapekka Lappi/Janne Ferm	Toyota Yaris WRC	3:06:47.6
19th	Ott Tänak/Martin Järveoja	Toyota Yaris WRC	3:26:51.4

ROUND 12

Rally Catalunya
25-28 October

Rd 12 #7 Latvala.

Rd 12 #8 Tänak.

Rd 12 #8 Tänak.

Rd 12 #9 Lappi.

At Rally Catalunya (Rally de España), the Gazoo Team failed to finish on the podium for the first time since the sixth round in Portugal. Ott Tänak was the highest-ranked Toyota driver on the team in sixth place, Esapekka Lappi finished in seventh, and Jari-Matti Latvala eighth. With all three drivers failing to make the top five, the result was a crushing defeat.

Round 12 of the WRC had 70 starters and was run over 18 tarmac and gravel stages covering 207 miles (332km). The format in Spain was similar to other rallies, with a lightweight Thursday, and a Power Stage to finish things off. Incidentally, the first stage on Saturday (SS8) was cancelled, taking almost nine miles (14km) off the total distance.

But even though Gazoo suffered a poor result in Spain, the performance of the drivers was not as bad as the numbers themselves suggest. Tänak and Latvala each recorded four stage wins, with Tänak leading the rally for seven stages in a row, and Latvala for four straight stages. That meant Toyota was in control for over 60 percent of the rally but missed out on a podium. Two major reasons – punctures and wet weather.

Featuring a mid-rally switch from gravel to tarmac surfaces, the event is known as the only 'mixed' rally, and as such, requires very special preparation and super-efficient suspension, brake, tyre and powertrain modifications during a tight 75-minute service period at the end of Day Two.

Many of the 'tarmac' roads in Spain have unpaved shoulders, so when drivers pick tight lines through corners, they will often risk hitting tyres on sharp exposed rocks and edges. Tänak suffered this fate and was forced to change tyres, relinquishing his chance of a podium finish. After winning SS10, Latvala finished Day Three in the lead, 4.7 seconds ahead of Ogier.

As the rain came down on Day Four, tyre choice was crucial. Loeb gambled and went for hard tyres, which eventually paid dividends later on as the track dried. Then, in SS17, Latvala, on semi-wets, lost control through a left-hander, touched the guard rail, suffered a puncture, and dropped to sixth, before falling again to eighth. Even though Tänak won the Power Stage, he still could only manage sixth, with Lappi in seventh and Latvala in eighth. Meanwhile, multiple Rally Catalunya winner Sébastien Loeb, who had initially risked a hard tyre choice on a slightly wet track, drove superbly, picking up three straight stage wins on the final day to claim the silverware.

Rally Catalunya *Overall results, with 53 finishers*

1st	Sébastien Loeb/Daniel Elena	Citroën C3 WRC	3:12:08.0
2nd	Sébastien Ogier/Julien Ingrassia	Ford Fiesta WRC	3:12:10.9
3rd	Elfyn Evans/Daniel Barritt	Ford Fiesta WRC	3:12:24.5
6th	Ott Tänak/Martin Järveoja	Toyota Yaris WRC	3:13:11.9
7th	Esapekka Lappi/Janne Ferm	Toyota Yaris WRC	3:13:24.6
8th	Jari-Matti Latvala/Miikka Anttila	Toyota Yaris WRC	3:13:34.4

ROUND 13

Rally Australia

15-18 November

Rally Australia was a triumph for the Toyota Gazoo rally team. Jari-Matti Latvala crossed the finishing line in first place, his first victory since Round 2 in Sweden last season. This win also secured the manufacturers' championship in only their second year back in WRC, and a celebratory mood surrounded the podium in the forests of Australia.

Known for its tough gravel surfaces, this event was a compact rally with 24 stages over 199 miles (319km). There were only 25 starters involved in Thursday's shakedown, before the real racing began on Friday. As expected, conditions were mostly dry with patchy showers on Day Two.

All three Toyota drivers shared the lead at

▲ *Rd 13 #7 Latvala.*

▼ *Rd 13 #8 Tänak.*

▼ *Rd 13 #9 Lappi.*

Rd 13
#7 Latvala.

various times, with Ostberg heading the field at one point, too, keeping the Japanese maker on its toes. Tänak, who won eight stages, and led at the end of Day Three, was forced to drop out with the end of the rally in clear sight, after landing heavily and damaging his gearbox. Teammate Latvala was in second place, just 21.9 seconds behind, and Lappi was in fourth.

Following Tänak's retirement, Latvala took the lead, but was challenged strongly by Hyundai's Hayden Paddon who was sitting in second, with Lappi in fourth. So there was immense pressure on Latvala and Lappi to secure the manufacturers' championship.

On the final day, Lappi won SS21, with rally leader Latvala posting the fastest times in SS22 and SS23 to give him victory Down Under. The points that Latvala and Lappi received for their first and fourth places were enough to secure the manufacturers' championship trophy for Gazoo.

As the 13-round championship of 2018 came to a close, the one and two slots were occupied by the same drivers as 2017 (Ogier perhaps counting himself a little lucky after Neuville failed to finish in Oz), but Toyota drivers now filled third through fifth. Lappi finished the season without scoring any victories. However, he had stood on the podium on three occasions, while Tänak won four rallies and Latvala one.

In addition, having overcome cooling system problems in rallies like Mexico, excessive mud accumulation in Wales, and traction issues, the Japanese manufacturer was able to lift the makers' trophy for the first time since 1999. As the team wound down from its decisive victory in Australia, it was announced that veteran Kris Meeke would be replacing Lappi for 2019.

Rally Australia *Overall results, with 15 finishers*

1st	Jari-Matti Latvala/Miikka Anttila	Toyota Yaris WRC	2:59:52.0
2nd	Hayden Paddon/Sebastian Marshall	Hyundai i20 Coupe WRC	3:00:24.5
3rd	Mads Ostberg/Torstein Eriksen	Citroën C3 WRC	3:00:44.2
4th	Esapekka Lappi/Janne Ferm	Toyota Yaris WRC	3:00:54.3
DNF	Ott Tänak/Martin Järveoja	Toyota Yaris WRC	—

2018 SUMMARY

The season reviewed in a way that provides a quick reference from a Toyota/Gazoo perspective, with driver performance, round by round (overall position, followed by the scoring Power Stage position in brackets), and year-end positions within the FIA WRC championship.

	Latvala	Lappi	Tänak
Rd 01	3rd (4th)	7th (10th)	2nd (6th)
Rd 02	7th (6th)	4th (1st)	9th (5th)
Rd 03	8th (2nd)	11th (6th)	14th (1st)
Rd 04	DNF (–)	6th (1st)	2nd (5th)
Rd 05	DNF (–)	8th (6th)	1st (4th)
Rd 06	24th (9th)	5th (1st)	DNF (–)
Rd 07	7th (7th)	3rd (6th)	9th (3rd)
Rd 08	3rd (3rd)	DNF (–)	1st (1st)
Rd 09	DNF (–)	3rd (3rd)	1st (2nd)
Rd 10	2nd (4th)	DNF (–)	1st (3rd)
Rd 11	2nd (1st)	3rd (5th)	19th (2nd)
Rd 12	8th (23rd)	7th (8th)	6th (1st)
Rd 13	1st (5th)	4th (2nd)	DNF (–)

Drivers

1st	Sébastien Ogier	Ford	219
2nd	Thierry Neuville	Hyundai	201
3rd	Ott Tänak	Toyota	181
4th	Jari-Matti Latvala	Toyota	128
5th	Esapekka Lappi	Toyota	126

Co-drivers

1st	Julien Ingrassia	Ford	219
2nd	Nicolas Gilsoul	Hyundai	201
3rd	Martin Järveoja	Toyota	181
4th	Miikka Anttila	Toyota	128
5th	Janne Ferm	Toyota	126

NB: Points totals include Power Stage bonuses for drivers and co-drivers.

Manufacturers

1st	Toyota	Toyota Gazoo Racing WRT	368
2nd	Hyundai	Hyundai Motorsport	341
3rd	Ford	M-Sport Ford World Rally Team	324

The 2019 Season

The 2019 season was held over 14 rounds, with a new gravel event in Chile (surprisingly, only run for the first time in the previous year), added to make the trip to South America more worthwhile. Otherwise, there were no changes to the calendar. For the record, while the WRC3 category was dropped for 2019, the Junior World Rally Championship continued to be held over five rounds.

2019 Season Rounds

Round	Dates	Surface
Monte Carlo Rally	24-27 January	Tarmac
Rally Sweden	14-17 February	Snow
Rally Mexico	7-10 March	Gravel
Tour de Corse	28-31 March	Tarmac
Rally Argentina	25-28 April	Gravel
Rally Chile	9-12 May	Gravel
Rally de Portugal	30 May-2 June	Gravel
Rally Italia Sardegna	13-16 June	Gravel
Rally Finland	1-4 August	Gravel
Rallye Deutschland	22-25 August	Tarmac
Rally of Turkey	12-15 September	Gravel
Wales Rally GB	3-6 October	Gravel
Rally Catalunya	24-27 October	Mixed
Rally Australia	14-17 November	Gravel

FIA rule changes and season prospects

Thankfully, there were very few changes to the rules for 2019. Special stage distances were officially reduced from 312 miles (500km) to a maximum of 219 miles (350km), although few events had gone near the limit imposed in 2010 anyway. The number of test days was cut by 25 percent to 42 per year, and 'personalised' car numbers could be issued to drivers (in the past they had been allocated according to championship positions from the previous season): Toyota drivers chose the numbers 5, 8 and 10. There was also some shuffling around in the lower classes, but these aren't really relevant to this book.

The same four manufacturers (and vehicles) fought for glory in the top WRC Class, although Citroën would campaign the entire season with just two cars, and Ford also cut back on its commitment, albeit to a lesser extent. In addition, several big names changed allegiances. Significantly, Ogier went to Citroën to join ex-Gazoo man Lappi, while Loeb moved across to Hyundai.

The Gazoo team cars and their drivers

The 380bhp Yaris WRC was basically unchanged for 2018, with only detail refinements. Even the paintwork was similar, although careful inspection revealed a subtle change in the rear spoiler assembly, along with a fresh rear diffuser and exhaust surround.

Jari-Matti Latvala (#10) and Ott Tänak (#8) were signed up for works driving duties once more (duly partnered by the same co-pilots – Miikka Anttila and Martin Järveoja, respectively), but Kris Meeke was called in to handle the third car for 2019, replacing Esapekka Lappi in the Toyota camp.

Kris Meeke.

Takamoto Katsuta was also named as a works WRC driver on occasion, after stamping his authority in the WRC2 Class.

Meeke (who drove the #5 car) was born in Northern Ireland in 1979. After a disappointing

The Toyota Yaris WRC for the 2019 season.

debut on the 2002 Rally GB, he duly entered several events over the following years, using a variety of vehicles. His big break came when Citroën offered him a works seat in 2013; he started to build up a respectable record, coming first with the DS3 WRC and then the C3 WRC, before a mixed season with the French maker in 2018. However, armed with a new co-driver for 2019 (Seb Marshall), it was hoped Meeke could show his speed in a more productive fashion within the Gazoo team.

Katsuta was born in 1993, and a fair bit younger than Meeke. He was mainly involved in the WRC2 category via Tommi Mäkinen Racing, but earned himself a Yaris WRC drive in 2019. Like Meeke, Katsuta had a new person in the seat beside him, in this case Daniel Barritt, who had partnered Elfyn Evans in a works Fiesta in the previous season. We will take a look at Katsuta's career in more detail later on ...

◄ *Rd 01 #5 Meeke.*

ROUND 01

Monte Carlo Rally

24-27 January

Marking the 87th running of the Monte Carlo Rally (affectionately known by enthusiasts as 'The Monte'), this year the action was held almost exclusively outside the principality. Based in the town of Gap, 16 stages were held over 201 miles (323km) on varying degrees of icy roads with occasional dry sections.

Some 84 teams started the rally, including three Toyotas, Fords and Hyundais, plus two Citroëns in the top World Rally Car category. In the 2017 Monte,

Rd 01 #10 Latvala.

Latvala had claimed a second place, while Tänak had also picked up a second in the 2018 event. Tänak won SS1 on Day One to take an early lead, while Latvala captured a stage victory on Day Two. It was shaping up to be an all-Toyota victory run, but the Gazoo team did not have everything its own way.

This season, the team strengthened its collaboration with Toyota Connected – a company that specialises in IT – and fully implemented the advanced IT tools developed by the company's European branch for the first time. As a result, the team was now able to carry out a more scientific analysis of course conditions, and the tools played an important role during the Rallye Monte-Carlo as well.

On Day Two, however, the sudden cancellation of SS3, a 12-mile (20km) special stage that Gazoo had been specifically preparing for, deprived the team of being able to demonstrate the Yaris' full potential on snow and ice. The team recovered later, but even though Tänak showed his dominance by winning six consecutive stages from SS9 to SS14, he still was not able to hold on to the lead.

Unforeseen punctures and wheel damage on SS7 saw Tänak lose two minutes, forcing him to relinquish the victory to Sebastien Ogier in his Citroën C3, with Tänak taking third place behind a charging Neuville. Meeke showed his mettle by winning the SS16 Power Stage on the final day with a super quick run, while Latvala had managed a series of solid performances to end Day Two in fourth overall, and was in a strong position to challenge for a podium finish, but slipped to fifth.

Rd 01 #8 Tänak.

Rd 01 #10 Latvala.

Monte Carlo Rally

Overall results, with 67 finishers

1st	Sébastien Ogier/Julien Ingrassia	Citroën C3 WRC	3:21:15.9
2nd	Thierry Neuville/Nicolas Gilsoul	Hyundai i20 Coupe WRC	3:21:18.1
3rd	Ott Tänak/Martin Järveoja	Toyota Yaris WRC	3:23:31.1
5th	Jari-Matti Latvala/Miikka Anttila	Toyota Yaris WRC	3:23:45.8
6th	Kris Meeke/Sebastian Marshall	Toyota Yaris WRC	3:26:52.1

ROUND 02

Rally Sweden
14-17 February

Based around the town of Torsby, 61 starters began Rally Sweden, with the event comprising 19 snowbound stages over 198 miles (317km). Two-time drivers' champion Marcus Grönholm competed in a GRX Team-entered Yaris, and although he was looked after by Gazoo staff as a one-off, he failed to make an impression.

Gazoo Racing president Shigeki Tomoyama believed that a win in this rally would prove pivotal in his team's fight for the 2019 championship. He was right. Tänak shared Tomoyama's intuition about the victory, and thought it crucial for him to win rallies that suited his driving style and his Yaris – and Rally Sweden was one of those rallies.

To maximise team morale prior to the event, Tänak sent a video message to Tomoyama in Japan, asking him to attend the rally in person to show support and encouragement. With a redesigned rear fender, heavy snowfall and mud were less likely to block up the rear fins, and aerodynamics were improved. However, snowfall was light due to higher than normal temperatures, meaning that large areas of

Rd 02 ▲ (Top) #8 Tänak ▲#10 Latvala. ▼#5 Meeke.

Rd 02 #8 Tänak.

green began to appear, creating less than ideal conditions.

On the morning of Day Two, the course conditions of the Special Stages, which ventured into neighbouring Norway, were relatively good. Tänak, who was third in the starting order, took advantage of hard-packed ice on the road surfaces to record two fastest times and take the rally lead. Latvala also performed strongly and finished the morning stages in third overall. By the afternoon, however, road surfaces had changed dramatically with snow melt and mud causing large ruts that hindered progress of the top order cars. Towards the end of Day Two, the two drivers ahead of Tänak lost control of their cars in the tricky conditions and plummeted down the standings, while the Toyota driver showed superb risk management to stay in second place.

With a superbly set-up car to challenge Day Three, Tänak reeled off a succession of second-fastest times that enabled him to gain the overall lead. Holding a 34-second advantage, Tänak made the most of the afternoon conditions and recorded a further three fastest stage times. Having built up a sizable lead, he eased off the pace to preserve his tyres and allow him to focus on the Power Stage the following day. Thanks to some clever tyre management and a cool head, Tänak blitzed the Power Stage, winning it by 3.5 seconds, adding a further five bonus points to the 25 he secured for winning the rally. The victory put him ahead in the drivers' championship and also gave Toyota a narrow lead in the standings.

Latvala, who broke Carlos Sainz's record for the most WRC starts, captured two stage wins but was sadly forced to restart after getting stranded on a snowbank. This dropped him right down the field, and he ultimately finished in 21st. Meanwhile, Kris Meeke, competing on snow in a Yaris for the first time, lacked confidence and was unable to show his true speed, but remained focused enough to snag a well-earned sixth place.

Rally Sweden *Overall results, with 55 finishers*

1st	Ott Tänak/Martin Järveoja	Toyota Yaris WRC	2:47:30.0
2nd	Esapekka Lappi/Janne Ferm	Citroën C3 WRC	2:48:23.7
3rd	Thierry Neuville/Nicolas Gilsoul	Hyundai i20 Coupe WRC	2:48:26.7
6th	Kris Meeke/Sebastian Marshall	Toyota Yaris WRC	2:49:08.8
21st	Jari-Matti Latvala/Miikka Anttila	Toyota Yaris WRC	3:02:14.4

ROUND 03

Rally Mexico

7-10 March

Staged in the Guanajuato region in central Mexico, Rally Mexico saw 23 starters compete over 21 stages covering 194 miles (310km). The Gazoo team had suffered poor results here for the past two years, but 2019 would be different.

In stark contrast to the icy Rally Sweden, Rally Mexico takes place in 30 degree heat at altitudes of over 2000 meters. Dry and dusty, with loose rocks everywhere, the high altitude means that engines lose significant power, with cooling performance compromised too, and the multiple twisty turns translate into full throttle driving for long periods.

With newly fitted radiators and electric fans developed by partner Denso, the three Yaris rally cars managed to record fastest times in nine out of the 21 stages, with Ott Tänak finishing second, Kris Meeke posting a fifth and Jari-Matti Latvala recording an eighth. This result enabled Tänak and co-driver Martin Järveoja to retain their position at the top of the drivers' championship while Gazoo stayed in the lead too.

Tänak struggled with loose gravel on Day Two, falling behind the leader by over 20 seconds. But he kept his cool and progressively narrowed the gap to the leading drivers with solid performances before posting the fastest time in SS7 and second fastest in the following two stages. This put him

Rd 03 ▲ #10 Latvala. ▼ #8 Tänak.

Rd 03 #5 Meeke.

in fourth place at the end of Day Two while Meeke did well to finish in third spot.

On Day Three in SS10, Meeke recorded his first fastest time of Rally Mexico and immediately took the rally lead but then suffered a puncture on SS11, lost 90 seconds, and fell to fifth overall. Latvala recorded stage wins on both SS11 and SS12, after having retired on Day Two with an electrical issue.

With a strong chance of grabbing second place overall, Tänak went on the offensive on Day Four and made an aggressive tyre choice, selecting four hard tyres and one medium. His strategy was a success as he won both of the morning Special Stages and duly claimed second. He was not able to make up the 24 seconds to the leader, Sébastien Ogier, who took the overall victory in his Citroën.

Rally Mexico *Overall results, with 15 finishers*

1st	Sébastien Ogier/Julien Ingrassia	Citroën C3 WRC	3:37:08.0
2nd	Ott Tänak/Martin Järveoja	Toyota Yaris WRC	3:37:38.2
3rd	Elfyn Evans/Scott Martin	Ford Fiesta WRC	3:37:57.9
5th	Kris Meeke/Sebastian Marshall	Toyota Yaris WRC	3:43:14.2
8th	Jari-Matti Latvala/Miikka Anttila	Toyota Yaris WRC	3:56:03.9

ROUND 04

Tour de Corse
28-31 March

The Tour de Corse is a fast tarmac classic held on the picturesque French island of Corsica. When it was first run in 1956, it was indeed a tour of the island, but as it evolved it became centred on a series of mountain roads that are notoriously twisty. Indeed, they demand a great deal of respect, as they have claimed several lives over the years, more or less sealing the fate of the Group B cars as a consequence.

Based in the town of Bastia, the Tour de Corse was held in dry conditions, had 95 starters and covered 14 stages over 217 miles (348km). The Gazoo team's results proved that this event was a rally of attrition as the Toyota drivers were fastest in six of the 14 stages and second fastest in another eight. However, even with Meeke winning the Power Stage, the team still missed out on a podium finish – the first time that season.

Rd 04 ▲ *#5 Meeke.*
◀ *#10 Latvala.*

Elfyn Evans (driving a Ford Fiesta) and Tänak led for most of the event, but Thierry Neuville, driving a Hyundai, inherited the win to put him narrowly ahead in the championship standings; Tänak and Toyota suddenly dropped to third

In fact, the Gazoo team was unable to place a single driver in the top five, the main reason being lost time due to air-loss from the cars' tyres. All three Yaris machines suffered from a variety of air-loss issues, with tyres punctured from running over sharp stones, and wheels damaged when overcoming height differences in the road surface or when hitting curbs.

Involved in a fierce battle for the lead with Evans on Day Three, Tänak, pushing hard in SS11, damaged his wheel rim as he cut a corner fighting for precious seconds. Having to stop to change his wheel, and losing two minutes in the process, was a theme of Gazoo's performance in Corsica.

Rd 04 ▲ #5 Meeke. *▼ #8 Tänak.*

Tour de Corse *Overall results, with 68 finishers*

1st	Thierry Neuville/Nicolas Gilsoul	Hyundai i20 Coupe WRC	3:22:59.0
2nd	Sébastien Ogier/Julien Ingrassia	Citroën C3 WRC	3:23:39.3
3rd	Elfyn Evans/Scott Martin	Ford Fiesta WRC	3:24:05.6
6th	Ott Tänak/Martin Järveoja	Toyota Yaris WRC	3:24:39.0
9th	Kris Meeke/Sebastian Marshall	Toyota Yaris WRC	3:28:05.3
10th	Jari-Matti Latvala/Miikka Anttila	Toyota Yaris WRC	3:29:43.6

ROUND 05

Rally Argentina
25-28 April

Staged in Villa Carlos Paz, only 25 starters competed in Rally Argentina. It was originally intended to be held over 18 stages taking in 217 miles (347km), although SS3 covering 19 miles (30km) was cancelled. Several days of heavy rain made conditions very tricky during the early part of the event.

Ott Tänak in his Yaris WRC started well by recording the quickest time during shakedown, with Meeke just 0.7 seconds behind in second. In fact, the two Gazoo drivers swapped fastest times in SS1 and SS2 with Tänak capturing the first win and Meeke posting the fastest time in SS2.

Toyota held onto the rally lead until the end of Day Two thanks to seven stage wins and several second places, but could still not manage to snag a podium finish, replicating their Corsica results. Meeke would go on to be the highest-placed Gazoo Racing driver in fourth overall; Latvala would finish fifth, and Tänak eighth. In 2018, Tänak had been the runaway winner, so his failure to get a podium was all the more disappointing.

After SS6, Meeke had difficulties coping with

Rd 05 ▲ #10 Latvala. ▼ #8 Tänak.

▼ Rd 05 #5 Meeke.

◀ *Rd 05 #10 Latvala.*

the changing surface conditions, and dropped from leader to fourth overall, before a puncture and a 10-second penalty that ended up costing him a podium spot.

Latvala had struggled during the first four rallies of the season. In Argentina, although he was third overall in the rally's early stages, he fell behind due to a loss of tyre pressure and lack of traction. He did improve though, posting three third fastest times from SS11 to SS13 in a row, and then a second fastest time in SS14, SS17 and SS18 – enough to place him fifth overall.

Tänak did well until his driveshaft broke on Friday, when he was just 13 seconds off the lead. But on SS13, the voltage of Tänak's battery dropped, significantly affecting his time and eventually forcing him to retire on Day Three. He restarted on Day Four to finish eighth overall. Neuville stayed out of trouble to inherit the lead and another win.

Rally Argentina *Overall results, with 21 finishers*

1st	Thierry Neuville/Nicolas Gilsoul	Hyundai i20 Coupe WRC	3:20:54.6
2nd	Andreas Mikkelsen/Anders Jaeger	Hyundai i20 Coupe WRC	3:21:43.0
3rd	Sébastien Ogier/Julien Ingrassia	Citroën C3 WRC	3:21:59.4
4th	Kris Meeke/Sebastian Marshall	Toyota Yaris WRC	3:22:00.8
5th	Jari-Matti Latvala/Miikka Anttila	Toyota Yaris WRC	3:22:15.7
8th	Ott Tänak/Martin Järveoja	Toyota Yaris WRC	3:35:19.4

ROUND 06

Rally Chile
9-12 May

This was the very first running of Rally Chile as a WRC round, and was well supported with 55 crews taking to the start. Massive crowds turned out to see the cars at Thursday's opening ceremony.

Based in the town of Talcahuano, the teams competed over 16 gravel stages covering 191 miles (305km), although the cars had to travel 779 miles (1246km) if one includes transport distances. Tänak began the rally with high hopes of victory and temporarily held the rally lead.

Even though driveshaft issues saw him fall down the standings, he was still able to recover the time he lost through a series of outstanding drives, giving him the chance to return to a position from which he could fight for the win. One reason for the exceptionally strong performance in Chile was that the parent company Toyota had placed extra efforts on beefing up the Yaris' reliability, as it saw this rally as especially critical in being able to win the championship.

One area to go under the microscope was the unexpected electrical system issue suffered in Argentina. Specialist Toyota R&D engineer,

Rd 06 ▲*#5 Meeke.* ▼ *#10 Latvala.* ▲ *#8 Tänak.*

Keiichi Kondo, was brought in from head office to troubleshoot the problems, and after close examination of the symptoms, one remedy implemented was to change the tightening torque values used when installing electrical system parts. This revision, in addition to several other upgrades, helped to raise the Yaris WRC cars' reliability significantly, which in turn, led to the victory.

Jari-Matti Latvala and Kris Meeke shared the best time on the opening Special Stage, while Tänak went fastest on SS2 to claim top spot in the rally standings – a position he maintained until the end of the rally. Indeed, Tänak was fastest

▲ *Rd 06 #8 Tänak.*

in six of Rally Chile's 16 Special Stages. He also claimed five bonus Drivers' Championship points by winning the final Power Stage, and, as a result, the Estonian driver rose to second in the overall standings, sitting just 10 points behind the leader, Sébastien Ogier.

Meeke rolled early on Saturday, but continued to charge without a windscreen. Neuville suffered a huge crash, but thankfully walked away okay. Meanwhile, Latvala was having an impressive run until he hit a rock and broke a driveshaft. In the end, Tänak was untouchable from SS2 onwards.

Rally Chile *Overall results, with 35 finishers*

1st	Ott Tänak/Martin Järveoja	Toyota Yaris WRC	3:15:53.8
2nd	Sébastien Ogier/Julien Ingrassia	Citroën C3 WRC	3:16:16.9
3rd	Sébastien Loeb/Daniel Elena	Hyundai i20 Coupe WRC	3:16:24.0
10th	Kris Meeke/Sebastian Marshall	Toyota Yaris WRC	3:24:27.2
11th	Jari-Matti Latvala/Miikka Anttila	Toyota Yaris WRC	3:26:53.0

ROUND 07

Rally de Portugal

30 May-2 June

Marking the 53rd running of the Rally de Portugal, some 60 starters entered the event, competing over 20 stages and covering 194 miles (311km) after a ceremonial start on Thursday. Held in the Porto region in dry conditions, SS14 and SS15 were cancelled, but knocked only three miles (4.5km) off the full route.

Due to many sections of the course being in such disrepair, many rally cars suffered severe damage from large stones dug up by corner cutting.

Rd 07 #8 Tänak.

Rd 07 #10 Latvala.

Ott Tänak retired on Day Two after suffering damage from stones, while Jari-Matti Latvala was also forced to retire for the day. It turned out to be an extremely difficult event for the Gazoo team, but the drivers learned to better anticipate changing conditions. They also employed a new, more efficient way to carry their spare tyres. Switching to an upright position that was more centrally located in the car, this new strategy moved the centre of gravity which helped to minimise the yaw moment of inertia, thus improving handling.

Winning five out of the 20 stages, Tänak set two fastest times in SS2 and SS3 to take an early lead and did not relinquish his stronghold, consolidating his victory with back-to-back fastest times in SS17 and SS18.

But it was not only Tänak who performed superbly. Although he was further down the

Rd 07 #5 Meeke.

Rd 07 #8 Tänak.

Rd 07 #8 Tänak.

running order, Latvala also set strong times – posting two fastest times – and finished Day One in second place overall. Pushing hard, Kris Meeke, too, was third, just 5.5 seconds behind Latvala, as the Yaris WRCs secured a clean sweep of the top positions. However, the Toyota drivers, especially Tänak, did not have it all their own way.

On Day Two, Tänak damaged his brake lines resulting in reduced braking force and lost time. Although managing to temporarily fix the issue himself, he was not able to extract all of the air from his brake lines and was forced to start SS9 without full brake force or feel. Overhearing Tänak's radio conversation with engineers, Team Principal Tommi Mäkinen, using his years of experience as a championship-winning driver, gave the Gazoo driver valuable advice – to stomp on the brakes multiple times – that enabled him to correct the problem and finish the stage with the second fastest time.

Throwing away a ton of points, Meeke retired when he lost a wheel after crashing into a tree on the PS (SS20). Just when it looked like Latvala was fighting for a podium finish, he suffered suspension trouble that pushed him down the rankings to finish seventh. Tänak dominated again, but Ogier's Power Stage win kept him at the top of the points table.

Rally de Portugal *Overall results, with 33 finishers*

1st	Ott Tänak/Martin Järveoja	Toyota Yaris WRC	3:20:22.8
2nd	Thierry Neuville/Nicolas Gilsoul	Hyundai i20 Coupe WRC	3:20:38.7
3rd	Sébastien Ogier/Julien Ingrassia	Citroën C3 WRC	3:21:19.9
7th	Jari-Matti Latvala/Miikka Anttila	Toyota Yaris WRC	3:31:51.0
DNF	Kris Meeke/Sebastian Marshall	Toyota Yaris WRC	–

ROUND 08

Rally Italia Sardegna
13-16 June

Based in Alghero, the Rally Italia Sardegna welcomed its 16th anniversary running in mid-June. With only the shakedown and one short stage on Thursday, the rally proper started with 90 entrants on Friday – contested in dry conditions (apart from the odd river crossing) over 19 stages and covering 194 miles (311km).

Ott Tänak had just won two rallies in a row so he lined up in Italy with high expectations,

Rd 08 #8 Tänak.

searching for his tenth victory in this his 100th WRC rally. But one serious issue remained – the damper troubles that afflicted Tänak and Latvala in Portugal. While Tänak had somehow managed to overcome the trouble and clinch victory, Latvala had been delayed significantly, losing the chance to challenge for the podium. With a high concentration of low-speed sections in Sardinia, cars are not able depend on their natural cooling systems, placing great stress on engines and cooling systems. Luckily Denso's work had remedied Toyota's issues allowing the Yaris to attack fully.

Rd 08 #5 Meeke.

Tänak started well on Day One by posting the fastest time in SS4 and second fastest in SS5, finishing the day in third place. On Day Two, with the starting order inverted, Tänak began in ninth position. Faced with a clean, grippy track, he upped his pace and won all six special stages putting him into the lead. Having built up a sizable gap to second place, Tänak eased off with a series of error-free drives on the final day, entering the final Power Stage with a 26 second lead.

But then disaster struck. Just as he started his run, the Estonian felt something wrong with his steering. The power assist was unstable and his steering suddenly became very heavy rendering the car almost uncontrollable. He spun out early on and lost a large amount of time. Even though the stage was only 6.89km in length, Tänak lost over two minutes, wiping out his lead and plunging him down to fifth place. Latvala had also suffered the same steering issue on Friday, forcing him to retire for the day, and finished in 19th overall. Meeke, for his part, drove dependably, and staring at a potential fourth place was forced to stop and change a tyre on Day Two, pushing him down to eighth at the end.

A sobering thought for Tänak was that in his despair, he still managed to hold onto a narrow four-point lead in the championship from Sebastien Ogier, as Dani Sordo in his Hyundai came out of Sardinia with an unexpected victory. Before moving on, we should also mention that Juho Hänninen had a works-supported Yaris for the event (#69), but sadly he was forced to retire the Tommi Makinen Racing machine.

Rd 08 #10 Latvala.

Rd 08 #5 Meeke.

Rally Italia Sardegna *Overall results, with 49 finishers*

1st	Dani Sordo/Carlos del Barrio	Hyundai i20 Coupe WRC	3:32:27.2
2nd	Teemu Suninen/ Marko Salminen	Ford Fiesta WRC	3:32:40.9
3rd	Andreas Mikkelsen/Anders Jaeger	Hyundai i20 Coupe WRC	3:32:59.8
5th	Ott Tänak/Martin Järveoja	Toyota Yaris WRC	3:33:57.3
8th	Kris Meeke/Sebastian Marshall	Toyota Yaris WRC	3:37:07.3
19th	Jari-Matti Latvala/Miikka Anttila	Toyota Yaris WRC	3:53:03.2

The Rally Estonia was run in mid-July as an FIA promotional event. It was duly won by the country's favourite rallying duo.

ROUND 09

Rally Finland

1-4 August

Held in the Keski-Suomi region, Rally Finland 2019 marked the 69th running of the legendary event in which cars often look like planes as they get airborne. In a format similar to Sardinia, some 61 starters contested 23 largely dry stages over 192 miles (308km).

In Italy, Tänak had endured loss and despair, being snatched from the jaws of victory, so for the Estonian, Finland was his chance to get even in this, Gazoo Racing's home event. Tänak and his teammates knew that their Yaris WRCs excelled on Finland's distinctive, hard-packed, high-speed gravel roads, and both the team and the drivers were full of confidence, especially after its engineers meticulously went over every component to avoid a repeat of Sardinia. Finland would be a defining moment for Gazoo.

On Day One, Jari-Matti Latvala recorded the fastest time in SS2 while Kris Meeke went fastest in SS3, with Latvala quickest again on SS4. Tänak, meanwhile, overcame the disadvantage of starting first and posted some very quick times to lead the rally standings by the end of SS2. He then went fastest on SS5, SS12, SS14, SS17, SS20 and SS22 – to consolidate his victory of Rally Finland. When Tänak went fastest in SS20, he had recorded his 50th stage win of the season, the Yaris WRC's 120th, and a remarkable 200th stage win for the team since its return to the WRC.

In fact, with Latvala setting blistering times too – winning SS6, SS7 and SS9, he took the fight right up to Tänak, with the lead changing four times throughout the event. Meeke was also flying in

Rd 09 #8 Tänak.

Finland, posting a fastest time in SS10 to finish in second spot on Day Two. However, there was high drama on SS14 when both Latvala and Meeke went off course at the same right-hand corner, colliding with a large rock in a ditch. Latvala damaged his wheel and bodywork, but was able to finish SS14 some 14 seconds behind Tänak, who won the stage. Latvala had dropped off the lead, but he remained in second overall. The situation was not so positive for Meeke, who, after damaging his suspension, was unable to continue and had to retire for the day.

Tänak was now 22 points clear of Ogier in the standings, with Toyota catching up on Hyundai (238 versus 262).

Rd 09 ▲ #5 Meeke. ▶ #10 Latvala.

Rd 09 #8 Tänak.

Rally Finland *Overall results, with 49 finishers*

1st	Ott Tänak/Martin Järveoja	Toyota Yaris WRC	2:30:40.3
2nd	Esapekka Lappi/Janne Ferm	Citroën C3 WRC	2:31:05.9
3rd	Jari-Matti Latvala/Miikka Anttila	Toyota Yaris WRC	2:31:13.5
DNF	Kris Meeke/Sebastian Marshall	Toyota Yaris WRC	–

ROUND 10

Rallye Deutschland
22-25 August

In this the 37th running of Rallye Deutschland, 52 crews (including a fourth works-assisted Yaris WRC for Katsuta) contested the 19 tarmac stages over 215 miles (344km) in warm and dry conditions throughout.

The Gazoo team's outing to Germany would prove to be its most successful yet, with a telling maiden 1-2-3 finish. When Ott Tänak completed the final stage, securing the rally victory and confirming the team's clean sweep of the podium, cheers and applause erupted from the team's area of the service park.

This year, the German roads were in poor condition, making drivers sense increased risks. In particular, the infamous Panzerplatte and Arena Panzerplatte stages, which take place inside the Baumholder military training ground, were in even worse condition than usual, in part due to the direction of travel being the reverse of most years.

Rd 10 #8 Tänak.

As Tänak fought with Neuville and Ogier for the top spot at the first Panzerplatte stage, the two rivals suffered punctures, forcing them to drop down the standings, and, as luck would have it, allowed Meeke and Latvala – who managed to avoid punctures – to rise into podium contention.

Rd 10 #10 Latvala.

Rd 10 #5 Meeke.

In all, Toyota drivers recorded the fastest times in eleven out of nineteen stages with all drivers winning at least one special stage, while Tänak maintained the rally lead from as early on as SS3.

In addition to his outright speed, Tänak's complete trust and confidence in the car's capability was key to securing his third Rallye Deutschland victory in succession. Meeke, meanwhile, had been fighting among the leaders over the last few rallies, but he had failed to score any meaningful results due to crashes caused by driver errors. In Germany, however, he completed the difficult event with outstanding race management, and secured his first podium finish since joining the Gazoo Racing WRT. So it was Tänak first, Meeke second and Latvala third, taking Toyota to within just eight points of Hyundai.

Takamoto Katsuta, a member of the Gazoo Racing Rally Challenge Program competed for the first time in a WRC car for the sole purpose of allowing him a chance to gain much-needed experience. With his job being to complete all the stages, he resisted the urge to push hard, and finished in tenth place.

Rallye Deutschland *Overall results, with 41 finishers*

1st	Ott Tänak/Martin Järveoja	Toyota Yaris WRC	3:15:29.8
2nd	Kris Meeke/Sebastian Marshall	Toyota Yaris WRC	3:15:50.6
3rd	Jari-Matti Latvala/Miikka Anttila	Toyota Yaris WRC	3:16:05.8
10th	Takamoto Katsuta/Daniel Barritt	Toyota Yaris WRC	3:23:49.0

ROUND 11

Rally of Turkey
12-15 September

Regarded as the slowest gravel round on the calendar, and as such, one of the toughest to win, Rally of Turkey saw 28 starters contest 17 stages in dry conditions over 194 miles (310km).

Tänak had won last year's Turkish event, while Latvala came second, giving Gazoo its best result of the 2018 season with a 1-2 podium finish. This year, however, the rally gods would not be on Toyota's side. On some of the worst road conditions of the calendar, Toyota engineers set about revising the Yaris WRC's suspension setup to handle the tricky surfaces.

Tänak came into the rally as the leader of the drivers' championship, and was first in the running order on Day Two. The roads were covered in loose gravel, making the conditions extremely slippery and risky, yet the Estonian driver managed to limit his losses to the leader to 25.3 seconds, finishing in fifth place. However, on SS6, his front tyre detached from its rim, and he was significantly delayed. In fact, on the previous Special Stage, Latvala had

Rd 11 #8 Tänak.

suffered damage to his front-right tyre too, as the team was hit with a succession of tyre troubles.

The team's poor showing in Turkey could be put down to three issues – punctures, mechanicals, and lack of performance. The team's three drivers recorded a total of six fastest times, and so were able to show the car's speed on a number of stages. Yet on other stages, the drivers were unable to gain sufficient traction, and they were not able to find the speed they had anticipated. Even though the team had undertaken thorough testing, the new suspension did not demonstrate its full potential. On Day Two, Tänak's ECU packed up, meaning that

Rd 11 #5 Meeke.

Rd 11 #10 Latvala.

he was not able to restart his car, forcing him to retire for the day.

In the end, Latvala finished sixth, and Meeke drove consistently to snatch a seventh. Tänak languished down in 16th but still managed to win the Power Stage, keeping his championship hopes alive while Hyundai pulled 19 ahead of the Japanese rivals. French car enthusiasts got a rare treat, with Ogier and Lappi leading for most of the rally before Ogier came out on top.

Rally of Turkey *Overall results, with 24 finishers*

1st	Sébastien Ogier/Julien Ingrassia	Citroën C3 WRC	3:50:12.1
2nd	Esapekka Lappi/Janne Ferm	Citroën C3 WRC	3:50:46.8
3rd	Andreas Mikkelsen/Anders Jaeger	Hyundai i20 Coupe WRC	3:51:16.6
6th	Jari-Matti Latvala/Miikka Anttila	Toyota Yaris WRC	3:53:11.2
7th	Kris Meeke/Sebastian Marshall	Toyota Yaris WRC	3:54:05.4
16th	Ott Tänak/Martin Järveoja	Toyota Yaris WRC	4:29:22.3

ROUND 12
Wales Rally GB
3-6 October

Known as one of the oldest rallies on the calendar, celebrating 75 years, Wales Rally GB welcomed 53 crews contesting 22 stages over the same distance as the Turkish event. Held in wet, muddy conditions, by and large, SS20 over Great Orme was cancelled, slicing off some three miles (5km) from the total distance.

In what can only be described as something of a roller-coaster ride for Tänak so far this season, the Estonian would bounce back from the disappointment of Turkey with a win in Great Britain. Thanks to a thorough mechanical

Rd 12 #10 Latvala.

overhaul of every component on the Yaris, especially the suspect ECU and the car's suspension setup, Toyota's drivers entered this rally with bags of confidence.

Meeke started his home rally superbly with fastest times in the shakedown and SS1, before setting the second quickest times in SS2 and SS3 to take an early lead. When Latvala crashed, he rolled his car down a bank and retired from the rally on SS7; Meeke felt a renewed sense of responsibility to bring his car home in one piece so he could earn precious points for the team to challenge Hyundai.

In hindsight, it was Tänak's superb driving in the two night stages of Day Two, SS9 and SS10 that allowed him to overtake Meeke for the rally lead and help set himself up to win the event. Before the night stages, Tänak had commented, "The most important thing at the Rally GB is confidence. If you lose confidence even a little, then your times will fall away significantly." He shone in those circumstances, while the Yaris WRC's suspension and drivetrain functioned as expected and fully delivered the engine's power to the road.

In a battle with Neuville for the win, that stayed close until the end, Tänak managed to win SS17, SS18, and the Power Stage, to pip the Hyundai driver by just 10 seconds at the finish. Tänak finished the rally in a commanding position with 240 points, 28 ahead of Ogier while Toyota was just eight points shy of Hyundai.

▲▼ *Rd 12 #8 Tänak.*

▲ *Rd 12 #5 Meeke.*

Wales Rally GB *Overall results, with 47 finishers*

1st	Ott Tänak/Martin Järveoja	Toyota Yaris WRC	3:00:58.0
2nd	Thierry Neuville/Nicolas Gilsoul	Hyundai i20 Coupe WRC	3:01:08.9
3rd	Sébastien Ogier/Julien Ingrassia	Citroën C3 WRC	3:01:21.8
4th	Kris Meeke/Sebastian Marshall	Toyota Yaris WRC	3:01:33.6
DNF	Jari-Matti Latvala/Miikka Anttila	Toyota Yaris WRC	–

ROUND 13

Rally Catalunya

24-27 October

Celebrating its 55th anniversary, the Rally Catalunya welcomed 61 starters (including Katsuta again) who competed over 17 stages, with the first on Friday. In dry conditions on challenging mixed tarmac and gravel surfaces, the rally covered 203 miles (326km).

Nine-time world champion Sebastien Loeb was the defending rally winner, but Gazoo drivers felt confident after a good performance in Wales. In fact, Tänak, after battling with Neuville, would finish in second place and be crowned world champion for the first time.

In the morning Special Stages on Day One, the Estonian was only able to record the fourth and fifth fastest times, finishing the session in third place overall. Then, in the afternoon stages, Tänak was unable to improve his times, falling to fifth overall with Neuville in the lead by 20 seconds. Then on Day Two, Tänak found his rhythm and recorded four straight stage wins, putting pressure on Neuville. The Hyundai driver, who led the rally standings, continued to perform consistently well, and at the end of the day led Tänak by 24 seconds.

On the final day, after discussion with his team, Tänak decided to go flat out for the win in the Power Stage, and finished 3.6 seconds faster than Neuville to clinch his first world championship.

Meeke meanwhile had crashed on Saturday trying to chase down a flying Loeb. In his second rally of the season, Katsuta got 33 minutes of penalties thrown at him, forcing him to drop down the field to 39th overall. Tänak was crowned champion, while Toyota sat only 18 points down on Hyundai.

Rd 13 #5 Meeke.

Rd 13 #10 Latvala.

Rd 13 #8 Tänak.

Rally Catalunya *Overall results, with 42 finishers*

1st	Thierry Neuville/Nicolas Gilsoul	Hyundai i20 Coupe WRC	3:07:39.6
2nd	Ott Tänak/Martin Järveoja	Toyota Yaris WRC	3:07:56.8
3rd	Dani Sordo/Carlos del Barrio	Hyundai i20 Coupe WRC	3:07:57.2
5th	Jari-Matti Latvala/Miikka Anttila	Toyota Yaris WRC	3:08:39.8
29th	Kris Meeke/Sebastian Marshall	Toyota Yaris WRC	3:49:59.6
39th	Takamoto Katsuta/Daniel Barritt	Toyota Yaris WRC	4:03:36.4

Rd 13 #8 Tänak.

ROUND 14

Rally Australia

14-17 November

Australia often provided a backdrop to Japan's early efforts at dominating the world of motorsport. Ultimately, just like the Safari Rally, the long-distance trials of the 1950s were an excellent proving ground, and victories could be used by PR departments to increase awareness in fledgling export markets. Rally Australia came much later, in 1988, first as an Asia-Pacific round and then a WRC one, but it has always been a firm favourite with the various teams.

Sadly, the 2019 edition was cancelled at the last minute due to a series of bushfires in New South Wales, and with no FIA contracts signed to take the event beyond 2019, this would ultimately be the last World Rally Championship round held in Australia, at least at time of writing. It was a sad end to a well-loved fixture on the calendar.

As far as the championship was concerned, while it made little difference to the driver standings (Tänak was so far ahead that he was untouchable), the cancellation of the event destroyed Toyota's chances of winning the title, which had been mathematically within reach prior to the trip Down Under. Tommi Mäkinen and his bosses back in Japan had every right to feel gutted ...

2019 SUMMARY

The season reviewed in a way that provides a quick reference from a Toyota/Gazoo perspective, with driver performance, round by round (overall position, followed by the scoring Power Stage position in brackets), and year-end positions within the FIA WRC championship.

	Latvala	Tänak	Meeke	Katsuta
Rd 01	5th (6th)	3rd (4th)	6th (1st)	- (-)
Rd 02	21st (7th)	1st (1st)	6th (6th)	- (-)
Rd 03	8th (9th)	2nd (6th)	5th (2nd)	- (-)
Rd 04	10th (6th)	6th (2nd)	9th (1st)	- (-)
Rd 05	5th (2nd)	8th (5th)	4th (6th)	- (-)
Rd 06	11th (3rd)	1st (1st)	10th (5th)	- (-)
Rd 07	7th (6th)	1st (3rd)	DNF (-)	- (-)
Rd 08	19th (4th)	5th (43rd)	8th (8th)	- (-)
Rd 09	3rd (5th)	1st (1st)	DNF (-)	- (-)
Rd 10	3rd (3rd)	1st (8th)	2nd (4th)	10th (11th)
Rd 11	7th (4th)	16th (1st)	8th (6th)	- (-)
Rd 12	DNF (-)	1st (1st)	4th (7th)	- (-)
Rd 13	5th (6th)	2nd (1st)	29th (8th)	39th (10th)
Rd 14	–	–	–	–

Drivers

1st	Ott Tänak	Toyota	263
2nd	Thierry Neuville	Hyundai	227
3rd	Sébastien Ogier	Citroën	217
6th	Kris Meeke	Toyota	98
7th	Jari-Matti Latvala	Toyota	94
25th	Takamoto Katsuta	Toyota	1

Co-drivers

1st	Martin Järveoja	Toyota	263
2nd	Nicolas Gilsoul	Hyundai	227
3rd	Julien Ingrassia	Citroën	217
6th	Seb Marshall	Toyota	98
7th	Miikka Anttila	Toyota	94
27th	Daniel Barritt	Toyota	1

NB: Points totals include Power Stage bonuses for drivers and co-drivers. It should also be noted that in the case of Katsuta and Barritt, most of the season was spent driving Ford Fiestas.

Manufacturers

1st	Hyundai	Hyundai Motorsport	380
2nd	Toyota	Toyota Gazoo Racing WRT	362
3rd	Citroën	Citroën Total WRT	284

The 2020 Season

The 2020 season was originally supposed to have 13 rounds on the calendar, with some interesting revivals amongst them (such as the Safari, Rally Japan, and a sortie to New Zealand) as thoughts of event rotation came back to the fore, but the COVID-19 outbreak saw to it that several events were cancelled. Even after replacements were found in a few cases, there were still only seven WRC rallies held in the end (including the WRC2 and WRC3 categories once more). The Junior World Rally Championship was ultimately contested over just four rounds this particular year.

2020 Season Rounds

Rally	Dates	Surface
Monte Carlo Rally	23-26 January	Tarmac
Rally Sweden	13-16 February	Snow
Rally Mexico	12-15 March	Gravel
Rally Estonia	4-6 September	Gravel
Rally of Turkey	18-20 September	Gravel
Rally Italia Sardegna	8-11 October	Gravel
Rally Monza	3-6 December	Tarmac

FIA rule changes and season prospects

There was little to report on this front for 2020, other than modifications to road order rulings, and a temporary ban on testing brought about by COVID-19. Ultimately, the FIA felt that the different restrictions in place from country to country could have given certain teams an advantage, which makes sense given the chaos caused during the early days of the outbreak.

Given this background, lockdowns and financial uncertainty, the facility to create additional 'teams' using the cars homologated in the manufacturer equipes was a welcome move at this stage of the proceedings. A French Hyundai team was formed to take advantage of the new 'WRC Team' ruling, although only the top two positions would count towards the championship in any one team, as before.

At the end of the day, it was a sensible way of getting more top-flight machines to enter events – a move that partially made up for an unexpected loss on the entry sheets. With Sébastien Ogier leaving the team after a difficult season, Citroën pulled out of the championship, although Petter Solberg drove a private C3 WRC in one round to add some variation to the paddocks, even if he wasn't allowed to score manufacturer points.

Anyway, behind the scenes, Toyota was quick to snap up the multiple World Champion, while Ogier's old teammate Lappi went to Ford. With the Frenchman joining the Japanese team, Tänak decided to go across to Hyundai, augmenting Neuville as the second full-time driver, while others took turns at piloting the third full-time works i20 Coupe.

The Gazoo team cars and their drivers

The new generation XP210 Yaris (based on the lightweight but very rigid GA-B platform) was announced in October 2019, going on sale in Japan and Europe soon after in FF and 4WD five-door hatchback form. It also spawned a Gazoo Racing version – the three-door GR Yaris – unveiled at the 2020 Tokyo Auto Salon, and in showrooms by the end of the year. This latter beast was the car that Toyota used for the homologation of its rally machine, which was expected to hit the WRC scene in 2021. Ultimately, the GR Yaris was not used as a works car until the 2022 season, but at least the scene has been set ...

Meanwhile, the existing car was rolled out for service once more, with several modifications made to make it lighter and more responsive for its fourth season. From the outside, one could be forgiven for thinking nothing had changed, for even the livery was almost identical, but careful inspection revealed subtle revisions to the rear wing assembly. As with all the major runners for 2020, the Yaris continued with Michelin as the supplier of its tarmac, gravel and snow tyres.

It was all-change in the driver line-up, however, with Sébastien Ogier, Elfyn Evans and Kalle Rovanperä being called up for full season duty in the works cars, joined on occasion by Takamoto Katsuta, as per last season. In addition, Jari-

The Yaris WRC for 2020.

An all-new driver line-up was announced for the 2020 season.

Matti Latvala had a single outing in the Swedish round, with his car officially entered by Latvala Motorsport.

Ogier was born in Gap, France, in December 1983. He didn't begin his rallying career until 2005, but still managed to win the 2007 Peugeot 206 Rally Cup one-make series and moved up to the JWRC in the following year. Teaming up with Julian Ingrassia in a Citroën C2, he duly won the 2008 title, and got his foot in the door with the works team as a result. He was eighth in the WRC title chase for 2009, improving to fourth and third over the following two seasons. Ogier then moved to Volkswagen Motorsport, and after a slow start with the Skoda Fabia, was then crowned World Champion with the VW Polo R WRC in 2013, 2014, 2015 and 2016. His fifth and sixth championships came courtesy of Ford before a move to Citroën in 2019, when he finished the season in a fighting third. Far from happy, though, the Frenchman decided it was time to sign up with Toyota.

Elfyn Evans comes from good rallying stock, being the son of Gwyndaf Evans. Not surprisingly, given his family history, he started his career with

Sébastien Ogier.

Ford, and stayed with the M-Sport team until the end of 2019. Kalle Rovanperä was another second generation rally driver, with an epic start to his career. We will take a look at these two youngsters later in the book.

As per 2019, the 27-year old Katsuta would be given a few drives in the #18 Yaris WRC, albeit signed for the Gazoo outfit this year rather than via Tommi Mäkinen Racing. Despite the new 'WRC Team' ruling, he was still not eligible to score manufacturer points for the main team or any other at this stage; the same was ultimately true of Latvala.

ROUND 01

Monte Carlo Rally
23-26 January

With 12,000 COVID deaths a week in France alone at the start of 2020, it was almost surreal to be holding the Monte against such a backdrop. But, like F1, teams were kept in a 'bubble' to enable the season to continue as best it could.

The Monte started with 88 entries and was run over 16 stages covering 190 miles (304km). The Gazoo Racing World Rally Team's all-new driver line-up (with Takamoto Katsuta entered in a fourth car) made a stunning start on Thursday's tricky night-time stages. Sébastien Ogier won his very first stage in the Yaris WRC and ended the night in second overall, with Elfyn Evans only two places behind, and top-level newcomer Kalle Rovanperä in seventh.

With a little lingering snow around, and heavier patches higher up, it was difficult to get the tyre choices right. Day Two belonged to Evans who won the first three stages – SS3, SS4 and SS5 – back-to-back to take the lead, before Ogier showed great pace late in the day to win SS6 and SS7 and pinch the lead back from his teammate. Rovenpera finished sixth overall, while Tänak's Hyundai debut ended suddenly with an accident on SS4.

Day Three proved to be a tough day for Toyota, seeing the lead change twice as Ogier and Evans battled for top spot with Neuville in a three-way fight. Evans picked up another stage victory in SS10 and managed to regain the lead, which he held until SS13 when he relinquished his number one spot to Neuville. Rovenpera held onto sixth, while Katsuta did well to pick up seventh.

Rd 01 #17 Ogier.

▲ *Rd 01 #69 Rovanperä.*

▲ *Rd 01 #18 Katsuta.*

Evans held top spot into the final day, but that dominance would be whittled away as Neuville found his rhythm and blitzed the last six special stages to take a commanding lead and eventually the victory. Ogier officially scored exactly the same time as Neuville on the PS, so picked up a joint-first, even though the Belgian was given the five points, with four for Ogier. In the end, Ogier came second, Evans third, Rovenpera fifth, and Katsuta could go home a happy man, finishing the event in seventh.

◀ *Rd 01 #17 Ogier.*

Monte Carlo Rally

Overall results, with 73 finishers

1st	Thierry Neuville/Nicolas Gilsoul	Hyundai i20 Coupe WRC	3:10:57.6
2nd	Sébastien Ogier/Julien Ingrassia	Toyota Yaris WRC	3:11:10.2
3rd	Elfyn Evans/Scott Martin	Toyota Yaris WRC	3:11:11.9
5th	Kalle Rovanperä/Jonne Halttunen	Toyota Yaris WRC	3:15:14.8
7th	Takamoto Katsuta/Daniel Barritt	Toyota Yaris WRC	3:22:25.5

Rd 01 #33 Evans.

ROUND 02

Rally Sweden

13-16 February

The Swedish Rally dates back to 1950, and is traditionally run in the winter months to provide an event held almost exclusively in snowy conditions. As such, this has always been one for the Scandinavians to show their prowess on studded tyres. Indeed, over half a century passed by before someone other than a Swede or Finn claimed the top spot on the podium.

The event was originally scheduled for 18 stages over a distance similar to that of the Monte, but

Rd 02 #33 Evans

Rd 02 #17 Ogier.

it was dramatically shortened to 11, with two SSs cancelled to give a total rally distance of just 93 miles (149km). Strangely however, there was hardly any snow, which led to exposed loose gravel in many places.

The event had 46 entries as Toyota boosted its presence to no less than five cars, thanks to an entry by Jari-Matti Latvala, who was disappointing, and ultimately retired early on with electrical problems. In contrast, Elfyn Evans made a faultless run from start to finish, putting him level with Neuville in the championship, and helping Toyota to jump into top spot. Rovanperä showed remarkable potential winning the first shakedown.

Evans won five stages over the event's three days putting him into the top spot, a position he did not relinquish. On Day One, he set the fastest times in SS1 and SS3 to take a dominant lead. On Day Two, as Evans extended his lead, Gazoo teammates Sébastien Ogier and Kalle Rovanperä pushed hard for third and fourth overall respectively, with the two drivers separated by just 0.5s as they battled for a place on the podium.

On Day Three, even though Neuville picked up SS8 and Rovanperä won the final Power Stage, Evans held onto his strong lead to pick up his first World Rally victory in just his second event and take the championship lead. Joining him on the podium was rookie sensation Kalle Rovanperä who captured a brilliant third, with Ogier in fourth and Katsuta in ninth.

Rd 02 #69 Rovanperä.

Rally Sweden *Overall results, with 42 finishers*

1st	Elfyn Evans/Scott Martin	Toyota Yaris WRC	1:11:43.1
2nd	Ott Tänak/Martin Järveoja	Hyundai i20 Coupe WRC	1:11:55.8
3rd	Kalle Rovanperä/Jonne Halttunen	Toyota Yaris WRC	1:12:03.3
4th	Sébastien Ogier/Julien Ingrassia	Toyota Yaris WRC	1:12:06.7
9th	Takamoto Katsuta/Daniel Barritt	Toyota Yaris WRC	1:13:42.7

Rd 02 #33 Evans.

▲ *Rd 03 #17 Ogier.*

ROUND 03

Rally Mexico

12-15 March

Rally Mexico was the last rally to follow original schedules as the COVID situation worsened. Some 36 crews started, including three Toyotas, three Hyundais and four Fords in the top category.

Based in the Guanajuato region, the rally was originally set to be held over 24 stages, covering 202 miles (325km). After the Shakedown and two street stages on Thursday, the rally got underway in earnest on Day One with Ott Tänak winning SS3 to take an early lead. That didn't last for long as Sébastien Ogier in his Yaris captured SS4 to steal the lead away from Tänak, a dominating lead he held until the end.

Day Two was a trouble-free day for the Toyotas with Ogier in first, Evans in third and Rovanperä in fifth. All three Yaris WRCs ran reliably throughout the day in the tough conditions posed by the altitude and high temperatures. The team's rookie driver, Rovanperä, suffered a damaged tyre in SS3 and took a cautious approach to complete the morning loop, but showed impressive progress in the afternoon, winning the León street test to remain in contention.

Rd 03 #33 Evans.

On Day Three, Ogier won SS13 to stay in the lead, but impressively managed to maintain that lead and take his first victory for the Gazoo WRC team, even though the two Hyundai pilots in Tänak and Neuville won all the following SSs on the final day. The win gave Ogier the championship lead.

The finish of the event was brought forward to Saturday evening – meaning that Sunday's stages (including the PS) were cancelled – a decision taken in the face of fast-changing travel restrictions connected with the global COVID virus outbreak, to ensure safe and timely travel home for officials, competitors and team personnel.

Rd 03 #69 Rovanperä.

Rd 03 #17 Ogier.

Rally Mexico *Overall results, with 21 finishers*

1st	Sébastien Ogier/Julien Ingrassia	Toyota Yaris WRC	2:47:47.6
2nd	Ott Tänak/Martin Järveoja	Hyundai i20 Coupe WRC	2:48:15.4
3rd	Teemu Suninen/Jarmo Lehtinen	Ford Fiesta WRC	2:48:25.5
4th	Elfyn Evans/Scott Martin	Toyota Yaris WRC	2:49:01.0
5th	Kalle Rovanperä/Jonne Halttunen	Toyota Yaris WRC	2:50:08.1

ROUND 04

Rally Estonia

4-6 September

Rally Estonia marked the return of the WRC after a half-year hiatus due to the COVID pandemic. Celebrating the 600th rally since the championship was founded back in 1973, this event was the tenth running of Rally Estonia, albeit its debut on the WRC calendar. Based in the town of Tartu, it was duly won by an Estonian, who was able to make the most of the largely dry conditions. There were quite a few fans to watch history being made, although they were forced to register their attendance online.

With 59 starters including four Toyotas, the rally comprised a first day Shakedown plus one short stage. Sébastien Ogier led the field after recording the joint-fastest time with Lappi. Then, Kalle Rovanperä won SS2 to snatch the rally lead from Ogier, but that was short-lived. Hyundai's

Rd 04 #33 Evans.

Rd 04 #17 Ogier.

Rd 04 #69 Rovanperä.

Ott Tänak quickly found his form by posting the fastest times in SS3 and SS4 to take a commanding lead that he held onto until the finish.

Toyota's drivers had been closely-matched for stage times on the high-speed gravel roads. Rovanperä's fastest time in SS2 was matched by Ogier who posted the quickest times in SS5 and SS7, but nothing Toyota could do was enough to unseat Tänak as the rally leader. Even though Evans, Rovanperä and Ogier took turns in winning every stage on Day Three, they could still not catch Tänak who had opened up a strong lead.

Along the way, each Gazoo driver had issues, with Evans suffering tyre trouble and Rovanperä being slugged with a one-minute penalty for a radiator removal infraction, problems that impacted on their overall performances.

Even with superb drives and fast times, the best Toyota could do in Estonia after 146 miles (233km) in SS distance was a third, fourth and fifth, with Gazoo Racing WRC Challenge Program driver Takamoto Katsuta placing fifth at one point after a strong day, but being forced to retire after crashing out on SS13.

Rally Estonia *Overall results, with 44 finishers*

1st	Ott Tänak/Martin Järveoja	Hyundai i20 Coupe WRC	1:59:53.6
2nd	Craig Breen/Paul Nagle	Hyundai i20 Coupe WRC	2:00:15.8
3rd	Sébastien Ogier/Julien Ingrassia	Toyota Yaris WRC	2:00:20.5
4th	Elfyn Evans/Scott Martin	Toyota Yaris WRC	2:00:35.5
5th	Kalle Rovanperä/Jonne Halttunen	Toyota Yaris WRC	2:01:12.3
DNF	Takamoto Katsuta/Daniel Barritt	Toyota Yaris WRC	–

ROUND 05

Rally of Turkey

18-20 September

The Rally of Turkey was brought forward to allow a postponed Italian sortie to fit into the calendar. It marked the 13th running of the event in this country and started with just 24 entries, of which ten were in the top category. Run in dry conditions, only 12 stages were held over

Rd 05 #69 Rovanperä. ▶

Rd 05 #17 Ogier.

Rd 05 #33 Evans.

Rd 05 #33 Evans.

three days (138 miles/221km) and with no spectators.

The Gazoo team was in a strong position after the opening two stages on Friday evening with Ogier third, Evans in fourth and Rovanperä fifth. Ogier posted the fastest times early on Day Two in SS3 and SS4 to take an early lead in the rally. Then as Neuville (Hyundai) won the next three special stages, he snatched the lead away from Ogier, maintaining the number one spot until the end of Day Two. All three Toyota drivers were within 2.7s of the lead, with Evans 0.8s behind Ogier, and Rovanperä a further 0.6s back.

On Day Three, Evans showed strong form to win the day's opening SS9 and take the lead away from Neuville. Surprisingly Evans pulled out all the stops, and managed to hold onto his lead and take the rally victory even though Neuville finished strongly by posting the fastest times in the last three SSs. That win propelled Evans to the top of the drivers' championship board and Toyota into first in the manufacturers' table. As for Ogier, his engine failed in SS11 and forced him to retire.

Rovanperä's impressive rookie season continued with a fourth-place finish – the 19-year-old's fifth top-five result from as many events at rallying's highest level. As it happens, Evans and his Finnish teammate posted the same time in the PS, but the point advantage went to the younger driver and his co-driver, Jonne Halttunen.

Rally of Turkey *Overall results, with 18 finishers*

1st	Elfyn Evans/Scott Martin	Toyota Yaris WRC	2:43:02.7
2nd	Thierry Neuville/Nicolas Gilsoul	Hyundai i20 Coupe WRC	2:43:37.9
3rd	Sébastien Loeb/Daniel Elena	Hyundai i20 Coupe WRC	2:44:02.1
4th	Kalle Rovanperä/Jonne Halttunen	Toyota Yaris WRC	2:45:38.6
DNF	Sébastien Ogier/Julien Ingrassia	Toyota Yaris WRC	–

ROUND 06

Rally Italia Sardegna
8-11 October

In a challenging year, thanks to COVID, this event was the 17th running of Rally Italia Sardegna, and was staged over four days, although the first was reserved purely for a shakedown. With 16 stages over 149 miles (239km), four Toyotas were entered amongst a field of 63 starters.

As a result of their positions at the top of the championship, Day One saw Elfyn Evans and Ogier having to run first and second on the gravel roads throughout the day's stages with team-mate Kalle Rovanperä not far behind in fourth. Evans set the best time in SS3 with Ogier in second, and they rounded out the morning in fourth and third overall respectively. But these times were not quick enough to challenge for the rally lead, held by Hyundai's Dani Sordo from

Rd 06 #17 Ogier.

Rd 06 #69 Rovanperä.

early on Day One, a lead he would maintain until the finish.

Rd 06 #33 Evans.

During the morning loop of four stages on Day Two, Ogier won both passes over the famous Monte Lerno test as he moved up into the podium positions. He was then also fastest over both of the afternoon stages to snatch second place overall at the end of the day, taking an advantage of 1.5 seconds into Sunday over his third-placed rival. No longer having to run first on the road as championship leader as he did on Friday, Evans could also compete for the leading times, and moved up from fifth to fourth overall.

Rovanperä crashed out of the rally on the second stage of the morning when he ran wide and struck two trees with the rear of the car, forcing him to retire from the event. Even though Ogier won SS13 and SS15, those victories were not quite enough to catch Sordo and Neuville in the Hyundais. In the end, Ogier finished in third with Evans in fourth, allowing Hyundai to jump ahead in the championship.

Rally Italia Sardegna *Overall results, with 50 finishers*

1st	Dani Sordo/Carlos del Barrio	Hyundai i20 Coupe WRC	2:41:37.5
2nd	Thierry Neuville/Nicolas Gilsoul	Hyundai i20 Coupe WRC	2:41:42.6
3rd	Sébastien Ogier/Julien Ingrassia	Toyota Yaris WRC	2:41:43.6
4th	Elfyn Evans/Scott Martin	Toyota Yaris WRC	2:42:39.8
DNF	Kalle Rovanperä/Jonne Halttunen	Toyota Yaris WRC	–
DNF	Takamoto Katsuta/Daniel Barritt	Toyota Yaris WRC	–

ROUND 07

Rally Monza
3-6 December

▼ *Rd 07 #17 Ogier.*

Rally Monza was a newcomer to fill out the calendar, and was based on a traditional event at the famous circuit. There were 92 starters tackling 16 stages over 149 miles (239km), as per Sardinia. However, SS10 was cancelled due to a crash that proved awkward to clear up, and SS12 was also cancelled due to heavy snow in the mountains north of Bergamo. That took 29 miles (47km) off the SS total distance.

Holding off a challenge from Sordo, Sébastien Ogier claimed the early rally lead with a stage win, with his

Rd 07 #33 Evans.

▲ Rd 07 #69 Rovanperä.

fellow Gazoo Racing World Rally Team drivers Elfyn Evans and Kalle Rovanperä also safely completing the stage inside the top five. In fog and low-grip, near-freezing temperatures, Ogier was third-fastest after three runs, with Rovanperä fourth and Evans in ninth. In fact, all Gazoo team drivers made it through the first full day of competitive action on Rally Monza without major drama and in a strong overall position in very challenging conditions.

With special studless snow tyres fitted, drivers' championship contenders Evans and Ogier both recorded a fastest time during the afternoon and closed up on the rally leaders as Lappi and Sordo both held early leads. Ogier ended the day ahead in third overall, 12 seconds from first place, with Evans 5.1 seconds behind him in fourth. Meanwhile, after damage caused him to stop on Thursday, Takamoto Katsuta restarted the morning showing great progress, and on SS5, he helped complete a first-ever 1-2-3-4 for Toyota, with all drivers finishing in the top four.

Avoiding trouble on Day Three in treacherous conditions on mountain roads, Ogier surged into the lead of Rally Monza. Teammate Evans was fastest in SS9 but heartbreakingly slid off the road on SS11 and could not continue. After being

Rd 07 #17 Ogier.

warned of the dangers by Evans, Ogier went on to win the stage and take the lead, before SS12 was cancelled for safety reasons due to the quantity of snow.

Having captured the lead on Day Three, Ogier won SS14 to take the overall victory, with Katsuta finally showing his mettle by posting the fastest time in the PS. After winning Rally Monza, Ogier and Ingrassia became seven-time world champions, but Toyota just missed out on the manufacturers' title by a slim margin of just five points to Hyundai.

Rally Monza *Overall results, with 71 finishers*

1st	Sébastien Ogier/Julien Ingrassia	Toyota Yaris WRC	2:15:51.0
2nd	Ott Tänak/Martin Järveoja	Hyundai i20 Coupe WRC	2:16:04.9
3rd	Dani Sordo/Carlos del Barrio	Hyundai i20 Coupe WRC	2:16:06.3
5th	Kalle Rovanperä/Jonne Halttunen	Toyota Yaris WRC	2:17:02.1
20th	Takamoto Katsuta/Daniel Barritt	Toyota Yaris WRC	2:27:41.3
29th	Elfyn Evans/Scott Martin	Toyota Yaris WRC	2:36:03.6

2020 SUMMARY

The season reviewed in a way that provides a quick reference from a Toyota/Gazoo perspective, with driver performance, round by round (overall position, followed by the scoring Power Stage position in brackets), and year-end positions within the FIA WRC championship.

	Ogier	Evans	Rovanperä	Katsuta
Rd 01	2nd (2nd)	3rd (4th)	5th (6th)	7th (7th)
Rd 02	4th (3rd)	1st (6th)	3rd (1st)	9th (9th)
Rd 03	1st (-)	4th (-)	5th (-)	- (-)
Rd 04	3rd (4th)	4th (2nd)	5th (1st)	DNF (-)
Rd 05	DNF (-)	1st (4th)	4th (3rd)	- (-)
Rd 06	3rd (3rd)	4th (4th)	DNF (-)	DNF (-)
Rd 07	1st (7th)	29th (3rd)	5th (6th)	20th (1st)

Drivers

1st	Sébastien Ogier	Toyota	122
2nd	Elfyn Evans	Toyota	114
3rd	Ott Tänak	Hyundai	105
5th	Kalle Rovanperä	Toyota	80
13th	Takamoto Katsuta	Toyota	13

Co-drivers

1st	Julien Ingrassia	Toyota	122
2nd	Scott Martin	Toyota	114
3rd	Martin Järveoja	Hyundai	105
5th	Jonne Halttunen	Toyota	80
13th	Daniel Barritt	Toyota	13

NB: Points totals include Power Stage bonuses for drivers and co-drivers.

Manufacturers

1st	Hyundai	Hyundai Motorsport	241
2nd	Toyota	Toyota Gazoo Racing WRT	236
3rd	Ford	M-Sport World Rally Team	129

The 2021 Season

The COVID-19 outbreak continued to play havoc with the calendar, and any notions of event rotation had to be kicked into touch once again. Four events planned for 2021 were cancelled (those set to take place in Sweden, Britain, Chile and Japan), but the FIA still managed to put 12 rounds together to create a decent spectacle in these trying times, even though it involved going back to Finland twice. At least some old favourites returned, while the Junior World Rally Championship was held over five rounds.

2021 Season Rounds

	Event	Dates	Surface
🇲🇨	Monte Carlo Rally	21-24 January	Tarmac
🇫🇮	Arctic Rally	26-28 February	Snow
🇭🇷	Croatia Rally	22-25 April	Tarmac
🇵🇹	Rally de Portugal	20-23 May	Gravel
🇮🇹	Rally Italia Sardegna	3-6 June	Gravel
🇰🇪	Safari Rally	24-27 June	Gravel
🇪🇪	Rally Estonia	15-18 July	Gravel
🇧🇪	Ypres Rally Belgium	13-15 August	Tarmac
🇬🇷	Acropolis Rally	9-12 September	Gravel
🇫🇮	Rally Finland	1-3 October	Gravel
🇪🇸	Rally Catalunya	14-17 October	Tarmac
🇮🇹	Rally Monza	18-21 November	Tarmac

FIA rule changes and season prospects

The 'WRC Team' ruling introduced last year was taken a stage further with the creation of a fourth world championship title – one for teams would be established to augment those already in place for drivers, co-drivers and manufacturers. With only seven rounds necessary to qualify (including a minimum of one outside Europe), this move would probably encourage more equipes to enter the series in the future, but for the time being, the FIA had to be thankful the WRC had managed to come through the pandemic in relatively good shape. Although it wasn't presented in the top category of the sport for 2021 (due to duplication), it should be noted that the 'team' moniker was used rather than the 'manufacturer' one in the WRC2 championship from 2020 onwards.

Meanwhile, starting intervals were increased from two to three minutes, and Power Stage bonus scores were extended to include manufacturers as well as drivers for 2021. The PS point allocations remained the same (first through fifth), but for the makers, only the two fastest cars from each brand would be allowed to add points to a team's final tally.

The Gazoo team cars and their drivers

As noted earlier, the arrival of the GR Yaris-based rally car was delayed, in large part due to the damage caused to the motor industry in the wake of the COVID-19 pandemic. Ultimately, with regulations set to change in 2022, the expense of developing a 'homologation special' to contest just a single season simply couldn't be justified, so the existing car was rolled out for service once more.

The leading specifications were carried over, although Toyota moved over to Pirelli tyres (as did the other teams – one Ford, and two Hyundai outfits), having previously used Michelin rubber on the Yaris rally car since its inception; other minor upgrades were carried out on a number of components to enhance reliability, but otherwise the 2021 model was much the same as its predecessor, including the distinctive tarmac and gravel wheel designs.

On the bodywork, the main intake up front looked quite different, but was actually nothing more than a trick of the eye caused by the 2021 car's new paint job. There was a new vent cut into the leading edge of the front wheelarch, however, along with fresh door mirrors, a revised rear diffuser, and some very subtle tuning on the rear spoiler assembly. In reality, it was the dramatic livery, now lacking Microsoft stickers, that was the most obvious change, with its white, red and black

The Toyota Yaris WRC for the 2021 season.

colouring revamped to give the vehicle a very edgy look.

After a difficult 2020, Jari-Matti Latvala decided to hang up his race overalls in order to replace Tommi Mäkinen as Team Principal. Latvala, like Mäkinen, was chosen for the role by Akio Toyoda, and was assisted by Project Director Yuichiro Haruna, Sporting Director Kaj Lindström, and Technical Director Tom Fowler. Mäkinen did not leave the Toyota fold altogether, however, for he was kept on the payroll as a motorsport advisor.

The same trio of drivers were named to pilot the three full works cars for 2021 (Ogier, Evans and Rovanperä), with Katsuta being called up to handle a fourth Yaris, as before, but this time for almost a full season. Now carrying #1 on his doors rather than #17, Ogier was due to retire at the end of last season, but decided to give it one more year,

New Team Principal, Jari-Matti Latvala.

Kalle Rovanperä.

which duly became another, and so on. Ogier's career was looked at in the last chapter, so this time we will run a profile on the youngest member in the team, Kalle Rovanperä.

Born in Finland in October 2000, Kalle is the son of Harri Rovanperä (who drove in the WRC from 1993 through to 2006). He made his debut at the end of 2017, competing in Britain and Australia, and surprised everyone by getting a seat in the Skoda team the following year. More Skoda WRC2 outings came in 2019, with his performance in Portugal (first in Class, and sixth overall) confirming the equipe's confidence in him. But a drive like that puts you in the spotlight, and Toyota duly signed the young lad for 2020, with Jonne Halttunen in the seat beside him.

For the record, Esapekka Lappi moved into the

WRC2 arena, but got back into the Yaris driving seat for his home round in Finland, entered via RTE-Motorsport. Meanwhile, Katsuta was present in almost every round, albeit with three different co-drivers over the season, and while he was still unable to score for the manufacturer, he was gaining experience and providing useful feedback for his masters.

ROUND 01

Monte Carlo Rally

21-24 January

With no spectators allowed, 79 starters commenced the Monte on January 21. Originally scheduled with 15 stages, the last one on Friday was cancelled, leaving 161 miles (258km) plus transport distance. Wet roads for Thursday's two SSs set the theme for this year's event, as snowy conditions prevailed throughout, making tyre choices difficult. Elfyn Evans said that it was tough at the beginning to get heat into the tyres as they attacked slippery roads through small villages.

The Gazoo team arrived in Monte Carlo full of confidence and brandishing a superb driver lineup that soon proved its mettle. Tänak in his Hyundai may have won the first two stages on Day One, but on Day Two Ogier seized the lead with three straight stage wins from SS3 though SS5. Rovanperä had started Day Two well but had a mechanical issue and lost precious seconds on the time control.

On Day Two, Evans won SS6 to briefly snatch the lead from Ogier, but the Frenchman proceeded to post the fastest time in SS7 and retake the lead to start Day Three on top of the standings. Day

Rd 01 #1 Ogier.

Rd 01 #33 Evans.

Three's slippery conditions proved challenging for all drivers, especially Ogier who complained about having "the lowest grip I've ever had in my career, so I could not push too much." Such modesty. Even in the trying conditions, Ogier was still able to consolidate his position by winning SS8 to extend his lead, while Evans was fastest in SS10, and Rovanperä and Katsuta performed well, finishing in the top six.

On Day Four, Ogier posted the quickest times in three of the four stages, including the tough Power Stage to maintain the lead, and went on to win the Monte outright. Meanwhile, Evans was not happy as he couldn't find his rhythm in the icy conditions and lost a lot of time. It was Ogier's 50th win, and seventh Monte (eighth if one includes a non-championship victory), while Evans also finished on the podium for a strong 1-2-4-6 finish.

▲ *Rd 01 #33 Evans.*

▼ *Rd 01 #69 Rovanperä.*

▼ *Rd 01 #1 Ogier.*

Monte Carlo Rally

Overall results, with 62 finishers

1st	Sébastien Ogier/Julien Ingrassia	Toyota Yaris WRC	2:56:33.7
2nd	Elfyn Evans/Scott Martin	Toyota Yaris WRC	2:57:06.3
3rd	Thierry Neuville/Martijn Wydaeghe	Hyundai i20 Coupe WRC	2:57:47.2
4th	Kalle Rovanperä/Jonne Halttunen	Toyota Yaris WRC	2:59:07.3
6th	Takamoto Katsuta/Daniel Barritt	Toyota Yaris WRC	3:03:35.0

ROUND 02

Arctic Rally
26-28 February

Based in Rovaniemi in the north of Finland, the Arctic Rally marked the first time that this event had been run as a round of the WRC, which was surprising as it had been held some 56 times in the past. Run in snowy and icy conditions, the 55 starters competed over ten stages covering 157 miles (251km).

The action started straight away on Friday after three short shakedowns with Hyundai's Ott Tänak taking an early lead. Rovanperä had high hopes for victory in his home rally, and started out strongly but made a few small mistakes that cost time. Ogier, meanwhile, was happy with the car's performance and tyre grip and managed to stay in reach of a podium finish, while Evans posted quick times in the first and second stages.

On Day Two, Tänak continued to dominate with three stage wins, while Evans and Rovanperä

◀ *Rd 02 #33 Evans.*

▼ *Rd 02 #1 Ogier.*

both showed their pace by each picking up a stage victory. Although Ogier also pushed hard, he ended up stuck on a snow bank on Saturday evening, and out of contention. The reason for not being able to catch Tänak, according to Evans, came down to front tyre grip, which the Welshman had struggled with all day. Rovanperä, who had also been suffering from understeer, made minor adjustments to the suspension that proved fruitful later on, allowing him to post the fastest time in SS7. Evans concluded that his car had flashes of good speed but was nowhere near consistent enough – an appraisal that was applicable to all Gazoo drivers. Katsuta meanwhile had done well to finish sixth overall, having got used to his car in the tough conditions. Tänak led from start to finish, but Rovanperä, with his second place, was now leading the championship.

Rd 02 #69 Rovanperä.

Arctic Rally *Overall results, with 51 finishers*

1st	Ott Tänak/Martin Järveoja	Hyundai i20 Coupe WRC	2:03:49.6
2nd	Kalle Rovanperä/Jonne Halttunen	Toyota Yaris WRC	2:04:07.1
3rd	Thierry Neuville/Martijn Wydaeghe	Hyundai i20 Coupe WRC	2:04:09.4
5th	Elfyn Evans/Scott Martin	Toyota Yaris WRC	2:04:51.1
6th	Takamoto Katsuta/Daniel Barritt	Toyota Yaris WRC	2:05:27.4
20th	Sébastien Ogier/Julien Ingrassia	Toyota Yaris WRC	2:14:55.8

ROUND 03

Croatia Rally

22-25 April

Based in Zagreb, the 2021 Croatia Rally marked the first time this event had been held as a WRC round. Attracting 65 entries the rally was held in dry conditions throughout. With only the shakedown held on the Thursday, some 20 stages covering 188 miles (300km) followed on Friday through Sunday.

In the early stages, Evans had been querying Gazoo's mixed tyre package, which was not performing as expected. On SS1, Rovanperä left the course, rolled down the bank and hit a tree, suffering considerable damage. Then Ogier nearly went off at the same corner. Neuville in his Hyundai i20 led for the entirety of Day One, picking up three fastest times to hold onto a commanding lead. Ogier and Evans fought back to

Rd 03 #69 Rovanperä.

Rd 03 #1 Ogier.

share the quickest time on SS3, before Ogier found his form and posted a hat-trick of fastest times during the last three stages of Day One.

Starting off Day Two in second place, Ogier went on to win the day's first stage, and in so doing, snatched the lead from Neuville. Meanwhile, there was a revolution happening in Takamoto Katsuta's camp when the Japanese driver dug deep to find outstanding form and pull off his first, and then second stage wins in WRC. With wins on SS9 and SS12, Ogier on the other hand, returned to service in Zagreb with a seven-second margin over Evans – the SS11 winner – with a larger gap back to third place.

On Day Three, Evans, who had been just seconds behind Ogier in the rankings, was fastest over the first two stages – SS17 and SS18, and burst into the rally lead. In a final-stage decider that went right down to the wire, Ogier and co-driver Ingrassia claimed the victory by just 0.6 seconds over their team-mates Evans and Martin in one of the WRC's closest ever finishes. Ogier's win put him at the top of the standings, and increased GR's lead over Hyundai. Toyota had recorded another strong one-two finish.

▲ *Rd 03 #33 Evans.*

▼ *Rd 03 #1 Ogier.*

Croatia Rally *Overall results, with 55 finishers*

1st	Sébastien Ogier/Julien Ingrassia	Toyota Yaris WRC	2:51:22.9
2nd	Elfyn Evans/Scott Martin	Toyota Yaris WRC	2:51:23.5
3rd	Thierry Neuville/Martijn Wydaeghe	Hyundai i20 Coupe WRC	2:51:31.0
6th	Takamoto Katsuta/Daniel Barritt	Toyota Yaris WRC	2:54:54.7
DNF	Kalle Rovanperä/Jonne Halttunen	Toyota Yaris WRC	–

ROUND 04

Rally de Portugal

20-23 May

While Toyota had four cars entered again, this rally marked the first appearance of a Citroën all year, with Sardinia being the only other event to feature the French carmaker. With dry weather throughout, some 77 entries began with a ceremonial start on Thursday, followed by 20 stages over 211 miles (338km), ending with a PS including the notorious Fafe jump.

Eight stages made up the opening day of the first gravel rally of the 2021 season, based mainly in the area around Arganil. An improved performance followed in the afternoon, beginning with Rovanperä posting the fastest time in SS4. Another stage win came for Ogier in a dramatic SS7 result that saw Evans awarded the same time. That victory allowed Evans to move up into second overall and he ended the day six seconds away from the leader. Katsuta had another impressive day driving a fourth Yaris WRC as

▲ *Rd 04 #69 Rovanperä.*

▲ *Rd 04 #1 Ogier.*

◀ *Rd 04 #33 Evans.*

▶ *Rd 04 #33 Evans.*

part of the TGR WRC Challenge Program, setting consistent times and finishing the day 9.4s behind Evans overnight. Ogier was 8.6s further back and 4.9s in front of Rovanperä.

Tänak, who had held onto the lead since snatching it from Sordo towards the end of Day One, proceeded to show his pace by knocking off three fastest times back-to-back at the start of Day Two. Evans meanwhile, moved up into second after posting a trio of second-fastest times in the morning loop. After winning SS12 and SS14, Evans took the lead from Tänak, before ramming his victory home on Day Three by going quickest in SS16, SS17 and SS19. Rovanperä had been running in sixth place overall prior to SS14, which he could not start because of technical reasons. However, he drove back to service where the team prepared his car for a restart.

Finishing a superb fourth place after a fast and consistent weekend, Takamoto Katsuta claimed the best result of his career to date. Ogier finished third and continued to lead the drivers' championship – two points ahead of Evans – while the team extended its lead in the manufacturers' standings. Another double podium finish for Gazoo.

Rally de Portugal *Overall results, with 44 finishers*

1st	Elfyn Evans/Scott Martin	Toyota Yaris WRC	3:38:26.2
2nd	Dani Sordo/Borja Rozada	Hyundai i20 Coupe WRC	3:38:54.5
3rd	Sébastien Ogier/Julien Ingrassia	Toyota Yaris WRC	3:39:49.8
4th	Takamoto Katsuta/Daniel Barritt	Toyota Yaris WRC	3:40:54.6
22nd	Kalle Rovanperä/Jonne Halttunen	Toyota Yaris WRC	4:00:36.4

ROUND 05

Rally Italia Sardegna
3-6 June

Rd 05 #1 Ogier.

Held in Olbia in Sardinia, some 55 starters competed in 20 stages over 189 miles (303km) after a ceremonial start on Thursday. With good weather all weekend, the sand-covered stages of Sardinia can be among the most demanding of the season for the driver who runs first on the road, but Ogier fought superbly against that disadvantage. He set the top-three times in five of the day's eight stages, and at one point moved up into second place overall.

Second in the championship, Portugal winner Evans did not feel as comfortable on Day One as his team-mates during the morning stages, but was able to improve his ranking throughout the afternoon and climbed up to fourth overall. Rovanperä showed potential in the morning, vying for stage wins and holding second place overall. Unfortunately, his day came

◀ *Rd 05 #69 Rovanperä.*

▲ *Rd 05 #33 Evans.*

▼ *Rd 05 #1 Ogier.*

to an abrupt end when he stopped in SS4 with suspension trouble. Katsuta was placed in sixth after another good performance.

Hyundai's Tänak meanwhile, had successfully posted five consecutive fastest times on Day One to take the lead.

On Day Two, Ogier was fastest on SS12 which allowed him to grab the lead away from the Estonian driver. Ogier then consolidated his position with three more back to back wins before Evans found form to pick up three of the last five stages. There were three Yaris WRCs in the top four positions, with TGR WRC Challenge Program driver Takamoto Katsuta on course to match his best-ever result of fourth overall that he achieved in Portugal.

This was Ogier's third victory from five events and saw both he and Toyota surge ahead in the points. Evans took second, despite nearly drowning his engine on the PS, and Katsuta duly captured fourth. In their best season so far, the Gazoo team once again picked up a superb 1-2-4 result to shoot to a 49-point lead over Hyundai. Meanwhile, Ogier now led the championship by 11 points over Evans, who was in turn 18 points ahead of Neuville.

Rally Italia Sardegna *Overall results, with 40 finishers*

1st	Sébastien Ogier/Julien Ingrassia	Toyota Yaris WRC	3:19:26.4
2nd	Elfyn Evans/Scott Martin	Toyota Yaris WRC	3:20:12.4
3rd	Thierry Neuville/Martijn Wydaeghe	Hyundai i20 Coupe WRC	3:20:31.6
4th	Takamoto Katsuta/Daniel Barritt	Toyota Yaris WRC	3:25:37.6
25th	Kalle Rovanperä/Jonne Halttunen	Toyota Yaris WRC	4:00:36.4

ROUND 06

Safari Rally
24-27 June

The Safari Rally will always stand as one of the true classics on the rally calendar. Based in Kenya, it was first run in 1953, and was a regular WRC fixture for the first three decades of the championship. Known for its mix of fast stretches and rough roads that can turn into a mud bath at the first sign of rain, the event has always called for strong, reliable vehicles that can be run almost flat-out in very demanding conditions.

Kicking off with one SS on the Thursday, some 53 starters competed in 18 stages held over 197 miles (315km). In addition to four Toyotas and five Hyundais, three Fords also entered the event in a three-way battle for line honours. In a highly competitive rally, the lead ended up changing six times over four days.

On Day One, Sébastien Ogier won the short opening super special stage ahead of his team-mates Kalle Rovanperä and Elfyn Evans to lead the field going into the rest of the event. Takamoto Katsuta became the highest-placed Yaris WRC driver on Safari Rally Kenya in second overall, while championship leader Sébastien Ogier occupied fourth overall. Later on in the day, Evans was running in fourth place until he stopped at the end of SS3 Kedong after hitting a large rock. He was unable to repair the damage in order to continue, but would restart the following day. Rovanperä set the fastest time in both SS4 and SS5 to briefly claim the rally lead, before getting stuck in deep ruts that forced him to be towed out – dropping him to seventh place overnight. Ogier lost time during the morning with a technical issue and fell to seventh, but recovered ground to finish the day in fourth. He and Katsuta set the joint fastest time in SS7 (Katsuta's first fastest time ever!), with the Japanese driver completing an impressive and trouble-free day in second place, just 18.8 seconds off the lead.

Rd 06 #1 Ogier.

Rd 06 #69 Rovanperä.

▲ *Rd 06 #33 Evans.*

▶ *Ogier congratulating Katsuta on his fine result.*

On Day Three, Ogier won three consecutive stages in intermittent rainy, muddy conditions, and then picked up another stage victory first thing on Day Four to snatch the lead from Neuville, who retired on SS15. But the rally was not over, as Katsuta burst into the lead, however briefly, for the first time in his career. Not to be outdone, Ogier dug deep to post a fastest time in SS17 and reclaim the lead from Katsuta and capture the overall victory.

Safari Rally — *Overall results, with 26 finishers*

1st	Sébastien Ogier/Julien Ingrassia	Toyota Yaris WRC	3:18:11.3
2nd	Takamoto Katsuta/Daniel Barritt	Toyota Yaris WRC	3:18:33.1
3rd	Ott Tänak/Martin Järveoja	Hyundai i20 Coupe WRC	3:19:20.8
6th	Kalle Rovanperä/Jonne Halttunen	Toyota Yaris WRC	3:29:04.7
10th	Elfyn Evans/Scott Martin	Toyota Yaris WRC	4:07:34.0

ROUND 07

Rally Estonia
15-18 July

Based in the town of Tartu, there were 49 entries competing over 24 stages that covered a total of 196 miles (314km). With only one short stage on Thursday, local lad Ott Tänak's hopes would ultimately be dashed early on by a series of wheel and tyre problems.

Meanwhile, Rovanperä recorded the fastest

▲ *Rd 07 #33 Evans.*

Rd 07 #69 Rovanperä.

Rd 07 #1 Ogier.

time in SS1, with team-mates Evans fourth and Ogier fifth. Rovanperä had the lead briefly but relinquished it to Tänak and Breen before regaining the top spot for the rest of the rally. The Finnish driver then went on to record five consecutive stage victories to thrust him into the lead. He then won the last stage on Day Two and the first on Day Three to consolidate his position out in front. Rovanperä was driving so well it didn't matter that Tänak posted fastest time on the next six stages.

Takamoto Katsuta was running in third overall after SS4, but retired on the following road section as a precaution after co-driver Dan Barritt reported neck and back pain following a heavy landing from one of the many large jumps.

Day Three saw Rovanperä further extend his lead. The 20-year-old from Finland began the day with a dominant performance in SS10, where he was over 10s quicker than anyone else over the longest stage of the rally, the 23.53-kilometre Peipsiääre test. By the end of the morning loop of four stages, his lead was up to 35.7s.

Gazoo drivers Ogier and Evans continued to be involved in a battle over third position as they tried to fight off Breen and Neuville. Ultimately they remained fourth and fifth respectively, with Ogier ending the day 17.9s away from third and Evans a further 23.4s behind him.

With Rovanperä literally flying, he became the youngest driver ever to win a round of the FIA World Rally Championship after he and co-driver Jonne Halttunen secured victory in Rally Estonia. The team's fifth consecutive win (and sixth from seven rounds so far this year) is the longest-ever WRC winning streak achieved by Toyota in its rallying history.

Rd 07 #69 Rovanperä. ▶

Rally Estonia *Overall results, with 38 finishers*

1st	Kalle Rovanperä/Jonne Halttunen	Toyota Yaris WRC	2:51:29.1
2nd	Craig Breen/Paul Nagle	Hyundai i20 Coupe WRC	2:52:29.0
3rd	Thierry Neuville/Martijn Wydaeghe	Hyundai i20 Coupe WRC	2:52:41.5
4th	Sébastien Ogier/Julien Ingrassia	Toyota Yaris WRC	2:52:53.1
5th	Elfyn Evans/Scott Martin	Toyota Yaris WRC	2:53:36.2
DNF	Takamoto Katsuta/Daniel Barritt	Toyota Yaris WRC	–

ROUND 08

Ypres Rally Belgium

13-15 August

In Ypres Rally Belgium, a remarkable 98 entries were registered, although only ten entered the top category. Teams competed in 20 stages covering 185 miles (296km). The good weather throughout made for some very fast stages. Katsuta started with a new co-driver, but an accident on Day Two (SS10) led to his retirement.

After Day One, all Gazoo drivers were breathing down a potential podium finish with Rovanperä in fourth, Evans fifth and Ogier sixth – which is no mean feat considering none of the drivers had ever competed before on the tricky asphalt stages around Ypres.

Hyundai drivers Breen, Tänak and Neuville all won stages on Day One and swapped the rally lead all day in a process resembling musical chairs. Evans had already climbed up into third overall on the morning's opening test Hollebeke, the longest of the rally at 25.86km, and later went on to set the fastest time in SS11. In the afternoon session, Ogier recorded stage wins in both SS13 and SS15, which

Rd 08 #1 Ogier.

▲ Rd 08 #33 Evans.

▼ Rd 08 #69 Rovanperä.

proved to be the only bright spots for Toyota in the whole rally. In the day's final stage it was Rovanperä who came close to a stage win of his own, setting the second-fastest time and finishing the day 3.3s behind Evans with just one second further back to Ogier.

With Neuville dominating the event, Rovanperä went on to seal third place by 6.5s over Evans and claim an impressive result as the event came to a close at the iconic Spa-Francorchamps circuit. Evans and his co-driver Scott Martin took fourth, while Ogier and Julien Ingrassia finished fifth.

Ogier was second-fastest on the rally-ending Power Stage (with Rovanperä fourth and Evans fifth) to gain additional points and strengthen his championship lead, which now stood at 38 points over Evans, who was tied on points with the driver in third. Toyota continued to lead the manufacturers' standings by 41 points.

Ypres Rally Belgium *Overall results, with 73 finishers*

1st	Thierry Neuville/Martijn Wydaeghe	Hyundai i20 Coupe WRC	2:30:24.2
2nd	Craig Breen/Paul Nagle	Hyundai i20 Coupe WRC	2:30:54.9
3rd	Kalle Rovanperä/Jonne Halttunen	Toyota Yaris WRC	2:31:07.3
4th	Elfyn Evans/Scott Martin	Toyota Yaris WRC	2:31:13.8
5th	Sébastien Ogier/Julien Ingrassia	Toyota Yaris WRC	2:31:20.0
DNF	Takamoto Katsuta/Keaton Williams	Toyota Yaris WRC	–

ROUND 09

Acropolis Rally
9-12 September

Marking the 65th running of the Acropolis Rally, this gravel event had 48 starters competing over a total of 15 stages covering 183 miles (292km) – minus Katsuta whose entry had been withdrawn. Under fine and sunny skies, a huge crowd greeted the teams from Toyota, Hyundai and Ford.

After a shakedown and the ceremonial start underneath the famous Acropolis in Athens on Thursday, the opening stage of the rally took place around Syntagma Square. Ogier was fastest by 0.6 seconds over Evans, with Rovanperä just 0.2s behind – with only one second covering the top six.

▲ *Rd 09 #33 Evans.*

Rd 09 #1 Ogier.

Rd 09 #69 Rovanperä.

Ogier retained his lead from SS1 with a strong performance in Day Two's opening stage before Rovanperä pinched the lead with stage wins in both SS3 and SS4. Ogier went on to take a stage win himself in SS5, and finished the day just 0.2s away from second overall, with Rovanperä finishing his first full day of this competition in the rally lead by 3.7s. It was a more difficult day for Evans, who was third by the end of the morning's opening test before encountering an issue when changing gears.

Rovanperä then went on to record four back-to-back fastest times on Day Three that helped him open up a lead of half a minute. With one day to go, the team still had two cars in the top three with Sébastien Ogier continuing to hold third overall.

Rain brought challenging conditions for the final day, but Rovanperä produced an incredible stage win in the day's opening Tarzan test, completing it 14.1s faster than anybody else, despite having a mixture of hard and soft tyres fitted to his car. He then went on to seal the victory in style on the shorter second running of Tarzan, with the fastest time in the Power Stage. In fact, the Yaris WRC locked out the top three places in the PS, with Evans second fastest and Ogier third.

While the event had been a little tamer than the classic Greek rallies of the past, thanks to a fifth double podium result of the year and the bonus points from the Power Stage, the team had increased its manufacturers' championship lead to 57 points.

Rd 09 #1 Ogier.

Rd 09 #69 Rovanperä.

Acropolis Rally *Overall results, with 42 finishers*

1st	Kalle Rovanperä/Jonne Halttunen	Toyota Yaris WRC	3:28:24.6
2nd	Ott Tänak/Martin Järveoja	Hyundai i20 Coupe WRC	3:29:06.7
3rd	Sébastien Ogier/Julien Ingrassia	Toyota Yaris WRC	3:29:35.9
6th	Elfyn Evans/Scott Martin	Toyota Yaris WRC	3:35:07.3

ROUND 10

Rally Finland

1-3 October

Based a lot further south than the Arctic Rally, Rally Finland was held over 19 stages covering 179 miles (287km). Staged in basically dry conditions, this event saw Toyota enter five cars, including one for Finnish home-grown driver Esapekka Lappi.

Three Yaris drivers formed part of a very close top five, covered by just 7.9 seconds at the end of the first day. Evans was third overall after an excellent stage win in the darkness of Friday's final test, just ahead of Lappi's privately-entered car in fourth and Rovanperä in fifth, with Ogier in seventh. Meanwhile, despite having another new co-driver, Katsuta posted the fastest time in SS1 to temporarily take the rally lead before a heart-stopping moment blunted his charge.

For Evans, the best performance came in the closing Oittila test run, after sunset, when he claimed a stage win. On the day he celebrated his 21st birthday, Rovanperä also showed speed on his home roads with second-fastest times on the repeat passes of the Ässämäki and Sahloinen–Moksi stages. He ended the day 1.8s behind Evans.

Rd 10 #33 Evans.

▲ *Rd 10 #1 Ogier*

► *Rd 10 #69 Rovanperä.*

Rd 10 #33 Evans.

Ogier did a great job in Oittila, bringing him to within 2.3s of the driver ahead overnight. Lappi had an impressive first day back in the Yaris WRC – also his first outing in the top class in 2021. Making the most of his improved road position compared to Friday, Evans was in outstanding form during the morning loop, winning all four stages. His SS8 win took him from third to first overall, and he opened up a lead of 5.6s. After winning SS14, he led the rally by 9.1s going into the final day.

Ogier showed improved pace during the afternoon after making changes to the setup of his Toyota Yaris WRC, and climbed up to fifth place on the overall leaderboard. Rovanperä went second-fastest to Evans in SS9, but his day ended on the following stage after he went off the road and hit a bank of sand. With Ogier down on power, Evans won three of the four final stages to maintain his lead and earn another victory for himself and Toyota, extending the maker's lead.

Katsuta and Rovanperä crashed out on Saturday, but both restarted way down the field. Evans was consistent all weekend and deserved this win. After Evans' win, Ogier was now just 24 points ahead of his team-mate. And although the gap was closing, Gazoo was still ahead, too.

Rally Finland

Overall results, with 37 finishers

1st	Elfyn Evans/Scott Martin	Toyota Yaris WRC	2:19:13.7
2nd	Ott Tänak/Martin Järveoja	Hyundai i20 Coupe WRC	2:19:27.8
3rd	Craig Breen/Paul Nagle	Hyundai i20 Coupe WRC	2:19:55.9
5th	Sébastien Ogier/Julien Ingrassia	Toyota Yaris WRC	2:22:08.1
34th	Kalle Rovanperä/Jonne Halttunen	Toyota Yaris WRC	3:22:05.4
37th	Takamoto Katsuta/Aaron Johnston	Toyota Yaris WRC	3:40:47.2

ROUND 11

Rally Catalunya

14-17 October

With some 83 starters, Rally Catalunya had 17 stages covering 175 miles (280km) after Thursday's shakedown. Largely dry but cool, the rally encompassed some night stages, with the odd shower making life difficult on tyre choices.

On Day One, Evans was just 0.7 seconds from the lead of the Rally de España at the end of a strong opening day for the Gazoo team, with Ogier making it two Yaris WRC drivers inside the top three. The Welshman made an excellent start to the asphalt event with the fastest time in all three of Friday morning's stages to temporarily head the leaderboard. Ogier, who led the drivers' championship by 24 points over Evans coming into the penultimate round, held third place throughout the day and finished it 19.4s away from the lead.

Katsuta had to stop after the first stage when he walloped a barrier coming out of tight corner, rearranging his car's front end. Although Evans set the pace early on, Neuville proved hard to beat on tarmac.

After a strong performance on Friday, Evans began Day Two only 0.7 seconds away from the rally leader, but was not able to repeat the same stunning form on a different set of stages, ending the day 16.4s behind.

Championship leader Ogier saw his advantage over fourth place reduced during the morning loop, but responded spectacularly

▲ *(Top) Rd 11 #33 Evans. (Above) #1 Ogier.*

Rd 11 #69 Rovanperä.

in the afternoon by setting the fastest time in both SS11 and SS12. Rovanperä remained in fifth place overall and set strong times, in particular through the two passes of the Savallà stage, gaining further experience on his first appearance on this event in a World Rally Car.

Evans had led the rally in the early stages but he could not find the pace to effectively compete with Neuville in his Hyundai, which dominated the event. Ogier was in contention for a podium finish all the way to the end, but just missed out on third position in a closely-fought battle through the final day's four stages – missing out to Sordo by 6.8 seconds. Evans had Ogier in his sights going into the last round ...

Rally Catalunya *Overall results, with 50 finishers*

1st	Thierry Neuville/Martijn Wydaeghe	Hyundai i20 Coupe WRC	2:34:11.8
2nd	Elfyn Evans/Scott Martin	Toyota Yaris WRC	2:34:35.9
3rd	Dani Sordo/Candido Carrera	Hyundai i20 Coupe WRC	2:34:47.1
4th	Sébastien Ogier/Julien Ingrassia	Toyota Yaris WRC	2:34:53.9
5th	Kalle Rovanperä/Jonne Halttunen	Toyota Yaris WRC	2:35:43.6
40th	Takamoto Katsuta/Aaron Johnston	Toyota Yaris WRC	3:27:10.1

ROUND 12

Rally Monza

18-21 November

Rally Monza was the 42nd running of the event and the 12th and final round of the 2021 WRC season. Mostly overcast and damp in places, and with some night work thrown into the equation, some 81 starters competed in 16 stages covering 158 miles (253km) following Thursday's shakedown at this rally held in Monza near Milan.

The drivers faced a demanding start to the rally, with a pair of stages in the mountains above Bergamo run in heavy fog that restricted visibility in places and contributed towards changeable grip levels. Ogier and Evans however, both excelled behind the wheel of the Yaris WRC, and between them managed to win the first five stages, giving Ogier the lead. Takamoto Katsuta was sixth overall, and was second-quickest in the day's closing circuit stage.

On Day Two, Ogier and Evans fought hard, trading fastest stage times and the lead of the rally. In fact, over the course of the event the lead changed no less than six times. Having come to Monza with a 17-point lead in the championship, Ogier and co-driver Julien Ingrassia were on target to win their eighth titles in the final event of their full-time WRC careers together. A podium finish would be enough for them to win.

They came into the final day of three tricky stages around Monza separated by just half a second – and then set identical times on the morning's opening test. An engine stall for Evans in the penultimate stage ultimately decided the rally victory in favour of Ogier. Meanwhile, poor Katsuta limped home on three wheels at one point on the last day, but made up for his mistake with an excellent PS performance; Evans was actually joint-third on the PS on times, but the extra points went to Sordo.

The win in Monza was the fifth of the season for Ogier and Ingrassia after victories in Monte Carlo, Croatia, Sardinia and Kenya, providing

Rd 12 #69 Rovanperä.

Rd 12 ◄ #1 Ogier. ▲ #33 Evans.

Rd 12 #1 Ogier.

them with the eighth title of their careers. This was the fifth time Toyota had won the manufacturers' championship – putting it joint third on the all-time list of titles – and the second since it returned to the sport in 2017 with the Yaris WRC.

Rally Monza *Overall results, with 67 finishers*

1st	Sébastien Ogier/Julien Ingrassia	Toyota Yaris WRC	2:39:08.6
2nd	Elfyn Evans/Scott Martin	Toyota Yaris WRC	2:39:15.9
3rd	Dani Sordo/Candido Carrera	Hyundai i20 Coupe WRC	2:39:29.9
7th	Takamoto Katsuta/Aaron Johnston	Toyota Yaris WRC	2:41:43.1
9th	Kalle Rovanperä/Jonne Halttunen	Toyota Yaris WRC	2:43:58.2

2021 SUMMARY

The season reviewed in a way that provides a quick reference from a Toyota/Gazoo perspective, with driver performance, round by round (overall position, followed by the scoring Power Stage position in brackets), and year-end positions within the FIA WRC championship.

	Ogier	Evans	Rovanperä	Katsuta
Rd 01	1st (1st)	2nd (3rd)	4th (2nd)	6th (12th)
Rd 02	20th (5th)	5th (6th)	2nd (1st)	6th (7th)
Rd 03	1st (1st)	2nd (4th)	DNF (-)	6th (8th)
Rd 04	3rd (3rd)	1st (5th).	22nd (4th)	4th (6th)
Rd 05	1st (4th)	2nd (12th)	25th (3rd)	4th (21st)
Rd 06	1st (4th)	10th (3rd)	6th (2nd)	2nd (8th)
Rd 07	4th (3rd)	5th (4th).	1st (5th)	DNF (-)
Rd 08	5th (2nd)	4th (5th)	3rd (4th)	DNF (-)
Rd 09	3rd (3rd)	6th (2nd)	1st (1st)	- (-)
Rd 10	5th (6th)	1st (1st)	34th (19th)	37th (4th)
Rd 11	4th (4th)	2nd (3rd)	5th (5th)	40th (8th)
Rd 12	1st (5th)	2nd (4th)	9th (22nd)	7th (2nd)

Drivers

1st	Sébastien Ogier	Toyota	230
2nd	Elfyn Evans	Toyota	207
3rd	Thierry Neuville	Hyundai	176
4th	Kalle Rovanperä	Toyota	142
7th	Takamoto Katsuta	Toyota	78

Co-drivers

1st	Julien Ingrassia	Toyota	230
2nd	Scott Martin	Toyota	207
3rd	Martijn Wydaeghe	Hyundai	176
4th	Jonne Halttunen	Toyota	142
7th	Daniel Barritt	Toyota	66
17th	Aaron Johnston	Toyota	12
44th	Keaton Williams	Toyota	0

Manufacturers

1st	Toyota	Toyota Gazoo Racing WRT	520
2nd	Hyundai	Hyundai Motorsport	462
3rd	Ford	M-Sport World Rally Team	199

NB: Points totals include Power Stage bonuses for all categories.

The 2022 Season

Despite lingering concerns over COVID-19, the FIA put together a strong calendar for 2022, made up of 13 high-level rounds spread evenly across the globe; the Ypres Rally was a worthy replacement for an event originally planned to be held in Britain. For the record, the Junior World Rally Championship was basically replaced by the WRC3 category for 2022, so took in the same 13 rounds as the main championship, now celebrating its 50th anniversary.

Season Rounds 2022

	Rally	Dates	Surface
	Monte Carlo Rally	20-23 January	Tarmac
	Rally Sweden	24-27 February	Snow
	Croatia Rally	21-24 April	Tarmac
	Rally de Portugal	19-22 May	Gravel
	Rally Italia Sardegna	2-5 June	Gravel
	Safari Rally	23-26 June	Gravel
	Rally Estonia	14-17 July	Gravel
	Rally Finland	4-7 August	Gravel
	Ypres Rally Belgium	18-21 August	Tarmac
	Acropolis Rally	8-11 September	Gravel
	Rally New Zealand	29 September-2 October	Gravel
	Rally Catalunya	20-23 October	Tarmac
	Rally Japan	10-13 November	Tarmac

FIA rule changes and season prospects

The rally arena entered a new era in 2022 with the eagerly-awaited introduction of Group Rally1 (RC1) regulations to replace existing World Rally Car codes. All lower categories (RC2 through RC5) in the so-called 'rally pyramid' had already been implemented, so RC1 was the last to be ushered in.

The basic idea was to encourage the use of advances in technology, bringing the WRC in line with the WEC via the use of hybrid electric power to augment existing 380bhp petrol engines. All teams used the same 100kW hybrid system, designed to recuperate kinetic energy under braking, and supply a 136bhp power boost at certain times (specific rules were established to cover this), as well as a pure EV mode on selected liaison sections. The latest cars had their minimum weight increased to 2772lb (1260kg), as the hybrid system added 185lb (84kg).

The new regulations were also aimed at reducing costs and enhancing the sport's 'green' credentials, so there were synthetic fuels for 2022, along with a limit of two engines per Rally1 car instead of the former three, a simplified turbocharger set-up, new five-speed gearboxes that lost their shift paddles, no active diffs, simpler suspensions, no liquid-cooled brakes, limits on the number of hybrid systems available per car, and an overhaul of the aerodynamics package. There was, however, some greater freedom on the use of tyres, cancelling out what were often huge advantages caused by being caught out with the wrong rubber due to limited availability, outlined in the previous rules.

With the arrival of these latest technical regulations, there were only three car types left running in the WRC now – the Ford Puma Rally1 (with Sébastien Loeb back behind the wheel in one car), the Hyundai i20 N Rally1, driven by an all-star line-up of familiar names, and a new version of the Toyota Yaris ...

The Gazoo team cars and their drivers

The Toyota GR Yaris Rally1 Hybrid was built around a spaceframe chassis, as required by the new rules in a bid to enhance safety. In many respects, it looked much like its predecessor, but careful inspection would reveal several small differences in the area surrounding the large intake up front, new lighting, revised aerodynamic appendages guiding air over the modified front wheelarches, and fresh grilles cut into the bonnet. New mirrors adorned the doors, with huge intakes positioned below the smaller rear side windows,

The Rally1 machines vying for 2022 WRC honours.

aft of the extended rear arches, which flowed from the hefty side skirts; the rear spoiler wing also featured a fresh design. Further changes were evident in the rear lighting units and a completely revamped section from the bumper line down. With the latest body and a wheelbase extended by some 119mm (4.7in), the car was now a fraction longer at 4225mm (166.3in), but the same width as before.

The new drivetrain took power to well over 500bhp, and there was a significant increase in torque, too. In line with Rally1 regs, whilst still four-wheel drive, the car lost its centre differential, and adopted a five-speed gearbox with a mechanical sequential shift beside the extended handbrake lever. The suspension remained a MacPherson set-up in principle, and although the brakes were the same size as last year (with different diameters for tarmac and gravel events), they lost their exotic liquid-cooling systems; wheel rims were carried over.

The driver line-up continued unchanged once more, although Sébastien Ogier had a new co-driver following Ingrassia's retirement (two by the end of the season), and Esapekka Lappi was brought back into the fold, taking turns with Ogier to be the third designated car alongside Evans and Rovanperä.

Lappi had driven for the Gazoo team in 2017 and 2018, so he knew what was expected of him, while Takamoto Katsuta was given a seat for the full season via the newly-formed Toyota Gazoo Racing

Elfyn Evans.

WRT NG outfit, with 'NG' standing for 'New Generation'; Katsuta's car was the only one in the equipe, but at least it was eligible to score for its maker, albeit separate from the main team in much the same way as the now-defunct French Hyundai 2C Competition outfit had been.

Having looked at Lappi's career earlier on in the book, along with that of Ogier and Rovanperä, Elfyn Evans is the only full-time driver left to cover at this stage. Born in Wales in December 1988, he is the son of Gwyndaf Evans who had a remarkable record on the British rallying circuit, his name becoming synonymous with Ford. Elfyn's first WRC event was in 2007, but he had to wait until 2011 before his next entry. The M-Sport team finally gave him a drive in a Fiesta RS WRC car in 2013, when he surprised everyone with a sixth in Italy – enough to secure him a full-time seat in Malcolm Wilson's outfit for 2014. A series of decent results followed, giving Evans fifth in the WRC standings in both 2017 and 2019, ultimately leading to him signing for Toyota in 2020.

The hybrid car for the 2022 season.

ROUND 01

Monte Carlo Rally
20-23 January

Marking the 90th running of the Monte Carlo Rally, some 74 entries competed, including four Toyotas. Two night stages were held on Thursday, with 17 SSs in total (185 miles/296km) before Sunday's finish. An unusually dry event prevailed, with just the odd patch of ice in shady spots being the norm, although snow and packed ice on the higher ground played havoc with tyre choices.

Toyota started well on Day One in this new hybrid era as Ogier won the first two stages with Evans in third overall. Rovanperä lost time after a spin in the opening stage to lie in 12th while Katsuta sat in ninth. On Day Two, Ogier and Evans were closely matched, finishing the day in second and third place. Ford's Loeb however won four stages in a row to snatch the lead from Ogier.

On Day Three, fastest times for Ogier in SS8, SS10 and SS11 once again gave the Frenchman the lead while Evans showed his pace with a win in SS9 before Rovanperä found form to capture the quickest times in SS12 and SS13, allowing him to move up to ninth; Katsuta was in eighth after some strong performances. The Gazoo team actually won every stage on Saturday, allowing Ogier to hang on to the lead as Loeb pushed hard.

Evans, meanwhile, set a fast pace over the most slippery section of SS11 only to be caught out on the fast descent during the Sisteron stage, and ended up in the scenery. With the help of spectators he was eventually able to rejoin and continue but lost around 20 minutes. Katsuta, who was holding onto fifth, also slid into a ditch in the icy conditions and fell to 13th. At the end of Day Three, Ogier's lead stood at 21.1s with four stages remaining.

Ogier had been on course to claim another Monte victory before a cruel twist of fate saw him suffer a flat front left tyre on the penultimate stage, a tragedy that, combined with a jump-start penalty on the PS, ultimately cost him the win. All three of the Gazoo drivers claimed stage wins over the weekend and the Yaris was fastest on nine of the 17 stages.

With the lead changing hands four times, the Monte turned out to be a battle between Ogier and Loeb from start to finish. With Loeb on top, Ford was in front – something not seen in a long time.

Rd 01 #33 Evans.

Rd 01 #69 Rovanperä.

Rd 01 #1 Ogier.

Monte Carlo Rally *Overall results, with 62 finishers*

1st	Sébastien Loeb/Isabelle Galmiche	Ford Puma Rally1	3:00:32.8
2nd	Sébastien Ogier/Benjamin Veillas	Toyota GR Yaris Rally1	3:00:43.3
3rd	Craig Breen/Paul Nagle	Ford Puma Rally1	3:02:12.6
4th	Kalle Rovanperä/Jonne Halttunen	Toyota GR Yaris Rally1	3:02:49.0
8th	Takamoto Katsuta/Aaron Johnston	Toyota GR Yaris Rally1	3:12:57.5
21st	Elfyn Evans/Scott Martin	Toyota GR Yaris Rally1	3:23:43.3

ROUND 02

Rally Sweden
24-27 February

Based in Vasterbotten County in the extreme north of the country, Rally Sweden got underway with some 45 starters in snowbound conditions. The shakedown and ceremonial start took place on Thursday, before 19 stages were run over 191 miles (306km). However, two stages were cancelled on Saturday, taking 26 miles (41km) off the SS distance. Lappi, whose background made him more suited to the icy roads, took over driving duties from Ogier in the Toyota camp, although the event ultimately turned out to be a triumph for Rovanperä.

On Day One, Evans, Lappi and Rovanperä all won stages and took a turn in the lead. Rovanperä ended the day strongly and took another stage win in SS7

Rd 02 #69 Rovanperä.

Rd 02 #33 Evans.

Rd 02 #69 Rovanperä.

to finish up second overall, only 4.3s from the lead. Evans ranked in third and Katsuta in sixth.

On Day Two, Evans led a Toyota lock-out of the top four positions on the technical Brattby stage, while Rovanperä reclaimed the overall lead – which he then extended with a stage win on the high-speed Långed test that followed.

Having moved up to second overall, Evans started the afternoon of Day Two by winning the repeat of Brattby and closing to within 1.2s of Rovanperä, who responded by posting the best time in the second pass over Långed – this time in the dark. Rovanperä finished the day with another stage win on the final test into Umeå to increase his lead. Lappi also performed well finishing in fourth. And with Katsuta positioned in fifth, Toyota had all four drivers inside the top five.

For most of the rally, all three of the team's drivers were part of a close fight for victory on the unfamiliar, high-speed, snow-covered roads. Evans was penalised 10s overnight on Saturday's final stage, after a misbehaving hybrid system deactivated due to an issue, and then he spun out and crashed, forcing him to retire.

The lead had changed hands many times in the first half of the event, although Rovanperä and Halttunen held onto the top spot from SS8 onwards to secure the third win of their WRC career. He also moved into the drivers' championship lead by 14 points.

Rd 02 #4 Lappi.

Rally Sweden *Overall results, with 36 finishers*

1st	Kalle Rovanperä/Jonne Halttunen	Toyota GR Yaris Rally1	2:10:44.9
2nd	Thierry Neuville/Martijn Wydaeghe	Hyundai i20 N Rally1	2:11:06.9
3rd	Esapekka Lappi/Janne Ferm	Toyota GR Yaris Rally1	2:11:15.5
4th	Takamoto Katsuta/Aaron Johnston	Toyota GR Yaris Rally1	2:13:04.3
DNF	Elfyn Evans/Scott Martin	Toyota GR Yaris Rally1	–

ROUND 03

Croatia Rally
21-24 April

The 46th running of Croatia Rally saw 63 entries competing over 20 stages. A total of 182 miles (292km) of stages were planned, although SS15 was cancelled, taking ten miles (16km) off the tally. This event, centered around Zagreb, turned out to be another masterful performance from Kalle Rovanperä, who dominated with his new Yaris Rally1 car.

In slippery, rain-drenched conditions, the Finnish driver won six stages on Day One to open up a one minute-plus lead over the rest of the field by the end of the day.

Facing unfavourable conditions running

Rd 03 #33 Evans.

▲ Rd 03 #69 Rovanperä. ▼ Rd 03 #4 Lappi.

further down the order, Elfyn Evans recorded the fastest time in SS3 but also lost close to two minutes during the morning loop after twice finishing a stage with a tyre off its rim. He finished in sixth position, one place ahead of Takamoto Katsuta. Esapekka Lappi's day came to an abrupt end when he clipped a large rock beside the road in the opening stage, damaging his front-right suspension.

Rovanperä's domination on Day Two was dampened in the third loop at Platak when rain and fog meant his tyre choice was not ideal, and although he lost time, he still managed to retain the lead over Tänak. Looking to recover from a difficult Friday, Elfyn Evans recorded the fastest time of Day Two's opening stage and moved up to fifth overall – also placing second on two of the morning's other tests. Lappi restarted and demonstrated great skill on his asphalt debut to win the morning's second stage and then the first two tests in the afternoon, only being denied a clean sweep of fastest times by Rovanperä's final stage effort. Katsuta ended two of the day's stages with a deflated tyre but remained on course to score points in sixth overall.

A sudden downpour on Day Three, and a wrong tyre choice from Rovanperä nearly cost him the rally as he conceded the lead temporarily to Tänak. This set up a thrilling showdown for the rally-ending Power Stage, where conditions were dry but with a lot of remaining mud. Rovanperä produced a stunning run, 5.6s quicker than Tänak and 21.8s faster than anybody else, to secure his second successive victory and a maximum points haul. That increased his championship lead after three rounds to 29 points. Evans, who was strangely off the pace in this event, finished in fifth, while Katsuta was sixth.

Croatia Rally

Overall results, with 56 finishers

1st	Kalle Rovanperä/Jonne Halttunen	Toyota GR Yaris Rally1	2:48:21.5
2nd	Ott Tänak/Martin Järveoja	Hyundai i20 N Rally1	2:48:25.8
3rd	Thierry Neuville/Martijn Wydaeghe	Hyundai i20 N Rally1	2:50:42.5
5th	Elfyn Evans/Scott Martin	Toyota GR Yaris Rally1	2:52:07.5
6th	Takamoto Katsuta/Aaron Johnston	Toyota GR Yaris Rally1	2:56:30.0
49th	Esapekka Lappi/Janne Ferm	Toyota GR Yaris Rally1	4:09:53.2

Rd 03 #69 Rovanperä.

ROUND 04

Rally de Portugal

19-22 May

Held in the Porto District, the rally got underway with 90 starters, including 12 Rally1 entries (five Fords, four Toyotas, and three Hyundais). Ogier was back in the Yaris, retaking his seat from Lappi. After a shakedown and one short stage on Thursday, the competitors battled over 21 stages covering 211 miles (338km).

Evans took the advantage of cleaner roads afforded by a later start, although Loeb was the early leader on the dry, dusty roads. Ultimately, though, Toyota's drivers won 16 of the 21 stages to completely dominate in Portugal, with Rovanperä winning his third straight rally.

On Day One, all four Yaris Rally1 drivers made it safely through without incident and within 3.5 seconds of the best time. Ogier was fastest of them in fifth with Rovanperä sixth and Evans ninth, while Takamoto Katsuta sat in seventh in his TGR WRT Next Generation entry.

On Day Two, between SS5 and SS9, Evans, Ogier and Rovanperä swapped fastest times as Evans held onto a narrow lead. Evans provided a strong start to the day for the team, winning the

Rd 04 #1 Ogier. ▶

◀ ▲ *Rd 04 #33 Evans.*

opening two stages and ending the loop only half a second from the lead. After winning several more stages the Welshman took the lead and held it until midway through Day Three. Meanwhile, championship leader Rovanperä was joint fourth overall with Ogier close behind in sixth. After winning SS5, Ogier suffered two flat tyres pushing him down the rankings. Katsuta enjoyed a strong day, aside from a brief spin in SS6, before going on to set the third-fastest time in both SS7 and SS8, completing a lock-out of the top three times for the Yaris Rally1.

On Day Three, Evans and Rovanperä traded fastest times during the morning loop of three stages, with Evans winning two of those tests to extend his overnight lead to 18.4 seconds. Rovanperä was stronger in the afternoon, winning the first two stages of the loop before taking the lead with an excellent second-fastest time when rain hit the repeat pass of Amarante. Katsuta also did well to pass Sordo and move up to third overall.

On Day Four, Rovanperä was fastest in the opening stage, and then went on to win the last two stages, including the Power Stage, to comfortably win his third consecutive rally and extend his lead to 46 points over Neuville. Toyota recorded a well-earned one-two finish (only Sordo's PS performance avoided a full Gazoo podium), with Evans finishing close behind the Finn.

▼ ▶ *Rd 04 #69 Rovanperä.*

Rally de Portugal *Overall results, with 53 finishers*

1st	Kalle Rovanperä/Jonne Halttunen	Toyota GR Yaris Rally1	3:44:19.2
2nd	Elfyn Evans/Scott Martin	Toyota GR Yaris Rally1	3:44:34.4
3rd	Dani Sordo/Candido Carrera	Hyundai i20 N Rally1	3:46:36.5
4th	Takamoto Katsuta/Aaron Johnston	Toyota GR Yaris Rally1	3:46:38.6
51st	Sébastien Ogier/Benjamin Veillas	Toyota GR Yaris Rally1	5:47:12.4

ROUND 05

Rally Italia Sardegna

2-5 June

A total of 59 crews registered to compete in the Alghero-based event's 21 stages. With SS8 and SS9 being cancelled, the actual distance was ultimately 175 miles (280km), with Thursday basically for spectators, and thc rally proper beginning Friday.

Thursday started with the pre-event shakedown, where all three Gazoo drivers placed inside the top five. Lappi looked immediately at home ahead of his first gravel rally; he set the second-best time in SS1, with Evans third and Rovanperä in fifth.

Day Two was a trying day, but started well for Toyota with Evans going fastest in SS2 to take the lead before having Lappi take the top spot from him with a quickest time. Then, after losing the lead to Tänak in SS4, Lappi won SS7 to regain the top spot, however briefly.

Championship leader Kalle Rovanperä faced a more difficult task opening the road on Sardinia's loose gravel than he did on the previous round in Portugal. He remained in touch with the leaders during the morning, before an over-zealous cornering moment damaged the rear wing on his car, denying him crucial downforce and an eighth overall. Katsuta, meanwhile, managed to finish one spot ahead as Evans had to stop after a heavy impact to the underside of his car, forcing significant time loss due to an ensuing cooling problem.

On Day Three, Lappi started in the lead but was forced out of contention after consecutive impacts damaged both rear corners on his car. Rovanperä was able to improve his times in the afternoon, placing in the top three on both passes of the Coiluna–Loelle stage to close up on fifth overall. Katsuta was one place behind Rovanperä even

Rd 05 ▲ #33 Evans. ▼ #4 Lappi.

though he had damaged his car. Having retired on Friday, Elfyn Evans restarted this morning with the challenge of running first on the road. He

Rd 05 #33 Evans.

Rd 05 #69 Rovanperä.

still set a strong third-fastest time in SS15, before sustaining suspension damage on the following test.

On Day Four, the four Gazoo drivers pushed hard, but various issues including small offs and spins meant that they were not able to match the times of Tänak, who grabbed the lead from Lappi in SS10 and never let up. The best Toyota could muster was a fifth from Rovanperä while Katsuta came in a commendable sixth.

Rally Italia Sardegna *Overall results, with 46 finishers*

1st	Ott Tänak/Martin Järveoja	Hyundai i20 N Rally1	3:10:59.1
2nd	Craig Breen/Paul Nagle	Ford Puma Rally1	3:12:02.3
3rd	Dani Sordo/Candido Carrera	Hyundai i20 N Rally1	3:12:32.1
5th	Kalle Rovanperä/Jonne Halttunen	Toyota GR Yaris Rally1	3:14:01.9
6th	Takamoto Katsuta/Aaron Johnston	Toyota GR Yaris Rally1	3:15:01.7
40th	Elfyn Evans/Scott Martin	Toyota GR Yaris Rally1	4:12:21.7
44th	Esapekka Lappi/Janne Ferm	Toyota GR Yaris Rally1	4:30:44.1

ROUND 06
Safari Rally
23-26 June

This was the 70th running for the only Africa-based event, with the Safari Rally welcoming 42 starters to compete over 19 stages covering a total of 222 miles (356km), or 765 miles (1224km) if one includes the transport distances. This tough rally saw Toyota record its best ever result thanks to a 1-2-3-4 finish, with Rovanperä capturing his fourth win in five events.

Ogier started strongly with a fastest time in the Kasarani super special stage on Day One putting him into the lead. Evans was fourth fastest, only 1.2s away. Rovanperä was 11th after he ran wide and damaged a tyre, but remained within 12s of the lead, with Katsuta in sixth.

Day Two was a perfect day for Toyota with Rovanperä, Ogier and Evans each taking turns in the lead, with the Yaris winning all but the morning's first stage. When Rovanperä won SS7

◀ Rd 06 #33 Evans.

▲Rd 06 #1 Ogier.

he snatched the lead from Ogier and held onto the top spot until the finish in a commanding performance. On a rally where he finished a career-best second last year, Katsuta was running in the same position after SS6.

Day Three saw heavy rain early on making conditions treacherous. The Toyota quartet, however, made it through the thick mud without major issues to hold a dream 1-2-3-4 position heading into the final day, with a gap of over eight minutes back to its nearest competitor in fifth place. Gazoo drivers then traded stage wins, first Evans won SS11, Rovanperä excelled in the mud winning SS12, and Ogier captured SS13, as Katsuta, who had been in second, slipped to third overall with consistent drives.

Even though Toyota only won one stage on Day Four, all four Gazoo drivers held their own to hold onto the top four spots. It was a landmark tenth victory for Toyota on the famous African event, and the first time it had achieved a 1-2-3-4 finish in the WRC to lock-out the podium – the first time since the very same rally in 1993. This win put Rovanperä 45 points ahead of Neuville, while Gazoo sat 62 points ahead of Hyundai.

Safari Rally *Overall results, with 25 finishers*

1st	Kalle Rovanperä/Jonne Halttunen	Toyota GR Yaris Rally1	3:40:24.9
2nd	Elfyn Evans/Scott Martin	Toyota GR Yaris Rally1	3:41:17.7
3rd	Takamoto Katsuta/Aaron Johnston	Toyota GR Yaris Rally1	3:42:07.6
4th	Sébastien Ogier/Benjamin Veillas	Toyota GR Yaris Rally1	3:42:35.2

Rd 06 ▲ *#69 Rovanperä.* ▶ *Filling the podium …*

ROUND 07

Rally Estonia

14-17 July

Rd 07 #69 Rovanperä.

Based in Tartu County, 42 teams tackled the 196 mile (314km) Rally Estonia over 24 stages. In an historic event, featuring a start and spectator stage (SSS) only on Thursday, Rovanperä would win his fifth rally in seven events, and Toyota would win a record 22 of the 24 stages. Lappi once again took over driver duties from Ogier.

On Day One, the only bright spot for Ford and driver Craig Breen was the sole stage win in SS1 and the briefly held rally lead. On Friday, Evans won five straight stages to take the top spot, a lead he held onto until the end of the day. Lappi lost time in the morning loop with a lack of confidence under braking because of a technical issue, but the team was able to resolve this during service and he produced a stronger performance in the wet afternoon conditions, moving up to fourth position overall. Katsuta was seventh overall as he too built up his confidence through the varied conditions.

Day Three saw Rovanperä, who had won the last three stages on Day Two, post the fastest times in the next seven stages to pinch the lead from Evans, and hold onto it until the finish. Evans began the day with his sixth stage win of the rally and was usually the closest driver to Rovanperä in the stage times, increasing his margin over third position to 42.4s in the process. Lappi was in fourth position overall before a tyre was knocked off its rim on the landing from a jump, forcing him to stop and replace it, while losing over two minutes and slipping to seventh place. Takamoto Katsuta continued to build on his pleasing performance and gained two positions to end the day in fifth overall.

On Day Four, Rovanperä was fastest in four of the six final stages allowing him to extend his lead and take the victory. Even though Lappi won SS22 and SS23 (the sudden downpour on the PS made it something of a lottery), he could still only finish in sixth place behind a strong finishing Katsuta. With this result, Rovanperä shot to an 83 point lead in the drivers' championship, while Toyota held onto an 87 point lead.

Rd 07 ◄ #33 Evans. ▼ #4 Lappi.

Rally Estonia *Overall results, with 33 finishers*

1st	Kalle Rovanperä/Jonne Halttunen	Toyota GR Yaris Rally1	2:54:29.0
2nd	Elfyn Evans/Scott Martin	Toyota GR Yaris Rally1	2:55:29.9
3rd	Ott Tänak/Martin Järveoja	Hyundai i20 Coupe WRC	2:56:24.7
5th	Takamoto Katsuta/Aaron Johnston	Toyota GR Yaris Rally1	2:58:42.4
6th	Esapekka Lappi/Janne Ferm	Toyota GR Yaris Rally1	2:59:18.1

ROUND 08

Rally Finland
4-7 August

The 71st Finland Rally was based in the Toyota Gazoo rally team's home city of Jyväskylä, and welcomed 44 starters. Held in dry conditions, crews competed over 21 stages covering 188 miles (301km) after SS5 was cancelled, with Thursday reserved for a shakedown and one stage only.

Championship leader Kalle Rovanperä set the fastest time on his fourth and final run over shakedown on Day One, half a second ahead of fellow Finnish driver Esapekka Lappi, with Takamoto Katsuta and Elfyn Evans making it four GR Yaris hybrids in the top five. In SS1, Katsuta was the quickest of the Toyota drivers, placing third overall and 0.1 seconds ahead of Jyväskylä native Rovanperä. Evans and Lappi were sixth and seventh respectively, both less than four seconds off Neuville's lead overnight.

Even though Lappi won four stages on Day Two, he could not catch Tänak, who snagged just three stage victories that day. Rovanperä and Evans faced more challenging conditions running first and third in the order due to their championship positions but also showed consistent and strong speed. Evans ended the day 19.3s behind the leader, with local favourite Rovanperä just 1.7s further back. Katsuta also enjoyed a strong day, claiming a win in SS6 on the short Harju test in the centre of Jyväskylä and occupied sixth overall.

Day Three started well for Toyota as Evans won the first stage of the day before losing time towards the end with damage to his left-rear suspension. Rovanperä blitzed the rest of Saturday's results by winning six out of eight stages to get within eight seconds of leader Tänak. Meanwhile, Lappi remained in a podium position in third, even though he was hampered in the afternoon with a damaged windscreen caused by a rock, and finished it 35.2s away. Katsuta remained in sixth as he put up a strong fight with Neuville for fifth, until a spin cost close to half a minute.

Rd 08 ◄ #4 Lappi. *▼ #33 Evans.*

▲ *Rd 08 #69 Rovanperä.* ▶ *#4 Lappi.*

On Day Four, Rovanperä won two of the four stages to further extend his championship lead with a well-calculated drive to second place behind a fast-finishing Tänak, as Toyota team-mate Lappi survived late drama to join him on the podium at their home rally. Gazoo finished with a strong 2-3-4-6, as Rovanperä moved to a 94 point lead over Neuville in the drivers' title chase.

Rally Finland *Overall results, with 34 finishers*

1st	Ott Tänak/Martin Järveoja	Hyundai i20 N Rally1	2:24:04.6
2nd	Kalle Rovanperä/Jonne Halttunen	Toyota GR Yaris Rally1	2:24:11.4
3rd	Esapekka Lappi/Janne Ferm	Toyota GR Yaris Rally1	2:25:25.3
4th	Elfyn Evans/Scott Martin	Toyota GR Yaris Rally1	2:25:42.2
6th	Takamoto Katsuta/Aaron Johnston	Toyota GR Yaris Rally1	2:27:13.6

ROUND 09

Ypres Rally Belgium
18-21 August

Based in the Flanders region, this event had 86 entries who competed over 20 stages covering 176 miles (282km). With a shakedown only on Thursday, Rovanperä started Day One well with the quickest time in the first stage, but was caught out by the notoriously tricky asphalt roads in the following test when he ran wide into one of the many ditches, causing his car to roll.

From SS2, Evans took the rally lead away from Rovanperä with some solid driving and a class win in SS4, before he lost the lead to Neuville late in the day after some rain tyre issues, and was given a 10-second penalty for arriving late to the

Rd 09 #69 Rovanperä.

day's final test. Lappi performed well to end the day in fourth overall, building a margin of 18.8s over his nearest rival. Katsuta was delayed by a transmission issue during the morning and, rolling his car slowly into the service area, fell outside of podium contention.

Evans began Day Two in third, 11.2s behind second-placed Tänak, and set about reducing that gap during the morning loop of four stages. His consistent pace in the dry conditions brought him to within 5.3s of the leader, and he narrowed the gap more after posting the fastest time in the second stage of the afternoon. Lappi moved up into third overall, and went into the final day with a minute-and-a-half in hand over fourth-placed Oliver Solberg.

After his SS2 rollover, Rovanperä was able to return to action and was immediately back up to speed, winning the first stage of the day. To show off the brand's efforts for zero emissions in SS11 team founder and ex-Toyota CEO Akio Toyoda, got behind the wheel of the new hydrogen-powered GR Yaris H2, a car that employed the same powertrain as the GR Corolla H2 that 'Morizo' had been racing in Japan's Super Taikyu Series.

After two early stage wins on Day Three, Evans ended strongly ahead of Lappi to record another double podium finish, with Evans just five seconds away from winner Ott Tänak. Rovanperä pushed hard in the final Power Stage to win it and take the sting out of the points loss, thus maintaining a 72-point margin over second place.

Ypres Rally Belgium — *Overall results, with 69 finishers*

1st	Ott Tänak/Martin Järveoja	Hyundai i20 N Rally1	2:25:38.9
2nd	Elfyn Evans/Scott Martin	Toyota GR Yaris Rally1	2:25:43.9
3rd	Esapekka Lappi/Janne Ferm	Toyota GR Yaris Rally1	2:27:20.5
5th	Takamoto Katsuta/Aaron Johnston	Toyota GR Yaris Rally1	2:31:45.0
62nd	Kalle Rovanperä/Jonne Halttunen	Toyota GR Yaris Rally1	2:24:11.4

▼ *Rd 09 #4 Lappi.*

▶ *#33 Evans.*

ROUND 10

Acropolis Rally

9-12 September

The Acropolis Rally has always been classed as one of the most demanding rallies, with crews having to tackle rough and rocky roads in the sweltering Greek heat. Many drivers have put it on a par with the Safari Rally, which says a lot for the conditions they have to contend with. First run in 1951, it was a regular European Rally Championship event for many years before becoming a World Rally Championship fixture. As it happens, it reverted to ERC status in 2014, but made its WRC comeback following the COVID-19 pandemic.

Welcoming 68 starters, the rally boasted 16 stages over 189 miles (303km), with dry conditions throughout. The rally got under way on the Thursday with an unusual Athens Olympic Stadium special stage. The slowish times of Toyota's four drivers in SS1 proved to be an omen for the team's average performance throughout the event, as Rovanperä walloped a tree on Saturday, Lappi suffered fuel feed problems, Evans had a turbo pop forcing him to retire, while Katsuta lost a tyre on Sunday.

Best of the Toyota drivers on Day Two was Lappi who won the team's only stage in this Greek rally to finish third, some eight seconds behind Loeb in his Ford (Malcolm Wilson's team actually had a decent run on this year's Acropolis). Struggling with the conditions, Rovanperä finished eighth, Evans was in ninth, and Katsuta tenth.

On Day Three, Lappi did well to temporarily get up into second place before a fuel system issue forced him to retire for the day. Through the attrition of others, Evans was able to climb from eighth to fourth, while Rovanperä damaged the rear of his car after running wide in SS9, losing

Rd 10 #4 Lappi.

◀ *Rd 10 #33 Evans.* ▲ *Rd 10 #69 Rovanperä.*

over 15 minutes as a result. Unlike his teammates, Katsuta avoided major issues and stayed in seventh overall.

After being in contention for a podium position, Evans had to retire on Day Four thanks to an engine-related problem. Lappi, who'd been running in second place on Saturday, suffered a technical issue and lost a lot of time giving him a final position of 22nd. Rovanperä, who finished in 15th, managed to set the second-fastest Power Stage time to claim four bonus points and remain 53 points ahead of Tänak. Interestingly, Katsuta was the highest finishing Toyota driver with a well-earned sixth.

Acropolis Rally *Overall results, with 53 finishers*

1st	Thierry Neuville/Martijn Wydaeghe	Hyundai i20 N Rally1	3:34:52.0
2nd	Ott Tänak/Martin Järveoja	Hyundai i20 N Rally1	3:35:07.0
3rd	Dani Sordo/Candido Carrera	Hyundai i20 N Rally1	3:36:41.7
6th	Takamoto Katsuta/Aaron Johnston	Toyota GR Yaris Rally1	3:41:13.1
15th	Kalle Rovanperä/Jonne Halttunen	Toyota GR Yaris Rally1	3:51:41.0
22nd	Esapekka Lappi/Janne Ferm	Toyota GR Yaris Rally1	3:59:31.0
DNF	Elfyn Evans/Scott Martin	Toyota GR Yaris Rally1	–

ROUND 11

Rally New Zealand

29 September-2 October

This rally was inaugurated in 1969, first becoming a WRC event in 1977. Although relatively new compared to the likes of the Monte, and the modern equivalent to the UK's RAC Rally, it is famous for its very fast gravel roads that some have likened to a river of marbles. It would turn out to be a triumphant rally for Rovanperä who won his first drivers' title.

Based around Auckland, the rally welcomed eleven top rank Rally1 teams to compete over 17 stages covering 175 miles (280km), with Ogier taking over driving duties from Lappi. With pre-event testing not permitted outside of Europe, the 3.54km shakedown on Thursday provided the first opportunity for teams to run their Rally1 cars on New Zealand roads and make adjustments. In SS1 (an SSS), Katsuta with a fourth was the quickest Yaris through the Pukekawa stage, closely followed by Evans, Rovanperä, and then Ogier in eighth.

With damp conditions on the Friday, Day Two proved a good one for Toyota as the latter three Gazoo drivers swapped fastest times, with Ogier snatching the lead away from Tänak midday, but then damage to Ogier's rear wing incurred on the day's last stage meant he ended the day third, 6.7s from the lead. Evans briefly held the lead in SS8 before Rovanperä took top spot on a wet Day Three, with a masterful SS9 victory and then four more stage wins to maintain his lead and win the rally. Katsuta meanwhile rounded out the day in eighth position overall.

Rd 11 #1 Ogier.

Ogier also produced a strong and consistent performance in the demanding conditions, moving up to second overall and creating a margin of 17.4s over third-placed Ott Tänak. Evans, who had the lead at the start of the day, was caught out in the second stage when he spun into a bank and rolled his car. Katsuta had climbed up into fifth position overall when he became the latest victim

Rd 11 ▲ (left) #33 Evans. ▲ #69 Rovanperä.
◀ #1 Ogier. ▼ #69 Rovanperä.

of the conditions and slid off the road in SS12.

After a commanding win in the final Power Stage, Rovanperä became the youngest ever winner of an FIA World Rally Championship title at the tender age of just 22 years and one day, having won six rallies in 2022. While Evans and Katsuta had to retire, at least Toyota finished with a one-two.

Rally New Zealand *Overall results, with 21 finishers*

1st	Kalle Rovanperä/Jonne Halttunen	Toyota GR Yaris Rally1	2:48:01.4
2nd	Sébastien Ogier/Benjamin Veillas	Toyota GR Yaris Rally1	2:48:36.0
3rd	Ott Tänak/Martin Järveoja	Hyundai i20 N Rally1	2:48:49.9
DNF	Elfyn Evans/Scott Martin	Toyota GR Yaris Rally1	–
DNF	Takamoto Katsuta/Aaron Johnston	Toyota GR Yaris Rally1	–

ROUND 12

Rally Catalunya

20-23 October

Based in Salou, after a shakedown on Thursday, Catalunya welcomed 67 entries to compete in 19 stages covering 184 miles (294km). It was a bit damp in places on Friday, but Ogier led at the end of the day, and duly stayed at the top of the standings to record his first win of the hybrid era and seal the title for Toyota.

As it happens, Ogier and Rovanperä won seven out of eight stages between them to ensure a one-two for Toyota at the end of a close-fought first day as the lead changed hands three times. Battling in the top five, Evans ended the penultimate stage of the day with a flat front-left tyre, losing more than half a minute and dropping a place to sixth. Katsuta suffered a similar issue in the same stage as he improved his pace during the day, ending it in eighth position overall.

Ogier had finished Day One with a win in SS8 to consolidate his lead, and then was fastest over three straight stages from SS10 on Day Two. Rovanperä was performing well and fighting for a podium finish with Neuville. Having dropped behind with tyre damage on Friday, Evans was battling closely with local hero Dani Sordo for fifth place during the morning, but lost ground in the afternoon. Katsuta had a good Saturday with some strong and consistent stage times and ended the day in eighth.

Ogier was a force of nature on Day Three when he won two stages back-to-back, including the final Power Stage that gave him a convincing victory in Rally Catalunya. With Rovanperä finishing in third, Toyota ended up in Spain with a double podium and the so-called World Rally 'treble' after Kalle Rovanperä won the drivers'

Rd 12 ▼ #33 Evans. *▶ #1 Ogier.*

title, Jonne Halttunen won the co-drivers' title, and Toyota captured the manufacturers' championship. Evans came in sixth and Katsuta seventh, giving the team a strong showing in Spain. In total, this was the sixth time that Toyota had topped the WRC's manufacturers' classification – the third time since it returned to the series in 2017.

▶ *#69 Rovanperä.*

Rally Catalunya *Overall results, with 57 finishers*

1st	Sébastien Ogier/Benjamin Veillas	Toyota GR Yaris Rally1	2:44:43.9
2nd	Thierry Neuville/Martijn Wydaeghe	Hyundai i20 N Rally1	2:45:00.3
3rd	Kalle Rovanperä/Jonne Halttunen	Toyota GR Yaris Rally1	2:45:18.4
6th	Elfyn Evans/Scott Martin	Toyota GR Yaris Rally1	2:46:35.0
7th	Takamoto Katsuta/Aaron Johnston	Toyota GR Yaris Rally1	2:47:03.0

▲ *Rd 13 #1 Ogier.*

ROUND 13

Rally Japan

10-13 November

In this long-awaited comeback, Rally Japan was now held in leafy Nagoya rather than the northern island of Hokkaido, and as such, much closer to Toyota's head office. Some 36 crews entered the event to compete in 19 stages, but three were cancelled, taking the actual SS distance down to 144 miles (231km).

With four Toyotas fighting four Fords and three Hyundais for WRC (Rally1) honours, Ogier (who'd changed his co-driver) took the lead on Day One after a win in SS1, Thursday's only stage.

Day Two belonged to Toyota as Rovanperä, Ogier and Evans took turns in the lead, each having won at least one stage. Starting his home round of the WRC for the first time, Katsuta ended the first day in seventh in his TGR WRT Next Generation entry.

On Day Three, Evans posted the fastest time in the opening stage, and increased his rally lead to 6.5 seconds. In the afternoon, the tables were turned and rival Thierry Neuville took over the lead in SS12, with Evans just four seconds behind after the Okazaki City super special that rounded out the day. Katsuta continued to perform well in his home rally and got up to fourth overall. Ogier set an impressive pace through the day, winning three of the five mountain stages, and fought back to fifth position.

Rovanperä began the day in third position overall, just 5.1 seconds from the lead, but dropped out of contention when he had to stop in SS8 to change a wheel after misjudging a corner and

◀ *Rd 13 #69 Rovanperä.*

hitting a wall; he ended up refitting a punctured tyre to limp home!

Toyota experienced late heartbreak on Day Four when Evans, who had been fighting for the win, ran wide in a corner forcing them to stop, change a wheel and drop to fourth; at least Katsuta moved up a spot as a result. Ogier showed excellent speed all weekend with his new co-driver Vincent Landais, and may have won had the pair not dropped 2m44s in Friday's first stage when they had to stop and replace a tyre. Rovanperä was also in the fight for victory until Saturday morning when he slid wide in one corner and made contact with a wall. In the pouring rain that blew in on Sunday afternoon, Katsuta was the only Toyota man on the podium. The wet wasn't going to spoil the feeling of walking away with both the drivers' and manufacturers' titles, though.

▲ *Rd 13 #69 Rovanperä.*

▼ *Rd 13 #33 Evans.*

Rally Japan *Overall results, with 32 finishers*

1st	Thierry Neuville/Martijn Wydaeghe	Hyundai i20 N Rally1	2:43:52.3
2nd	Ott Tänak/Martin Järveoja	Hyundai i20 N Rally1	2:45:03.4
3rd	Takamoto Katsuta/Aaron Johnston	Toyota GR Yaris Rally1	2:46:03.6
4th	Sébastien Ogier/Vincent Landais	Toyota GR Yaris Rally1	2:46:15.9
5th	Elfyn Evans/Scott Martin	Toyota GR Yaris Rally1	2:47:57.4
12th	Kalle Rovanperä/Jonne Halttunen	Toyota GR Yaris Rally1	2:54:33.1

2022 SUMMARY

The season reviewed in a way that provides a quick reference from a Toyota/Gazoo perspective, with driver performance, round by round (overall position, followed by the scoring Power Stage position in brackets), and year-end positions within the FIA WRC championship.

	Ogier	Lappi	Evans	Katsuta	Rovanperä
Rd 01	2nd (5th)	- (-)	21st (2nd)	8th (6th)	4th (1st)
Rd 02	- (-)	3rd (7th)	DNF (-)	4th (4th)	1st (2nd)
Rd 03	- (-)	49th (12th)	5th (3rd)	6th (13th)	1st (1st)
Rd 04	51st (7th)	- (-)	2nd (5th)	4th (6th)	1st (1st)
Rd 05	- (-)	44th (4th)	40th (3rd)	6th (5th)	5th (2nd)
Rd 06	4th (3rd)	- (-)	2nd (6th)	3rd (9th)	1st (8th)
Rd 07	- (-)	6th (4th)	2nd (2nd)	5th (5th)	1st (1st)
Rd 08	- (-)	3rd (10th)	4th (2nd)	6th (6th)	2nd (1st)
Rd 09	- (-)	3rd (6th)	2nd (2nd)	5th (5th)	62nd (1st)
Rd 10	- (-)	22nd (5th)	DNF (-)	6th (20th)	15th (2nd)
Rd 11	2nd (3rd)	- (-)	DNF (-)	DNF (-)	1st (1st)
Rd 12	1st (1st)	- (-)	6th (6th)	7th (5th)	3rd (3rd)
Rd 13	4th (7th)	- (-)	5th (21st)	3rd (16th)	12th (30th)

Drivers

1st	Kalle Rovanperä	Toyota	255
2nd	Ott Tänak	Hyundai	205
3rd	Thierry Neuville	Hyundai	193
4th	Elfyn Evans	Toyota	134
5th	Takamoto Katsuta	Toyota	122
6th	Sébastien Ogier	Toyota	97
9th	Esapekka Lappi	Toyota	58

Co-drivers

1st	Jonne Halttunen	Toyota	255
2nd	Martin Järveoja	Hyundai	205
3rd	Martijn Wydaeghe	Hyundai	193
4th	Scott Martin	Toyota	134
5th	Aaron Johnston	Toyota	122
6th	Benjamin Veillas	Toyota	85
9th	Janne Ferm	Toyota	58
11th	Vincent Landais	Toyota	43

Manufacturers

1st	Toyota	Toyota Gazoo Racing WRT	525
2nd	Hyundai	Hyundai Motorsport	455
3rd	Ford	M-Sport World Rally Team	257
4th	Toyota	Toyota Gazoo Racing WRT NG	138

NB: Points totals include Power Stage bonuses for all categories. Landais earned the majority of his points tally with Ford in 2022, before co-driving for Ogier. According to the FIA's official website, the 'Team' award went to Toyota Gazoo Racing WRT NG, but it was hardly publicised.

Kalle Rovanperä (right) and Jonne Halttunen at an FIA gala event.

The 2023 Season

The anticipated Saudi Arabian round never materialised, leaving the WRC to be contested over 13 events, as per 2022. However, quite a few changes were made to give an interesting recipe for the season. For the record, the Junior World Rally Championship was back to five rounds, once again returning as an independent series distanced from the WRC3 category.

Rally	Dates	Surface
Monte Carlo Rally	19-22 January	Tarmac
Rally Sweden	9-12 February	Snow
Rally Mexico	16-19 March	Gravel
Croatia Rally	20-23 April	Tarmac
Rally de Portugal	11-14 May	Gravel
Rally Italia Sardegna	1-4 June	Gravel
Safari Rally	22-25 June	Gravel
Rally Estonia	20-23 July	Gravel
Rally Finland	3-6 August	Gravel
Acropolis Rally	7-10 September	Gravel
Rally Chile	28 September-1 October	Gravel
Central European Rally	26-29 October	Tarmac
Rally Japan	16-19 November	Tarmac

FIA rule changes and season prospects

The FIA kept things straightforward for the same three manufacturer teams that had contested the 2022 championship (the Toyota and Hyundai works outfits ran three cars able to score points in all events, while Ford's M-Sport had two). In the post-season dealing, the big news was Ott Tänak moving over to Ford, with Esapekka Lappi effectively taking his place at Hyundai.

Test day limits were now laid out in stone to level the playing field, while longer repair times were allowed on the top-flight cars; revised evening service times were also slated. There were simplified tyre quantity rules, with a maximum of seven changes per rally, and 28 tyres the maximum amount allowed per car. The only other change of note was the penalty for every stage missed due to a hybrid unit fault, being reduced from ten minutes to two.

The Gazoo team cars and their drivers

Compared to last year's vehicle, the 2023 Yaris Rally1 was changed in a handful of details only. The intake system was tweaked to release more torque, and traction was enhanced by modifications to the differential units. There was also some optimisation of the cooling and aerodynamics, with different air ducts beneath the side windows, and minor revisions to the huge rear spoiler. Paintwork was similar to that of the 2022 car, which itself was much the same as the works car from the previous season. A big difference, however, making the new model easy to identify, was the loss of the DMG Mori logo on the bonnet and flanks.

It was back to three main drivers again for 2023, with Ogier, Evans and Rovanperä assigned to take their helm once more – all three pilots having been the main works wheelmen since 2020. In addition, Takamoto Katsuta was on hand to help

Takamoto Katsuta.

out with driving duties, as he had been since his WRC debut with Gazoo in 2019 (indeed, he was appointed the team's points scorer in place of Ogier in Sweden, Portugal, Estonia, Finland and Chile this particular year), while Jari-Matti Latvala couldn't resist an outing on his home turf, in the Rally Finland.

As it happens, Katsuta is the only driver we haven't had a close look at so far, so will provide a few lines to cover his career here. Born in Nagoya, in March 1993, the Japanese driver started off in single-seaters, but moved across to rallying in 2014. Tommi Mäkinen duly took him under his wing, and declared him ready for a WRC debut in 2016. Eventually he was given the chance to drive in the Yaris WRC car in 2019, which led to him having quite a few outings in 2020, and the continuation of his contract following on from that.

The Toyota Rally1 machine for the 2023 season. The tail shot is Rovanperä's car for Rally Japan, as this angle was not provided in the press pack. Note the cooling fan in the rear valance area – sometimes two were used.

ROUND 01

Monte Carlo Rally
19-22 January

The 91st running of the 'Monte' took place in mostly dry weather, with 75 starters competing over 18 stages covering 202 miles (325km). After the pre-event shakedown held on Thursday morning, the rally commenced as usual from Monaco's iconic Casino Square. From there, the crews headed directly into the mountains above the Principality for two stages in the dark, the first of which finishing on the famous Col de Turini.

Carrying on from the Gazoo team's championship-winning performance of the previous year, Sébastien Ogier set the pace on Days One and Two with five straight stage wins to take an early lead that he would not relinquish. Evans remained close to Ogier through the first two stages, but in SS5 lost over 40 seconds and dropped to fifth place when he reached the finish with a flat right-rear tyre. He fought back immediately in the afternoon when he led a GR Yaris Rally1 1-2-3-4 in SS6.

Toyota dominated the stage times on the first full day of the Monte, with Ogier leading Rovanperä on Friday night. Kalle Rovanperä made a solid start to the defence of his championship title with a pair of fifth-fastest times, while Takamoto Katsuta was an excellent fourth-quickest in the first stage, but was slowed by a handbrake issue through the many hairpins on the second stage, and sat ninth overall. Ogier was fastest once more in SS7 before Rovanperä took his first stage win of the season in the day's final test.

On Day Three, Toyota continued to hold first and second places in the Monte, with Ogier leading Rovanperä by 16 seconds. The Finnish driver picked up his 100th stage win in SS9 while Ogier maintained a 30-second lead. Evans continued to fight back from time lost to a flat tyre on Friday morning, moving up into fourth place ahead of Ott Tänak's M-Sport Ford. Katsuta claimed sixth place in the morning's first stage and continued his consistent pace through the day.

On Day Four, Ogier and Rovanperä traded fastest times over the last five stages to dominate the Monte and finish with a one-two result, with Evans coming in fourth and Katsuta finishing in sixth. Ogier ultimately took an unprecedented

Rd 01 #17 Ogier.

Rd 01 #69 Rovanperä.

Rd 01 #33 Evans.

Rd 01 #69 Rovanperä.

Rd 01 #18 Katsuta.

ninth Monte win, with eight of those victories counting towards the WRC. He had changed his car to #17 at the start of the season – perhaps retaining #1 would have been the right thing to do? Meanwhile, it was also Toyota's fifth Monte win with a fifth different model of car.

Monte Carlo Rally *Overall results, with 67 finishers*

Pos	Crew	Car	Time
1st	Sébastien Ogier/ Vincent Landais	Toyota GR Yaris Rally1	3:12:02.0
2nd	Kalle Rovanperä/Jonne Halttunen	Toyota GR Yaris Rally1	3:12:20.8
3rd	Thierry Neuville/Martijn Wydaeghe	Hyundai i20 N Rally1	3:12:46.6
4th	Elfyn Evans/Scott Martin	Toyota GR Yaris Rally1	3:13:14.4
6th	Takamoto Katsuta/Aaron Johnston	Toyota GR Yaris Rally1	3:15:34.6

ROUND 02

Rally Sweden

9-12 February

Marking the 70th running of Rally Sweden, the event got under way in Västerbotten County with 51 starters, including three works Toyotas, competing over 18 stages and covering 188 miles (301km). As the only pure winter event in the WRC, the competition started on Thursday in snowbound conditions with one stage only – a night sprint won by Rovanperä, giving him the early lead.

That number one spot was short-lived as Ott Tänak found his rhythm and snatched the lead in SS2. While Tänak temporarily gave the lead to Breen in the mid-sections, the Ford man recaptured the top spot in SS14 to finish first.

Day Two saw the Gazoo team trying to fight back following a tough first day, with Elfyn Evans in fourth place and Kalle Rovanperä in fifth. Rovanperä grabbed a fastest time in SS3 but could not catch Tänak. Just a few seconds behind in fifth was Takamoto Katsuta who also had a strong morning, claiming a stage win in SS4. Unfortunately, in SS5 he was caught out by the snowbanks along the road, causing him to barrel roll the car in dramatic fashion. In a first for Toyota, customer-driver Lorenzo Bertelli, in a works-assisted car, spent a lot of time in the trees (and finished 14th).

On Day Three, Rovanperä was fighting for a podium finish, and by winning three stages that day, he pushed his way in third in a battle with Neuville. Evans spun early on in the afternoon and fell to fifth, while Katsuta returned to the rally after his crash.

Neuville squeezed passed Rovanperä into third after winning the first two stages of Day Four, and that's where the Toyota driver finished – in fourth. Evans finished in fifth, struggling to find grip, while Katsuta was unable to finish the event.

With an extra three bonus points for the third-fastest time on the rally-ending Power Stage, Rovanperä remained second in the drivers' championship, only three points behind leader Ott Tänak (M-Sport Ford). Tänak gave his new team its first win in a long time, but Toyota still led the manufacturers' title chase.

Rd 02 #33 Evans.

Rd 02 #18 Katsuta.

Rd 02 #69 Rovanperä.

Rd 02 #33 Evans.

Rally Sweden *Overall results, with 45 finishers*

1st	Ott Tänak/Martin Järveoja	Ford Puma Rally1	2:25:54.5
2nd	Craig Breen/James Fulton	Hyundai i20 N Rally1	2:26:13.2
3rd	Thierry Neuville/Martijn Wydaeghe	Hyundai i20 N Rally1	2:26:14.5
4th	Kalle Rovanperä/Jonne Halttunen	Toyota GR Yaris Rally1	2:26:19.6
5th	Elfyn Evans/Scott Martin	Toyota GR Yaris Rally1	2:27:18.5
DNF	Takamoto Katsuta/Aaron Johnston	Toyota GR Yaris Rally1	–

ROUND 03

Rally Mexico
16-19 March

Mexico was the first gravel round of the 2023 season, providing a major test for the new generation of hybrid-powered Rally1 cars with its high altitude, high temperatures and rocky roads. As the 19th running of Rally Mexico, the event started with 31 entries competing over 23 stages, although SS15 was ultimately cancelled, dropping the overall distance to 186 miles (297km). Dry throughout, Thursday's shakedown and the first two stages were held over cobble streets in the evening.

After the shakedown, Rovanperä recorded the joint fastest time with Esapekka Lappi, while Ogier was third quickest and Evans fifth. Rovanperä had the second-fastest time in both passes and was 1.7 seconds from the lead overnight. Ogier was tied

Rd 03 #33 Evans.

for fourth overall, 2.8s off the leader, with Evans just half a second further back in sixth. Making his Mexico debut, Katsuta struggled to find his legs but managed to hold ninth overall.

On Day Two, Ogier was fastest in two stages but was not able to grasp the rally lead away from Lappi. In the 30°C heat and altitude of 2700m above sea level, not to mention the bumpy roads, all Gazoo entries did well by finishing inside the top five. Ogier was fastest over both passes of the Ortega stage, and was in a very close fight for the lead with Lappi's Hyundai. Evans drove solidly, moving up into third with Rovanperä fifth. Katsuta spun in SS5 and left the road, disabling his car for the day.

On Day Three, Ogier won the day's first stage, while Evans also performed brilliantly as they climbed into first and second place overall. Ogier, who'd snatched the lead from Lappi earlier in the day after the latter crashed out, then posted the quickest time in SS16 as Evans and Neuville fought for second place. Rovanperä gained fourth position after Lappi's exit as he looked to secure valuable points towards his championship defence.

Day Four saw Ogier win the Power Stage and come away with a record seventh victory in Mexico. It also saw Toyota capture a double podium finish as Neuville pushed Evans out of second place by just 0.4 seconds in the closing stages of the rally – suspension maladies costing him dearly. Rovanperä finishing in fourth helped Gazoo lock out three of the top four positions, with Katsuta in 23rd. Despite missing the Sweden round, Ogier was now in the championship lead, three points ahead of Neuville, while Gazoo was 27 points ahead of Hyundai, and 54 clear of Ford.

Rd 03 #69 Rovanperä.

Rd 03 #17 Ogier.

Rd 03 #17 Ogier.

Rally Mexico *Overall results, with 28 finishers*

1st	Sébastien Ogier/ Vincent Landais	Toyota GR Yaris Rally1	3:16:09.4
2nd	Thierry Neuville/Martijn Wydaeghe	Hyundai i20 N Rally1	3:16:36.9
3rd	Elfyn Evans/Scott Martin	Toyota GR Yaris Rally1	3:16:37.3
4th	Kalle Rovanperä/Jonne Halttunen	Toyota GR Yaris Rally1	3:18:04.7
23rd	Takamoto Katsuta/Aaron Johnston	Toyota GR Yaris Rally1	4:20:43.9

ROUND 04

Croatia Rally
20-23 April

Based in Zagreb, this event was the 47th staging of the Croatia Rally. Welcoming 55 entries and covering 20 stages over 188 miles (301km), the shakedown and opening ceremony were held on the Thursday, with the real action beginning on Friday.

Ogier made a strong start with the fastest time in SS1 to take an early lead before having to stop to change a tyre in SS2. Neuville took the lead with a win in SS2, and maintained the number one spot until Day Two. Ogier's team-mate Kalle Rovanperä suffered a similar problem after an impact in the same compression on the road. Evans took up the gauntlet on behalf of the team, moving up into second place overall, and ending the morning loop just over 16 seconds behind Neuville's Hyundai; Katsuta performed well to finish in sixth.

Evans, who had picked up a win in SS8 at the end of Day One, snatched the lead away from Neuville at the start of Day Two after the Belgian crashed out. Ogier and Rovanperä fought back from setbacks on Friday with strong

Rd 04 #17 Ogier.

◀ *Rd 04 #33 Evans.*

▼ *#69 Rovanperä.*

performances, winning seven of the eight stages between them and both gaining three positions during the day. Ogier had received a one-minute penalty overnight for an infraction on Friday, but went on to win three stages and climb back up to fourth overall, while Katsuta held onto his sixth place.

A well-managed drive enabled Evans and co-driver Martin to claim their fifth win with TGR-WRT and their first since Rally Finland in 2021. After gaining the lead on Saturday morning, Evans increased his advantage in tricky conditions in the evening to 25.4 seconds, and extended that margin to over half a minute in the first of Sunday's four tests. This allowed a more cautious approach to the final stages, with a winning margin of 27s. Ogier and Rovanperä did well in the closing stages of the rally to pick up three wins apiece, with Rovanperä finishing in fourth, Ogier in fifth and Katsuta locking out sixth.

This win allowed Evans to tie with Ogier on 69 points at the top of the rankings. Together with their fellow podium finishers, Evans and Martin dedicated the result to their friend and fellow competitor Craig Breen, who tragically lost his life in the build-up to the event.

Croatia Rally

Overall results, with 48 finishers

1st	Elfyn Evans/Scott Martin	Toyota GR Yaris Rally1	2:50:54.3
2nd	Ott Tänak/Martin Järveoja	Ford Puma Rally1	2:51:21.3
3rd	Esapekka Lappi/Janne Ferm	Hyundai i20 N Rally1	2:51:52.9
4th	Kalle Rovanpera/Jonne Halttunen	Toyota GR Yaris Rally1	2:52:12.6
5th	Sébastien Ogier/ Vincent Landais	Toyota GR Yaris Rally1	2:52:22.3
6th	Takamoto Katsuta/Aaron Johnston	Toyota GR Yaris Rally1	2:53:16.8

Rd 04 #33 Evans.

Rd 05 #69 Rovanperä.

ROUND 05

Rally de Portugal

11-14 May

This Portuguese rally was first run in 1967, and for many years was known as the TAP Rally, due to its sponsorship from the national airline, as well as the Port Wine Rally in recognition of the country's finest export.

The event started with 83 entries, but only eight top-flight cars (three Toyotas and Hyundais, plus two Fords). Portugal followed the same format as Croatia, but with 19 stages rather than 20 over three days, and covering 203 miles (325km). Ogier did not compete, and the rally turned out to be one of extremes for Toyota, with Rovanperä victorious while Evans and Katsuta struggled to finish.

In dry but tough conditions, Rovanperä took the lead from SS5 with three stage wins on Day One. Stepping into the team's main three-car line-up for the second time this season, Takamoto Katsuta made an encouraging start to the day and was level with Rovanperä for fourth position after two stages. An alternator issue unfortunately knocked him out for the rest of the day, dropping him down the standings. For Evans, it was one of his most challenging events as, although he was competing strongly in fifth early in the day, he would go off the road and crash in SS7, effectively retiring him from the event.

Following a strong performance on Friday's opening day from second on the road, Rovanperä came into the longest day of the rally with a 10-second lead that he doubled with a storming drive in the first stage of the day, going quickest by 12 seconds. Takamoto Katsuta returned to action under restart rules and managed to post the second-best time in SS15 in slippery conditions.

Reigning world champions Rovanperä and

◀ *Rd 05 #33 Evans.* ▲ *Rd 05 #18 Katsuta.*

Jonne Halttunen, who had held the lead from the mid-sections of Day One, picked up two wins on Day Three to take their first victory of the season – the win and PS bonus points taking them into the lead of the standings by 17 points.

Tänak in his Ford had been flying, but was hit by bad luck on Day One and then again on Day Two. With Neuville also suffering after a turbo popped, Toyota was now 32 points clear of closest rival, Hyundai.

Rally de Portugal *Overall results, with 47 finishers*

1st	Kalle Rovanperä/Jonne Halttunen	Toyota GR Yaris Rally1	3:35:11.7
2nd	Dani Sordo/Candido Carrera	Hyundai i20 N Rally1	3:36:06.4
3rd	Esapekka Lappi/Janne Ferm	Hyundai i20 N Rally1	3:36:32.0
33rd	Takamoto Katsuta/Aaron Johnston	Toyota GR Yaris Rally1	4:37:06.5
DNF	Elfyn Evans/Scott Martin	Toyota GR Yaris Rally1	–

Rd 05 #69 Rovanperä.

ROUND 06

Rally Italia Sardegna
1-4 June

Held in the Province of Sassari, the rally got under way with 71 starters but only nine Rally1 cars, including four Toyotas. The shakedown and one stage (an SSS) were held on Thursday, followed by 18 more to take the stage distance to 201 miles (321km). In this highly competitive event, the lead changed no less than eight times – Ogier led four times, but ultimately missed out on the win.

Sardinia's gravel rally is characterised by hot and dry conditions but rain threatened to add a slippery element this year. Ogier was the quickest of the Toyota drivers, third-fastest after three runs over the short mixed-surface stage. Takamoto Katsuta, who was lucky to stay in the rally Friday after going straight rather than turning left, was quickest through SS3 putting him in fourth, while both Rovanperä and Ogier each won a stage on Day Two. Evans lost precious time with a tyre deflation right at the end of SS7, where he dropped around 40s overall and slipped to sixth.

Ogier picked up a stage win in SS10 on Day Two to take the lead away from Lappi but that was short-lived when he slipped off the road in rainy conditions and had to retire for the day just as Neuville came storming back with two fastest times, and snatching the lead in SS14.

Rd 06 ▲ *#33 Evans.* ▼ *#17 Ogier.*

Starting Day Three in fourth place, Rovanperä benefitted from Ogier's misfortune to move up into third position overall. Evans was one place behind Rovanperä, in fourth overall, despite losing more than two minutes when he damaged the front of his car in another deep water-splash

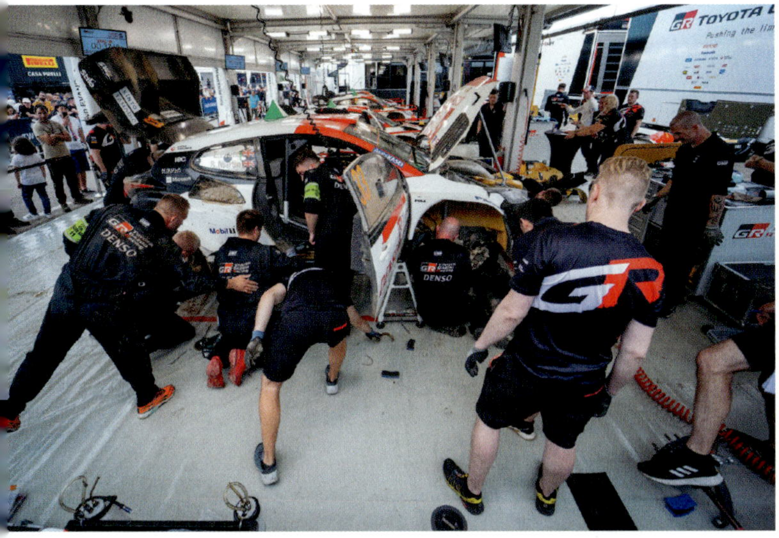

▲ *Rd 06 #69 Rovanperä.*

on SS10. Katsuta began the day in fifth after a strong Friday but was forced to stop with radiator damage from a strong hit in the water-splash at the end of SS8.

On Day Four, a clever drive by Rovanperä to avoid trouble, gave him a podium finish that allowed him to add to his lead in the drivers' championship, while Evans ensured there were two Yaris cars in the top four at the finish. Ogier had led the rally with a strong drive before a series of unfortunate events on Saturday that culminated in him sliding off the muddy road in SS14. After an eventful PS, he finished in 14th, with Katsuta in 40th.

Rally Italia Sardegna *Overall results, with 59 finishers*

1st	Thierry Neuville/Martijn Wydaeghe	Hyundai i20 N Rally1	3:40:01.4
2nd	Esapekka Lappi/Janne Ferm	Hyundai i20 N Rally1	3:40:34.4
3rd	Kalle Rovanperä/Jonne Halttunen	Toyota GR Yaris Rally1	3:41:56.7
4th	Elfyn Evans/Scott Martin	Toyota GR Yaris Rally1	3:45:21.9
14th	Sébastien Ogier/ Vincent Landais	Toyota GR Yaris Rally1	3:59:51.8
40th	Takamoto Katsuta/Aaron Johnston	Toyota GR Yaris Rally1	4:50:12.4

ROUND 07

Safari Rally

22-25 June

Centred around Naivasha, the 71st running of the Safari Rally started with a shakedown on Wednesday, followed by one stage (a SSS) Thursday, and then another 18 to cover 222 miles (356km) in all, or 744 miles (1191km) including transport distances. This rally would turn out to be one of Toyota's greatest ever rallying triumphs with the team winning all but four stages and monopolising the podium with a 1-2-3-4 finish.

Rd 07 #69 Rovanperä.

Ogier finished Day One just 0.1s behind Tänak in his Ford, temporarily giving the lead to the Estonian driver. Rovanperä was just behind Ogier with the third-best time, while Evans was fifth and Katsuta held seventh.

Day Two saw Toyota dominate the podium positions after a strong performance on the first full day, with Ogier leading Rovanperä and Evans. Ogier won four stages to snatch the lead from Tänak, a lead he would never relinquish. Rovanperä had clocked the fastest time in SS4 to come within just 2.5 seconds of Ogier. Evans was a further 10 seconds behind Rovanperä in third while Katsuta finished in the top five.

Day Three was a memorable day for Toyota as it held the top four places going into the final day and was set to lock out the podium. Ogier picked up two stage wins to consolidate his number one spot, Rovanperä was fastest three times, and Katsuta even picked up a stage win in SS12 to stay in the hunt for some silverware after an afternoon rain storm made the roads very slippery, although ironically dust had been the main problem for most of the rally. Poor Elfyn Evans had dropped from third to fourth at the start of the day after his car slowed following a water-splash, but later took back third from Katsuta.

On Day Four Tänak picking up two stage wins was not enough to prevent Toyota capturing a clean sweep of the top four positions with Ogier

Rd 07 #33 Evans.

and his battered car winning by 7 seconds over a fast-finishing Rovanperä. Evans was third and Katsuta fourth.

The 1-2-3-4 finish came 30 years to the month since Toyota first recorded such a result in Kenya with the Celica ST185. In the standings, Rovanperä now had 139 points against Neuville's 102 (the Finn was also 41 points ahead of teammate Evans), with Toyota 48 clear of Hyundai.

▶ *Rd 07 #17 Ogier.*

Safari Rally *Overall results, with 20 finishers*

1st	Sébastien Ogier/ Vincent Landais	Toyota GR Yaris Rally1	3:30:42.5
2nd	Kalle Rovanperä/Jonne Halttunen	Toyota GR Yaris Rally1	3:30:49.2
3rd	Elfyn Evans/Scott Martin	Toyota GR Yaris Rally1	3:33:41.0
4th	Takamoto Katsuta/Aaron Johnston	Toyota GR Yaris Rally1	3:34:06.3

Another full podium for Toyota ...

ROUND 08

Rally Estonia

20-23 July

Marking the 13th running of Rally Estonia, the event commenced with 50 starters, including eight Rally1 cars. The rally was fought over 21 stages covering 188 miles (300km), with a shakedown and just one stage on Thursday.

Known as one of the fastest fixtures on the calendar, Estonia saw Evans hold onto a joint lead with Lappi after SS1 on Day One. Tänak

Rd 08 #18 Katsuta.

Rd 08 #33 Evans.

may have won the next three stages, but he was out of the running soon after that when an engine swap brought a five-minute penalty. Neuville led the rally on Friday until light rain started. Meanwhile, Rovanperä, who had won the shakedown, was pushing hard for a podium finish; Katsuta was fifth, within 2.6s of the lead.

Rovanperä was in fine form on the first full day of Rally Estonia, flying into the lead on the fast forest stages, winning SS5 and SS6, allowing him to demote Neuville. Evans was running second behind Rovanperä and was not far behind his team-mate across the morning loop, which he completed in third overall. Katsuta was performing solidly finishing in seventh.

On Day Three, Rovanperä was unbeatable along Estonia's fast forest roads on a sensational Saturday as he opened up a commanding lead ahead of the dry final day. He was fastest in all eight of these forest stages as he gradually extended his lead from just three seconds to 34 by the end of the day. Evans was locked in an incredibly close battle for third position throughout the day with Esapekka Lappi in his

Rd 08 ◀▶ #69 Rovanperä.

Hyundai, while Katsuta retained his seventh place despite suffering a drivetrain problem.

Rovanperä maintained his total dominance of the event by winning all four stages on Day Four to storm to victory for the third year in a row, extending his lead to 55 points over Evans. Rovanperä recorded a remarkable run of 13 consecutive stage wins from Saturday morning until the rally-ending Power Stage on Sunday afternoon – becoming the first driver to have such a streak of fastest times on a WRC round since Sébastien Loeb in Germany 15 years ago. Meanwhile Toyota now had a comfortable 57-point advantage over Hyundai.

Rally Estonia *Overall results, with 44 finishers*

1st	Kalle Rovanperä/Jonne Halttunen	Toyota GR Yaris Rally1	2:36:03.1
2nd	Thierry Neuville/Martijn Wydaeghe	Hyundai i20 N Rally1	2:36:55.8
3rd	Esapekka Lappi/Janne Ferm	Hyundai i20 N Rally1	2:37:02.6
4th	Elfyn Evans/Scott Martin	Toyota GR Yaris Rally1	2:37:09.9
7th	Takamoto Katsuta/Aaron Johnston	Toyota GR Yaris Rally1	2:39:13.3

ROUND 09

Rally Finland
3-6 August

The 72nd running of Rally Finland saw 66 starters, including Latvala (#97) in a fourth Toyota as a one-off drive. Held in semi-wet conditions (basically dry but with a lot of damp areas and some standing water), the rally was staged over a total of 22 stages covering 201 miles (321km).

In its home Finnish city of Jyväskylä, Toyota Gazoo Racing started well with Rovanperä temporarily handing the lead to Tänak before quickly winning five stages back-to-back on Day One, holding the lead until SS8 when Evans snatched the number one spot. Evans was only 3.9 seconds away from Rovanperä after the morning loop, while Katsuta was fastest of all in Laukaa and fighting for the podium. Rovanperä continued to

Rd 09 #69 Rovanperä.

Rd 09 ◀ #18 Katsuta. ▲ #33 Evans.

set the pace in the first two stages after mid-day service, but was caught out in the second pass of Myhinpää, sliding towards a ditch that caused his car to roll, retiring it for the day. Evans finished Friday with an advantage of 6.9 seconds over second-placed Neuville (Hyundai). Katsuta was in third and Latvala was in fifth.

Evans dominated Day Three by winning seven straight stages to create a comfortable lead over Neuville. Katsuta, who impressively set the pace in the day's tricky Vekkula finale, won SS18. Rovanperä was not able to rejoin the competition on Day Three after his earlier roll, while Latvala remained in fifth position overall on his comeback behind the wheel.

On Day Four, Evans became only the third driver from outside of Finland to win the event on multiple occasions, as he and co-driver Scott Martin repeated their 2021 triumph on the fastest rally in the FIA World Rally Championship. Posting the fastest times in three of the last four stages, Welshman Evans looked at home in his Yaris all weekend, closely matched with team-mate and local hero Kalle Rovanperä on Friday until the Finn had to retire following a crash.

Second in the championship standings, Evans' maximum score meant that he was now 25 points down on leader Rovanperä with four rallies remaining. Katsuta scored his fourth WRC podium after a strong and confident performance on the roads around Jyväskylä, while Latvala finished fifth after taking part in his home event for the first time since 2019 – at the invitation of TGR-WRT Chairman Akio Toyoda, who took on his Team Principal duties in the service park.

Rally Finland *Overall results, with 49 finishers*

1st	Elfyn Evans/Scott Martin	Toyota GR Yaris Rally1	2:33:11.3
2nd	Thierry Neuville/Martijn Wydaeghe	Hyundai i20 N Rally1	2:33:50.4
3rd	Takamoto Katsuta/Aaron Johnston	Toyota GR Yaris Rally1	2:34:48.0
DNF	Kalle Rovanperä/Jonne Halttunen	Toyota GR Yaris Rally1	–

ROUND 10

Acropolis Rally

7-10 September

Now in its 67th year, the Acropolis welcomed 69 entries, including three Rally1 Fords and Hyundais, and four Toyotas. Run over 15 stages covering 169 miles (271km), Thursday was set aside for the shakedown and one stage (a SSS) as the sun started to go down in Athens, although the SD sessions were cancelled due to flash flooding.

In a rally where the lead changed five times, Rovanperä eventually found his form to dominate the latter stages and clinch victory. He'd taken an early lead on Day One, only to relinquish it to Neuville as his starting position left him at a disadvantage, cleaning the rough roads for others to follow. Sébastien Ogier was sixth, with Takamoto Katsuta setting the same time. Elfyn Evans was 11th, but still within 2.8s of the lead.

On Day Two, Toyota's drivers found their form and finished second, third and fourth behind Neuville. Ogier and Rovanperä had both won a stage but it was not enough to take back the lead. Evans was 5.5s further back, climbing up from sixth to fourth with a strong time in SS6, while Katsuta was sixth overall.

Early on Day Three, Ogier took the lead from Neuville in SS7 before handing it back to the Belgian in SS8. Suspension maladies hit both the Frenchman and the Belgian, although they were ultimately able to restart. Rovanperä then won four consecutive stages to end the day and lead by a sizable margin. Elfyn Evans and Dani Sordo fought hard for second place, with Evans taking SS13 and Sordo posting the quickest time in SS14. Katsuta was in fifth.

Rovanperä, however, managed to avoid issues on Day Four while also setting a string of fastest times to gain a lead of more than two minutes at the end of Saturday. The third win and maximum score of the season for Rovanperä and co-driver Jonne Halttunen represents a perfect bounce back from retirement in Finland, and increased Rovanperä's lead to 33 points ahead of Evans, who squeezed past Sordo in the final stages to finish in second place for a superb one-two for Toyota.

Rd 10 #69 Rovanperä.

Rd 10 #33 Evans.

▲ *Rd 10 #17 Ogier.* ▶ *#69 Rovanperä.*

On his first appearance since June's Safari Rally Kenya, Ogier was leading the rally until Saturday afternoon's tyre and suspension trouble put an end to his charge. Katsuta, who had been close to the Evans-Sordo battle, finished sixth after wheel damage forced stoppages.

With this victory Toyota now had a near 100-point advantage over their Korean rivals.

Acropolis Rally *Overall results, with 52 finishers*

1st	Kalle Rovanperä/Jonne Halttunen	Toyota GR Yaris Rally1	3:00:16.7
2nd	Elfyn Evans/Scott Martin	Toyota GR Yaris Rally1	3:01:48.4
3rd	Dani Sordo/Candido Carrera	Hyundai i20 N Rally1	3:01:52.6
6th	Takamoto Katsuta/Aaron Johnston	Toyota GR Yaris Rally1	3:07:37.6
10th	Sébastien Ogier/ Vincent Landais	Toyota GR Yaris Rally1	3:12:00.1

ROUND 11

Rally Chile
28 September-1 October

In only the second running of Rally Chile, 51 entries competed over 16 stages covering 200 miles (321km) across the Biobio region. Running second on the road based upon his championship position, Evans made a strong start in the morning, claiming the rally lead with the fastest times in SS2 and SS3.

In the afternoon, grip seemed harder to come by at the front of the order, and Evans slipped to third, giving up the lead to Teemu Suninen, but was still within 12 seconds of the leader overnight. As championship leader, Kalle Rovanperä had to drive first and open the road, but was running just one place behind team-mate and main title rival Evans, in fourth overall, until the final stage of the

◀ *Rd 11 #69 Rovanperä.*

▼ *#33 Evans.*

day when a half-spin demoted him to fifth. After a big moment, Takamoto Katsuta improved his pace in the afternoon and was just 6.9s further back in sixth place.

On Day Two, Evans began in third overall after a strong drive on Friday from a challenging road position, and took second place in Saturday morning's opening stage – where Kalle Rovanperä also regained fourth overall after setting the fastest time. However, unexpectedly high tyre wear would take a toll on the grippier soft-compound rubber fitted to the GR Yaris cars for the morning, causing all three chargers to lose significant time, with Evans in fourth, Rovanperä fifth, and Katsuta sixth.

All drivers chose only hard-compound tyres in the afternoon, and Rovanperä was fastest again in the repeat of the opening Chivilingo SS10 test, just ahead of Evans, while Rovanperä and Katsuta rounded out the top six. Tänak and Neuville found their form in Chile, with Tänak snatching the lead in SS5 and never relinquishing it, while Neuville fought hard by winning SS13 through SS15 on the trot for second place.

Evans, who led the rally for the first few stages, and looked like fighting for the win, suffered from tyre wear on extremely abrasive stages on Saturday. Ultimately, Rovanperä still held on to a 31-point lead over Evans, while Toyota finished 106 points ahead of Hyundai, duly retaining its crown as manufacturer champions. But with 60 points still available in the drivers' title chase, either Rovanperä or Evans could take home the drivers' trophy.

Rally Chile *Overall results, with 36 finishers*

1st	Ott Tänak/Martin Järveoja	Ford Puma Rally1	3:06:38.1
2nd	Thierry Neuville/Martijn Wydaeghe	Hyundai i20 N Rally1	3:07:20.2
3rd	Elfyn Evans/Scott Martin	Toyota GR Yaris Rally1	3:07:45.0
4th	Kalle Rovanperä/Jonne Halttunen	Toyota GR Yaris Rally1	3:08:49.1
5th	Takamoto Katsuta/Aaron Johnston	Toyota GR Yaris Rally1	3:11:19.6

Rd 11 ▲ #18 Katsuta.

ROUND 12

Central European Rally

26-29 October

Taking on an unfamiliar name, the first-ever running of the Central European Rally welcomed 67 entries, including four from Toyota in Rally1. Based in Passau, Germany, some stages were also held in the Czech Republic and Austria. Two stages were held on the Thursday (the last in damp night conditions) after the shakedown, with the remaining 16 over the following three days. Although the cars only competed over 194 miles (310km), the teams had to traverse huge distances to reach all the stages, taking the event to over 1000 miles (1691km to be exact) in total.

On Day One, Sébastien Ogier was second-fastest in SS1 and then fifth in SS2 to lie third. Kalle Rovanperä was just one position and 0.1s behind in fourth, while Elfyn Evans was eighth after a

Rd 12 ▲ *#17 Ogier.* ▶ *#69 Rovanperä.*

brief overshoot at a junction in SS2. Takamoto Katsuta held onto sixth.

On Day Two heavy rain added to the demands on the narrow but fast Czech roads. Rovanperä rose to this challenge, winning all three of the morning's stages. He capitalised on his road position at the front of the order, taking the lead on SS4 and arriving in Prachatice at lunchtime with a lead over Evans of 29.2 seconds. Ogier suffered an early setback in SS3 with a damaged wheel, losing around 40s. He was in sixth overnight, with Katsuta fifth in his WRC Challenge Program-supported entry.

On Day Three, everything started to fall apart for Rovanperä and Evans as they watched their hopes at winning literally wash away in the rain. Holding onto a thin lead over Evans, and with Neuville closing in fast, Rovanperä lost control on wet roads and spun out under heavy braking on SS10, shrinking his lead from 36 seconds to ten.

Evans meanwhile had started the day third overall and taken a stage win in SS9. Unfortunately, his championship hopes would be dealt a major blow in SS11 when he too slid off the road, and was forced to stop with damage to his car and restart under the SR rules. Ogier was up to fourth place and 31s behind Tänak after winning the first two stages of the afternoon loop. Fifth-placed Takamoto Katsuta also showed improved performance in the afternoon, when he was always driving among the top-four stage times.

Even though Neuville went on to win the event in his Hyundai, with Evans claiming the biggest share of the PS bonus, a second place finish for Rovanperä and co-driver Haltunnen was enough to secure their back-to-back WRC drivers' titles in the penultimate round. Toyota had already won its trophy, of course ...

▲ *Rd 12 #33 Evans.* ▼ *Another title in the bag ...*

Central European Rally *Overall results, with 54 finishers*

1st	Thierry Neuville/Martijn Wydaeghe	Hyundai i20 N Rally1	2:52:39.9
2nd	Kalle Rovanperä/Jonne Halttunen	Toyota GR Yaris Rally1	2:53:37.5
3rd	Ott Tänak/Martin Järveoja	Ford Puma Rally1	2:54:32.7
4th	Sébastien Ogier/ Vincent Landais	Toyota GR Yaris Rally1	2:54:48.5
5th	Takamoto Katsuta/Aaron Johnston	Toyota GR Yaris Rally1	2:55:28.2
31st	Elfyn Evans/Scott Martin	Toyota GR Yaris Rally1	3:32:38.1

ROUND 13

Rally Japan
16-19 November

Evolving from a round of the APRC, the Rally Hokkaido was renamed the Rally Japan in 2004, and was immediately included on the WRC calendar. Initially based on Japan's north island (as its original name suggests), it was strangely not used by the FIA from 2011 to 2019; COVID then delayed its comeback for another two years before it made a welcome return to WRC favour in 2022, now based on the main island of Honshu near Toyota's HQ just outside Nagoya. Perhaps the home advantage worked, as Toyota came away with a one-two-three finish.

Marking the eighth running of the event, Rally Japan was scheduled for 22 stages, although the number dropped to 21 over 176 miles (282km) after SS4 was cancelled. At his home event, after the rally opener inside Toyota Stadium, Katsuta was fifth-fastest, followed by Rovanperä in sixth, Ogier eighth and Evans ninth, all within five seconds of the lead.

On Day Two, Evans started superbly by winning SS2 and SS3 and snatching the lead away from Neuville, a lead that he held onto until the checkered flag. The Brit maintained a strong pace in the afternoon, despite the bad weather, and with nearest rival Neuville (Hyundai) retiring in SS6, Evans returned to Toyota Stadium after SS7 with a lead of 50.9s over Ogier. Meanwhile, Katsuta seemed like a man possessed at his home event, as the Japanese driver pushed hard to capture three consecutive fastest times from SS5 through SS7, and then an SS10 victory giving him a ninth overall in spite of a damaged radiator.

Rd 13 #33 Evans.

Rd 13 #17 Ogier.

◀ *Rd 13 #69 Rovanperä.*

▼ *Rd 13 #33 Evans.*

On Day Three, Gazoo still held the top three positions with Evans in the lead after winning two straight stages, followed by Ogier and Rovanperä. Even when Japan threw hail and snow at Evans, he still managed to hold his lead over Ogier. Katsuta again starred with another hat-trick of wins from SS13 through SS15.

On the final day, which started damp with a little snow on the ground but eventually dried out, Toyota scored a dream finish on home territory to complete a season of success in style, with Elfyn Evans claiming victory ahead of Sébastien Ogier and Kalle Rovanperä. TGR-WRC Chairman Akio Toyoda joined the winners on the podium, while Katsuta, who picked up no less than nine stage wins, finished in an admirable fifth despite picking up penalties.

The Gazoo team's dominance this season by winning nine out of thirteen rallies, gave it all three titles – the manufacturers', drivers' and co-drivers' championships.

Rally Japan *Overall results, with 28 finishers*

1st	Elfyn Evans/Scott Martin	Toyota GR Yaris Rally1	3:32:08.8
2nd	Sébastien Ogier/ Vincent Landais	Toyota GR Yaris Rally1	3:33:26.5
3rd	Kalle Rovanperä/Jonne Halttunen	Toyota GR Yaris Rally1	3:33:55.3
5th	Takamoto Katsuta/Aaron Johnston	Toyota GR Yaris Rally1	3:35:19.1

2023 SUMMARY

The season reviewed in a way that provides a quick reference from a Toyota/Gazoo perspective, with driver performance, round by round (overall position, followed by the scoring Power Stage position in brackets), and year-end positions within the FIA WRC championship.

	Ogier	Evans	Rovanperä	Katsuta
Rd 01	1st (5th)	4th (3rd)	2nd (1st)	6th (22nd)
Rd 02	– (–)	5th (2nd)	4th (3rd)	DNF (–)
Rd 03	1st (1st)	3rd (6th)	4th (4th)	23rd (7th)
Rd 04	5th (3rd)	1st (7th)	4th (2nd)	6th (4th)
Rd 05	– (–)	DNF (–)	1st (1st)	33rd (4th)
Rd 06	14th (5th)	4th (4th)	3rd (1st)	40th (3rd)
Rd 07	1st (4th)	3rd (6th)	2nd (3rd)	4th (7th)
Rd 08	– (–)	4th (2nd)	1st (1st)	7th (8th)
Rd 09	– (–)	1st (1st)	DNF (–)	3rd (4th)
Rd 10	10th (7th)	2nd (2nd)	1st (1st)	6th (8th)
Rd 11	– (–)	3rd (2nd)	4th (1st)	5th (5th)
Rd 12	4th (3rd)	31st (1st)	2nd (8th)	5th (4th)
Rd 13	2nd (5th)	1st (7th)	3rd (6th)	5th (4th)

Drivers

1st	Kalle Rovanperä	Toyota	250
2nd	Elfyn Evans	Toyota	216
3rd	Thierry Neuville	Hyundai	189
5th	Sébastien Ogier	Toyota	133
7th	Takamoto Katsuta	Toyota	101

Co-drivers

1st	Jonne Halttunen	Toyota	250
2nd	Scott Martin	Toyota	216
3rd	Martijn Wydaeghe	Hyundai	189
5th	Vincent Landais	Toyota	133
7th	Aaron Johnston	Toyota	101

Manufacturers

1st	Toyota	Toyota Gazoo Racing WRT	548
2nd	Hyundai	Hyundai Motorsport	432
3rd	Ford	M-Sport World Rally Team	287

NB: Points totals include Power Stage bonuses for all categories. Although advertised by the FIA as up for grabs, the 'Team' title was not awarded.

The 2024 Season

The World Rally Championship remained held over 13 rounds, although the Safari Rally took the slot occupied by last year's Mexican sortie, while new gravel events in Poland and Latvia basically replaced the Rally Estonia. The WRC2 and WRC3 calendar was the same, although teams didn't need to enter each round, in a bid to reduce costs. The JWRC continued to be contested over five of the rallies, held in southern Europe and Scandinavia.

2024 Season Rounds

Rally	Dates	Surface
Monte Carlo Rally	25-28 January	Tarmac
Rally Sweden	15-18 February	Snow
Safari Rally	28-31 March	Gravel
Croatia Rally	18-21 April	Tarmac
Rally de Portugal	9-12 May	Gravel
Rally Italia Sardegna	30 May-2 June	Gravel
Rally Poland	27-30 June	Gravel
Rally Latvia	18-21 July	Gravel
Rally Finland	1-4 August	Gravel
Acropolis Rally	5-8 September	Gravel
Rally Chile	26-29 September	Gravel
Central European Rally	31 October-3 November	Tarmac
Rally Japan	21-24 November	Tarmac

FIA rule changes and season prospects

In a surprise move, Ott Tänak went back to Hyundai as Ford kept its mainstream campaign to include just two Pumas, joining Thierry Neuville again as the main threat to Toyota; like the Gazoo team, the Hyundai outfit would shuffle the drivers around in its third vehicle.

There were no major technical changes for the start of 2024, other than some tweaks to the tyre regs. However, the points scoring system in the top WRC category was completely revised, with 18, 15, 13, 10, 8, 6, 4, 3, 2 and 1 point(s) being awarded based on Saturday's positions, assuming the cars finished on the final day to collect them. In addition, Sunday's stage times would be added to give an extra 7, 6, 5, 4, 3, 2 and 1 point allocation, while the Power Stage continued to yield up to five bonus points.

Once the season got rolling, it was announced that the plug-in hybrid unit would be ditched for 2025 (two years earlier than planned), and a new set of Rally1 regulations was on the horizon for the following year. Both moves were aimed at reducing costs and attracting new teams into the WRC fold. Greater variation in future rally formats was also mooted, albeit whilst retaining a Sunday Power Stage finish.

The Gazoo team cars and their drivers

Although the new paint scheme made the 2024 cars look quite different from those used in 2023, there were actually minimal changes made to the body. The grilles under the rear side windows were introduced during the last season, and the wheel centre dressing pieces on the tarmac-spec rims had often been seen before. Indeed, spot-the-difference junkies would be kept entertained for hours trying to find any significant revisions. On the mechanical front, the leading specifications were carried over, but the engine was tuned to give better torque characteristics, and improved response low down.

Jari-Matti Latvala was still the Team Principal, with Tom Fowler heading the technical boffins. The driver and co-driver line-up was the same as that for 2023, although Kalle Rovanperä stated before the season started that he wouldn't be entering every round. Likewise, Ogier also had a limited programme, as per the previous year, meaning that Evans and Katsuta would be the only ones taking in the full calendar.

For the record, having first broken cover at the 2022 Rally Japan, the GR Yaris Rally2 model was now available, with four customer teams using it in the WRC2 category from the very start of the season. Rally2 cars were limited to around 290bhp, by the way, so were quite a lot less powerful than their Rally1 brethren.

The Yaris was given an all-new livery for the 2024 season.

The limited edition road cars launched in early 2024.

Interestingly, two 8,450,000 yen limited edition road cars were announced in January 2024, with sales of the 100-off 'Ogier Edition' and more colourful 'Rovanperä Edition' (also restricted to 100 units) duly starting in the spring. Feedback from the drivers resulted in a number of interior and exterior changes, and a special 4WD switch, allowing owners to adopt the set-up favoured by the two star drivers.

ROUND 01

Monte Carlo Rally

25-28 January

Marking the 92nd running of the Monte, some 68 starters, including Ogier, Evans and Katsuta competed over 17 special stages in mainly dry conditions with the odd ice patch; the stage distance covered 203 miles (324km).

At the traditional start ceremony in the iconic Casino Square on the Thursday, Sébastien Ogier and Kalle Rovanperä helped to reveal their special edition GR Yaris models, which featured input from TGR-WRT's two world champion drivers. In

Rd 01 #33 Evans.

Rd 01 #17 Ogier.

the two night stages held that day, Elfyn Evans posted the fastest times to take an early lead. He led by 15.1s over Thierry Neuville (Hyundai), with Ogier in third position just 6.5s further back. Takamoto Katsuta rounded out the top six in the overall standings, 46.3s away.

Evans performed superbly throughout Day One and Two, finishing every stage inside the top three to hold onto a narrow lead until the start of Day Three. Ogier began Day Two third overall and claimed his first stage win in SS4 before a stunning time in SS5 where he was 11.2s faster than anyone else – a performance that moved him up into second. Takamoto Katsuta finished the day in 12th after falling foul on a particularly icy corner in the morning's first stage, requiring spectator help to get back on the road.

Going into Saturday, Ogier was firmly in the fight for the victory, just three seconds behind Evans. Hyundai's Thierry Neuville stole the lead from Evans with three fastest times in SS6, SS7 and SS9, delegating Evans to third after the Brit

Rd 01 #18 Katsuta.

suffered a hybrid issue, forcing him to lose power and pace. Ogier then won back-to-back stages (SS12 and SS13) to record the 700th stage win of his WRC career towards the end of Day Three, and briefly snatch the lead. After banking good points under the championship's new format by ending the penultimate day in third, Evans continued to push hard on Sunday when additional points were on offer for the fastest drivers.

But somehow Neuville found some extra pace on Day Four and posted four consecutive fastest times (including the PS) to take back the lead from Ogier and win the rally. With Ogier in second and Evans third in the overall results, TGR-WRT led the manufacturers' championship by one point, with Ogier six points behind Neuville in the drivers' title chase. Neuville couldn't expect an easy run to glory, though, even when two of his main rivals weren't competing over a full season ...

Monte Carlo Rally *Overall results, with 64 finishers*

1st	Thierry Neuville/Martijn Wydaeghe	Hyundai i20 N Rally1	3:09:30.9
2nd	Sébastien Ogier/ Vincent Landais	Toyota GR Yaris Rally1	3:09:47.0
3rd	Elfyn Evans/Scott Martin	Toyota GR Yaris Rally1	3:10:16.1
7th	Takamoto Katsuta/Aaron Johnston	Toyota GR Yaris Rally1	3:17:59.4

ROUND 02

Rally Sweden

15-18 February

Based in the Vasterbotten County in northern Sweden (bordering Norway), the rally welcomed 57 entries, including Lorenzo Bertelli in a private Rally1 Yaris, although he was unable to score for the manufacturer. With snowy conditions throughout, the event boasted 18 stages over a total of 188 miles (301km), although it was four times that if you include liaison distances.

Rovanperä won the only stage on Day One, and then the first stage on Friday morning to hold a 5.7 second lead over team-mate Katsuta after SS3. Unfortunately, Rovanperä spun in SS4 after contact with a snow bank, causing radiator damage and forcing him to throw in the towel for the day and return on Day Three. Meanwhile, Katsuta was enjoying one of his best performances ever as he won SS4, allowing him to take an early lead on Day Two. Evans suffered a high-speed spin in SS3 but recovered to finish the day in third. Then, Hyundai's Esapekka Lappi posted four straight fastest times from SS5 onwards to snatch the top spot away from Katsuta – a lead that he held onto until the checkered flag. Meanwhile, Evans ended Friday in fifth.

Day Three saw Katsuta just three seconds behind Lappi, but after over-extending himself, the Japanese driver slid into a snowbank and was unable to continue that day. Evans fought back, moving up from fifth to third overall after a win in SS12. With points now awarded based upon the positions at the end of Saturday, Evans was set to score 13 points, with additional points up for grabs for finishing the rally.

Rovanperä restarted following Friday's off, and scored a stage win in the morning's second test as he prepared to target points on Sunday. Day Four saw Evans storming into second place after a

Rd 02 #69 Rovanperä.

Rd 02 ▲ #18 Katsuta.
▶ #33 Evans.

win in SS17, and a close second in the rally-ending Power Stage. That was enough to top the 'Super Sunday' classification, giving the Welshman and his co-driver Scott Martin a total of 24 points from the weekend – more than any other crew.

Having both led the rally briefly, Rovanperä and Katsuta were victims of the snowbanks, and fell to 39th and 45th respectively. Driving the fourth Yaris Rally1, privateer Lorenzo Bertelli eventually reached the finish in tenth place overall. The result narrowed Neuville's title lead over Evans to just three points, while Toyota and Hyundai were now tied on 87 points apiece thanks to PS bonuses.

Rally Sweden

Overall results, with 50 finishers

1st	Esapekka Lappi/Janne Ferm	Hyundai i20 N Rally1	2:33:04.9
2nd	Elfyn Evans/Scott Martin	Toyota GR Yaris Rally1	2:33:34.5
3rd	Adrien Fourmaux/Alexandre Corio	Ford Puma Rally1	2:33:52.8
39th	Kalle Rovanperä/Jonne Halttunen	Toyota GR Yaris Rally1	3:21:36.8
45th	Takamoto Katsuta/Aaron Johnston	Toyota GR Yaris Rally1	3:32:09.4

ROUND 03

Safari Rally

28-31 March

Marking the 72nd running of the Safari Rally, this event saw only 28 cars entered, including the same three works Toyotas as those in Sweden, but joined by three Hyundais and three Fords in the Rally1 category. The event was held over a total of 19 stages covering 230 miles (368km) in largely dry and dusty conditions, with light rain on occasion.

The all-important shakedown was held on the Wednesday, with Hyundai's Neuville winning Thursday's only stage to take an early lead with Rovanperä in third, Katsuta in fourth, and Evans in sixth. Then on Day Two, Rovanperä showed his resilience around the Lake Naivasha and Kedong tests by winning every stage on the first full day to steal the lead away from Neuville, with team-mates Evans and Katsuta right behind. Evans was fifth after the morning loop, elevating himself above Katsuta and into second place in the day's final stage. There was 3.9s between them overnight, with fourth-placed Thierry Neuville (Hyundai) 6.5s further back.

On Day Three, despite being unhappy with the car's setup, Rovanperä held onto his lead with a day to go, as Katsuta followed in second, with Evans in fourth. Katsuta went from tragedy to triumph early on Day Three after he sustained a double puncture to lose over a minute, dropping to third, but then found superior pace to win both runs along the Soysambu test to get back his second place. Evans also had to stop to change a tyre early in the morning's first stage, losing nearly two minutes and falling to fourth. He then won SS12 but suffered yet another puncture to drop another place. Under the new scoring system for 2024, points were awarded based on the positions held at the end of Saturday, so this was not an ideal situation.

Rovanperä won the legendary Safari Rally for the fourth year in a row, with the Finnish driver leading Katsuta in a one-two finish in this most demanding of African events. The result demonstrated the reliability of the GR Yaris, which employed an updated suspension package as well as a distinctive snorkel system to tackle the Kenyan outback – a modern take on an iconic feature of Safari-specification cars of the past. Katsuta achieved his third podium result from four starts in Kenya, while Evans finished a strong fourth. It was Ford's first Safari podium in over 20 years, but the new scoring system allowed Neuville (who had a good Sunday run) to extend his lead over Evans to six points.

Rd 03 #18 Katsuta.

Rd 03 ▼ #69 Rovanperä. ▶ *#33 Evans.*

Rd 03 The podium in Africa ...

Safari Rally *Overall results, with 22 finishers*

1st	Kalle Rovanperä/Jonne Halttunen	Toyota GR Yaris Rally1	3:36:04.0
2nd	Takamoto Katsuta/Aaron Johnston	Toyota GR Yaris Rally1	3:37:41.8
3rd	Adrien Fourmaux/Alexandre Corio	Ford Puma Rally1	3:38:29.1
4th	Elfyn Evans/Scott Martin	Toyota GR Yaris Rally1	3:40:24.2

ROUND 04

Croatia Rally

18-21 April

Coming into this Zagreb-based rally, Elfyn Evans and Scott Martin were the defending winners of an event that began with a ceremonial start on Thursday, and SS1 on Friday. With some 67 entries, the rally included 20 stages covering 177 miles (283km), but only eight cars were competing in the Rally1 category, including two Fords, three Toyotas and three Hyundais.

In a rain-affected event (even when it didn't rain on Saturday, wet weather was expected, making tyre choices a real gamble), there would be no less than six leader changes with Neuville and Evans swapping the top spot for much of the rally, locked in a magnificent battle. On Day One, Neuville started out strong, winning four stages to take an early lead. In the morning, Ogier faced challenging conditions running sixth in the road order, so did well to hold onto third through the morning. But in the afternoon, he drove superbly to win SS7 and SS8 by a staggering 9.2s, helping him to close in on the leader. Katsuta was in sixth place overall, finishing a demanding day on a strong note with the fourth-best time in SS8.

Team Gazoo had two cars involved in an exciting fight for victory with one day remaining.

Rd 04 #17 Ogier.

As the lead chopped and changed, Evans began the day tied for the rally lead with Hyundai's Neuville, and Ogier just 6.6 seconds behind, breathing down their necks in third. Neuville won five stages on Day Two to snatch the lead away from Evans, while the Brit managed to win SS13, enabling him to finish the day just 4.9 seconds behind the Belgian. Ogier was a further six seconds back in third, while Katsuta demonstrated his improved pace to set several top-four stage times and remain in sixth position overall.

On a thrilling final day, the victory in Croatia was up for grabs. Neuville had held onto a narrow lead over Evans until both drivers, pushing hard, spun out and lost precious seconds, while Ogier, who enjoyed a clean run, claimed the lead on the third last stage of the day. He would maintain this

Rd 04 ◀ #18 Katsuta. ▼ #33 Evans.

lead to the finish, marking his 100th podium in WRC. Evans survived his spin with minimum lost time, enabling him to finish in second, while Katsuta found his rhythm and picked up the fastest times in SS17 and SS19 to finish in fifth. Neuville maintained a six-point lead over Evans, while Toyota overtook Hyundai by seven points thanks to a one-two finish.

Rd 04 #17 Ogier. ▶

Croatia Rally *Overall results, with 62 finishers*

1st	Sébastien Ogier/ Vincent Landais	Toyota GR Yaris Rally1	2:40:23.6
2nd	Elfyn Evans/Scott Martin	Toyota GR Yaris Rally1	2:40:33.3
3rd	Thierry Neuville/Martijn Wydaeghe	Hyundai i20 N Rally1	2:41:09.4
5th	Takamoto Katsuta/Aaron Johnston	Toyota GR Yaris Rally1	2:42:19.1

ROUND 05

Rally de Portugal
9-12 May

Rd 05 #17 Ogier.

In the 57th running of the Rally de Portugal, some 67 cars entered a rally that included 22 stages covering 221 miles (337km) in total. Toyota made an interesting move to put Rovanperä in the third scoring works car alongside Evans and Ogier, leaving Katsuta out in the cold – according to the rules, he couldn't score for the maker in a fourth vehicle, although his result would still be added to his drivers' championship tally. Three Hyundais and two Fords made up the rest of the Rally1 contingent.

In the opening SSS on Day One (a short street test in the coastal city of Figueira da Foz, and Thursday's only stage), Ogier was second fastest, with Katsuta fourth, Rovanperä fifth, and Evans in eighth.

Rd 05 ▲ *#33 Evans.* ▶ *#69 Rovanperä.*

On Day Two, Toyota locked out the top three places with Rovanperä in the lead, followed closely by Ogier, with Takamoto Katsuta holding third. As it happens, the Japanese driver won SS2 to snatch the lead away from Neuville, but that would be short-lived. By the afternoon, Rovanperä was flying and took over the lead from Katsuta in SS6 after some particularly inspiring steering. Ogier too was motoring, having picked up wins in SS6 and SS9 to maintain second. Katsuta also remained in the podium placings, just 3.7s away from Ogier and 0.7s in front of Ott Tänak. Meanwhile, with a tyre off the rim in SS7, Evans lost precious time and fell to eighth overall.

On Day Three, Ogier was fastest in SS11 and SS13, allowing him to steal the lead from Rovanperä. The Finn ran wide and clipped a tree stump, upending the car and postponing his restart until the following day. Katsuta, who began the day in third, sustained rear suspension damage when he hit a bank in SS12, forcing him to join Rovanperä. Ogier briefly gave up the number one spot to Tänak in SS12, but quickly recaptured it, and then held onto it until the finish thanks to additional wins in SS16 and SS17. Recovering places after losing time on a tough Friday, Evans reached the end of Saturday in sixth position overall.

On Day Four, after a foggy start to the morning, Ogier secured a second successive win with his record-breaking sixth victory at the Rally de Portugal. Elfyn Evans and Scott Martin finished sixth overall, while Katsuta ended up in 29th, with Rovanperä 31st. Escaping a few hairy moments, Neuville now led Evans by 24 points, while Toyota was four points down on Hyundai.

Rd 05 ▼ *#17 Ogier.* ▶ *#18 Katsuta.*

Rally de Portugal *Overall results, with 34 finishers*

1st	Sébastien Ogier/ Vincent Landais	Toyota GR Yaris Rally1	3:41:32.3
2nd	Ott Tänak/Martin Järveoja	Hyundai i20 N Rally1	3:41:40.2
3rd	Thierry Neuville/Martijn Wydaeghe	Hyundai i20 N Rally1	3:42:42.1
6th	Elfyn Evans/Scott Martin	Toyota GR Yaris Rally1	3:48:08.3
29th	Takamoto Katsuta/Aaron Johnston	Toyota GR Yaris Rally1	4:52:06.1
31st	Kalle Rovanperä/Jonne Halttunen	Toyota GR Yaris Rally1	5:02:26.7

ROUND 06

Rally Italia Sardegna

30 May-2 June

With the opening ceremony taking place in Alghero located in the island's north-west, the 21st running of the Sardinian event saw three Toyotas, three Hyundais and two Fords competing amongst 81 entrants over 16 dry and dusty stages that covered 166 miles (266km).

In a rare tight schedule in which the competitive action was crammed into just over 48 hours, the shakedown took place on the Friday morning before the rally proper began after lunch. Ogier made a storming start to post the quickest time in the opening Osilo-Tergu stage, a drive that gave him the early lead. As it turned out, this rally would become a titanic tit-for-tat battle between Ogier and Tänak with the lead changing five times and the win going down to the wire. Katsuta was fourth overall after making a consistent start, with Evans back in sixth after suffering tyre damage in SS1.

After Friday afternoon's opening leg of four stages, Ogier brought his lead of 4.5 seconds into Day Two, although a tyre coming off a rim in the morning's first stage eradicated that advantage. He briefly conceded the lead to Tänak in SS7 but would regain the top spot in SS9, and then hold onto the lead via three straight stage wins. Katsuta moved up into third position overall at the end of the morning loop, but hopes of a podium finish were dashed by a transmission-related issue that forced him to stop in SS9. Evans drove a clean day on the demanding stages and was rewarded with fourth place at the end of Saturday. New rules stipulated that drivers needed to be at the finish on Sunday to clinch any points banked on Saturday evening.

Rd 06 #33 Evans.

Rd 06 ▲ #18 Katsuta.
▶ #17 Ogier.

Ogier led the rally into the final day, and by the Power Stage, the Toyota driver was six seconds ahead of Tänak. Ogier looked to be doing enough to secure victory until he began losing air from a tyre over the rough final section. It meant that he and co-driver Vincent Landais ultimately missed out by just 0.2s in a finish that equals the closest ever in FIA World Rally Championship history. Evans reduced his gap to the championship leader to 18 points after finishing fourth overall.

Rally Italia Sardegna *Overall results, with 68 finishers*

1st	Ott Tänak/Martin Järveoja	Hyundai i20 N Rally1	3:06:05.6
2nd	Sébastien Ogier/ Vincent Landais	Toyota GR Yaris Rally1	3:06:05.8
3rd	Dani Sordo/Candido Carrera	Hyundai i20 N Rally1	3:08:31.4
4th	Elfyn Evans/Scott Martin	Toyota GR Yaris Rally1	3:08:43.4
35th	Takamoto Katsuta/Aaron Johnston	Toyota GR Yaris Rally1	3:47:33.7

ROUND 07

Rally Poland
27-30 June

As one of the most established rallies on the rallying calendar, Rally Poland celebrated its 80th running and its first staging of a WRC event since 2017 with a Toyota one-two victory. The rally had 42 entries, including nine Rally1 works cars, with the third (new) Ford pilot putting in an exceptional performance in a Puma without hybrid assistance, to finish in fifth. It was not a good advert for petrol-electric technology! Meanwhile, Rovanperä replaced an injured Ogier (who suffered a concussion caused by a traffic accident) at the last minute, giving him no time to prepare. And yet, he still went on to win the 189-mile (303km) event ...

The first competitive stage on Day One saw Evans set the third-fastest time, just 1.3 seconds off the pace, with Takamoto Katsuta only 0.3s further back in fourth. Rovanperä was seventh, just 2.1s away from the overnight lead.

On Day Two, Rovanperä and Evans were both involved in a close fight for the lead, sitting in second and third respectively. Rovanperä was third-fastest in the day's first stage with Evans being second-fastest in the next test, which was one of several that had to be either interrupted or

▲ *Rd 07 #69 Rovanperä.* ▼ *#18 Katsuta.*

cancelled due to concerns over spectator safety. A clever tyre choice by Toyota enabled Rovanperä to win SS5 and take the lead from Hyundai's Andreas Mikkelsen before handing the number one spot back to him in SS6. Evans finished in third, with Katsuta setting the joint-best time in SS8 to end the day in eighth overall.

As the good weather continued, Day Three belonged to Rovanperä, as the master driver won six out of the seven stages to maintain his lead. Evans unfortunately suffered a tyre issue in the first stage of the afternoon loop that cost him

Rd 07 #33 Evans.

several seconds and dropped him to third place with Katsuta remaining in eighth.

Although scoring well under the new points system, Tänak had to restart after hitting a deer, but it was Hyundai teammate Mikkelsen that pushed the Toyotas the hardest. No-one could touch Rovanperä, though, who claimed eight out of the 19 stages to win in Poland, and celebrate a one-two finish with Evans, who had to deal with a slight tyre deflation in the Power Stage. With the runner-up spot secured, Evans now sat just 15 points behind Neuville, while Hyundai held onto a narrow ten-point margin over Toyota.

Rd 07 #69 Rovanperä.

Rally Poland *Overall results, with 40 finishers*

1st	Kalle Rovanperä/Jonne Halttunen	Toyota GR Yaris Rally1	2:33:07.6
2nd	Elfyn Evans/Scott Martin	Toyota GR Yaris Rally1	2:33:35.9
3rd	Adrien Fourmaux/Alexandre Corio	Ford Puma Rally1	2:33:50.3
8th	Takamoto Katsuta/Aaron Johnston	Toyota GR Yaris Rally1	2:35:34.3

ROUND 08

Rally Latvia

18-21 July

Established in 2013, Rally Latvia had been part of the European Rally Championship for a good while, initially as a snow event, but later a gravel one following a shift in fixture dates. This was Rally Latvia's first running since gaining WRC status, though, so it is significant from that point of view. Run over 20 stages covering 188 miles

◀ *Rd 08 #69 Rovanperä.* ▼ *#17 Ogier.*

▲ *Rd 08 #33 Evans.*

▶ *#18 Katsuta.*

(300km), some 38 starters, including four Toyotas (Katsuta would score in the drivers' championship only), lined up for the start.

In SS1 on Day One, there was a mix of gravel tyre choices between the teams, but Rovanperä ended up fastest by 2.4 seconds over Ogier and the rapid Belgian, Thierry Neuville (Hyundai); Evans was fifth and Katsuta sixth. However, the big news on Day One was Mārtiņš Sesks again, on home ground and now with hybrid power.

Entering Day Two, Rovanperä showed no mercy by winning four stages to consolidate his healthy 15-second lead over local favourite Sesks, driving for Ford. Sébastien Ogier had a strong return to action after missing the previous round in Poland, and set the fastest time in SS5 to be just 5.9s away from second place overnight. Katsuta did well, particularly in the afternoon, where he was second-fastest to Ogier in SS5, and to Rovanperä in SS8 – that last time was good enough for him to gain fourth overall. Unfortunately, Evans faced some tough conditions running second on the loose gravel roads and sat in seventh.

On Day Three, Rovanperä and Ogier occupied the top two positions with a day remaining. Rovanperä more than doubled his advantage to 34.8s over Sesks with three stage wins out of four in the longer first loop. Ogier took second place from Sesks in the third test of the day, even though he ran wide into a ditch. Evans was in sixth position overall, while Katsuta was between Evans and Neuville in seventh.

With 11 stage victories (notching up a tally of 200 along the way), Rovanperä held on to win Rally Latvia after leading from start to finish, with Ogier coming in second for a memorable Toyota one-two; Evans finished in fifth and Katsuta sixth. With its strong podium result, Toyota took maximum manufacturers' points from the overall standings, plus second and third in the separate Super Sunday classification. With the Power Stage results also factored in, the team closed to within one point of the championship lead, as Evans climbed to within 13 points of Neuville.

Rally Latvia *Overall results, with 32 finishers*

1st	Kalle Rovanperä/Jonne Halttunen	Toyota GR Yaris Rally1	2:31:47.6
2nd	Sébastien Ogier/ Vincent Landais	Toyota GR Yaris Rally1	2:32:26.8
3rd	Ott Tänak/Martin Järveoja	Hyundai i20 N Rally1	2:32:52.1
5th	Elfyn Evans/Scott Martin	Toyota GR Yaris Rally1	2:33:30.3
6th	Takamoto Katsuta/Aaron Johnston	Toyota GR Yaris Rally1	2:33:54.6

ROUND 09

Rally Finland

1-4 August

Boasting the fastest average speed of any event on the calendar, Rally Finland included 20 stages covering 191 miles, or 306km. Among the 77 starters (with some interesting names in Rally2) was local man Sami Pajari making his Rally1 debut in a Yaris, while multiple world champions Rovanperä and Ogier both sported unique liveries inspired by their own Special Edition GR Yaris production models.

On Day One in SS1, Katsuta posted the second-fastest time on the greasy Harju spectator stage, with Ogier in fourth, just ahead of Rovanperä, and Evans in eighth; Sami Pajari was ninth.

Day Two saw Toyota lock-out the top three with Rovanperä leading, followed closely behind by Evans and Ogier. There was very little to separate home hero Rovanperä and two-time event winner Evans during the morning loop, where they claimed two stage wins each. Rovanperä then won two afternoon stages to open up an eight-second lead. Ogier was also strong and finished the day just 0.6s behind Evans. Sami Pajari sustained damage in a high-speed spin in the morning, but impressed with his performance during the afternoon, including a maiden stage win in SS9 to end the day in sixth overall. Meanwhile, Katsuta

Rd 09 #69 Rovanperä.

Rd 09 ▲ #33 Evans. ▶ #18 Katsuta.

was running in fourth place until SS5 when he crashed into a tree, damaging the right-rear of his car.

Rovanperä upped the ante on a damp Day Three by posting four straight stage wins to consolidate his lead to 44 seconds over Ogier. Evans was closing in on Rovanperä when a misjudged corner saw him damage his driveshaft, causing him to lose significant time as he limped home. Pajari was in fifth, and did exceptionally well to finish the rally in fourth, while Katsuta had fallen well down the standings.

Even though Rovanperä seemed assured of the win on Day Four, with speeds increasing as the roads dried out, he made a fatal mistake on one of the last corners of the penultimate stage when he hit a large rock in a high-speed left-hander, sending his car crashing into the trees. That incident allowed Ogier to not only take the victory, but also enabled him to climb up to second in the drivers' championship, 27 points off the lead. Meanwhile, Toyota sat 20 points adrift of Hyundai.

Rd 09 #17 Ogier.

Rally Finland *Overall results, with 55 finishers*

1st	Sébastien Ogier/ Vincent Landais	Toyota GR Yaris Rally1	2:25:41.9
2nd	Thierry Neuville/Martijn Wydaeghe	Hyundai i20 N Rally1	2:26:22.0
3rd	Adrien Fourmaux/Alexandre Corio	Ford Puma Rally1	2:26:56.0
41st	Takamoto Katsuta/Aaron Johnston	Toyota GR Yaris Rally1	3:17:26.7
DNF	Kalle Rovanperä/Jonne Halttunen	Toyota GR Yaris Rally1	–
DNF	Elfyn Evans/Scott Martin	Toyota GR Yaris Rally1	–

ROUND 10

Acropolis Rally

5-8 September

The Acropolis saw new WRC hybrid unit safety measures introduced – or more strictly enforced, to be accurate – for the first time. From now on, if a certain number of heavy shocks are registered, the hybrid unit had to go back to Compact Dynamics for repair or replacement, adding yet more pennies to the already horrifying budget.

Marking the 68th running of the Acropolis, some 70 cars were entered in a rally comprised of 15 stages covering 191 miles (305km). With rough, hot and dry conditions lasting throughout the event, the Greek rally became a rare nightmare for the Toyota Gazoo team as all its cars finished outside the top 15.

After Katsuta excelled in the shakedown, Day One saw Ogier make the most of his extra Pirelli tyre grip to win two of the morning's three stages and take a short-lived lead. Katsuta, who had just won SS2, misunderstood a pace-note on the third stage that resulted in him damaging the right-rear of his car, forcing him to stop. Evans had to change a wheel and tyre in SS1, before a turbo issue restricted the available power for the remainder of the loop. Ogier began the afternoon with another stage win to increase his advantage, but would

Rd 10 #17 Ogier.

also be slowed down by a turbo-related problem at the end of the day.

The highlight of Day Two (Saturday) was Ogier's triple stage wins that saw him move up to third overall. After losing around nine minutes on Friday, Evans was climbing the leaderboard before a slow-speed roll in a hairpin on SS11.

On the final day, Toyota was fighting for a podium until disaster hit. Firstly, Ogier was pushing hard in the final Power Stage when he sustained a puncture that forced him to run wide at the following corner and roll over. Evans lost

Rd 10 #18 Katsuta.

significant time with a number of issues, but reached the finish and took points for third in the Super Sunday classification and the PS, while Katsuta claimed fifth on Super Sunday and in the Power Stage; Pajari was actually Toyota's top finisher in a Rally2 car.

After all the carnage, Ogier was now 38 points behind Neuville, who had had his own troubles in Greece, while Toyota languished some 35 points behind its Korean rival. Seeing both the drivers' and manufacturers' titles slipping away, Latvala went on record stating that having three full-time wheelmen was the only way forward in the future. Next season's roster announcement will be an interesting one, that's for sure ...

Rd 10 #33 Evans.

Acropolis Rally *Overall results, with 52 finishers*

1st	Thierry Neuville/Martijn Wydaeghe	Hyundai i20 N Rally1	3:38:04.2
2nd	Dani Sordo/Candido Carrera	Hyundai i20 N Rally1	3:39:51.0
3rd	Ott Tänak/Martin Järveoja	Hyundai i20 N Rally1	3:41:01.5
16th	Sébastien Ogier/ Vincent Landais	Toyota GR Yaris Rally1	4:01:48.7
18th	Elfyn Evans/Scott Martin	Toyota GR Yaris Rally1	4:02:49.7
30th	Takamoto Katsuta/Aaron Johnston	Toyota GR Yaris Rally1	4:19:26.4

ROUND 11

Rally Chile
26-29 September

After the disastrous result in Greece, the Toyota Gazoo outfit arrived in Chile ready to redeem itself. And the outcome couldn't have been more different, with every Yaris driver winning multiple stages whilst taking turns at leading the event. Rally Chile saw 42 teams entered, competing over 16 stages covering 192 miles (307km). Katsuta was

The four Yaris Rally1s for Chile, with Ogier's nearest the camera, then the Evans machine, Rovanperä's car, and Pajari's white model just behind.

Rd 11 #69 Rovanperä.

Rd 11 ▲ #33 Evans. ▼ #69 Rovanperä

forced to give up his seat to Pajari for this event, but he was not able to earn points for the team anyway.

With a shakedown and ceremonial start on Thursday, the real action started on Friday. Ogier took an early lead with a rapid time in the first stage, which was then cancelled for the following cars because of spectator safety concerns. Evans went on to win SS2, and took over the lead in SS3 after Ogier ran wide into a bank and had to stop to change a wheel. Rovanperä was fastest in SS3 and ended the morning in second place, with Pajari making a strong start to his second event at rallying's top level to secure the top three places for Toyota. Rovanperä lost a few seconds with a spin in the first stage of the afternoon, but stayed in the top three, while Pajari was just 2.1s further back in fourth place; Evans managed to head the field until SS10.

At the end of Day Two, Rovanperä led Evans in a one-two with a day to go. Leading by three seconds at the start of Saturday, Evans continued his strong form in the morning with two stage wins out of three. Rovanperä took second place and closed to within 1.8s of his team-mate when he went quickest by 9.7s in SS8, but Evans responded by going eight seconds faster than anyone else in the following test, where rain and fog hit and tyre management proved key. Rovanperä had gone fastest in SS8, which allowed him to snatch the lead from Evans in SS11 – a position he maintained until the finish. Meanwhile, Sami Pajari showed maturity to avoid issues in the tricky conditions and finish in sixth position overall.

Toyota celebrated a maximum score on a challenging Rally Chile, as Rovanperä claimed victory ahead of Evans. Rovanperä's 15th win together with Toyota drew him level with fellow two-time champion Carlos Sainz as the drivers who've achieved the most FIA WRC victories for the Japanese manufacturer. When the dust settled, Neuville had stretched his lead over Ogier to 41 points, while Toyota narrowed the gap with Hyundai to just 17.

Rally Chile *Overall results, with 37 finishers*

1st	Kalle Rovanperä/Jonne Halttunen	Toyota GR Yaris Rally1	2:58:59.8
2nd	Elfyn Evans/Scott Martin	Toyota GR Yaris Rally1	2:59:23.2
3rd	Ott Tänak/Martin Järveoja	Hyundai i20 N Rally1	2:59:43.7
36th	Sébastien Ogier/ Vincent Landais	Toyota GR Yaris Rally1	4:26:02.9

ROUND 12

Central European Rally
31 October-3 November

Rd 12 #33 Evans.

The penultimate round of the 2024 championship blasted off for only the second time in Prague, Czech Republic, before crossing the border into Germany and Austria on Day Three, and then returning to Germany on Day Four. Thierry Neuville, who was heading for his maiden title, held a 29-point lead over Ott Tänak, with Sébastien Ogier sitting 12 points further back in third. With 43 entries, the rally was comprised of 18 stages and covered 189 miles (303km).

In the lull between Chile and the CER, Rovanperä confirmed that he'd be ready for a full season with Toyota in 2025, but it still remained to be seen who would join him in the line-up at this stage. For this rally, Ogier was driving instead of Rovanperä, backed up by Evans and Katsuta, with Pajari in a fourth car.

On Day One, Sébastien Ogier set the quickest time in SS1 to take an early lead, just ahead of team-mate Takamoto Katsuta. By day's end, the Japanese driver was fourth overall, and just two seconds off the lead. Elfyn Evans held seventh, with Sami Pajari a further three seconds back in eighth.

Day Two saw the drivers taking on the slippery Czech roads with Ogier lucky, after a slide, to win SS3 and hold onto the lead. That was short-lived, however, as Neuville pinched the number one spot in SS5, holding onto it until the end of the day. At this point, Ogier was in second, Evans third, Katsuta fourth, and Pajari in fifth.

A nightmare stage in Austria awaited the drivers on Day Three, though. On a wet track, rally leader Neuville spun a full 360 degrees to lose 30s and his lead. Indeed, things got so bad that Ford's Adrien Fourmaux, who slid off into the scenery, described the conditions as undriveable! Katsuta also tried out his lawn-mowing skills but survived. Crossing back into Germany, conditions worsened still further. But while some drivers were wiped out, Evans and Ogier excelled, swapping stage wins between SS8 and SS14, and allowing Ogier to take back the lead from Neuville on SS11.

The final day saw more carnage as Pajari slid off the road and rolled three times, while Mikkelsen smashed into a hay bale. Ogier's five second lead over Tänak was gone when the Frenchman overshot a corner, losing over ten seconds. Then, with the finish in sight, Ogier slid wide and hit a tree, thus throwing away his chance of the win and the world championship. Tänak claimed the

Rd 12 ◀ #18 Katsuta. ▼ #17 Ogier.

victory, depriving Neuville of his maiden title – that would have to wait for Japan. Meanwhile, Evans picked up a second place, and Katsuta was fourth. Toyota was now just 15 points behind Hyundai, in need of a big win at the team's home rally to clinch the title.

Central European Rally *Overall results, with 40 finishers*

1st	Ott Tänak/Martin Järveoja	Hyundai i20 N Rally1	2:37:34.6
2nd	Elfyn Evans/Scott Martin	Toyota GR Yaris Rally1	2:37:41.6
3rd	Thierry Neuville/Martijn Wydaeghe	Hyundai i20 N Rally1	2:38:14.4
4th	Takamoto Katsuta/Aaron Johnston	Toyota GR Yaris Rally1	2:38:55.6
DNF.	Sébastien Ogier/ Vincent Landais	Toyota GR Yaris Rally1	–

ROUND 13

Rally Japan
21-24 November

Rd 13 #33 Evans

Just before Rally Japan, Jari-Matti Latvala announced his desire to take a step back from full-time management to be able to spend more time in the historic rally arena. In the past, Akio Toyoda had stepped in to cover for him, but with Latvala wanting more time away from the office for 2025, we'll have to wait and see how the logistics work out on this one. For now, though, Toyota still had a mathematical chance of claiming the manufacturer's title, and fate would tip the odds in its direction, coming from behind for a miracle win.

The last WRC round to use hybrid cars in Rally1, Rally Japan started with 44 entries, including eight Rally1 cars competing over 21 stages covering 189 miles (303km). On Day One's SD around Kuragaike Park, Sébastien Ogier was third-quickest, with Takamoto Katsuta fourth and Elfyn Evans seventh. In the SSS inside Toyota Stadium, Katsuta beat championship leader Thierry Neuville in the face-off to finish the day in third place; Evans was just behind in fourth, with Ogier in fifth.

On Day Two, Evans was in a battle for the number one spot with Ott Tänak as they traded fastest times and the rally lead, with Evans finishing the day 20 seconds behind Tänak. Both Ogier and Katsuta suffered tyre trouble and lost precious time in a stage featuring a supposed haunted tunnel, but the two drivers made spectacular comebacks with the Japanese driver in fourth after winning SS8 and SS9, and the Frenchman in fifth at day's end.

On Day Three, Tänak, who had taken the rally lead away from Evans in SS5, strengthened his position and looked like snatching the driver's championship away from the ailing Neuville, who was back in seventh. But then Evans won SS10 and started to smell his first victory of the season. Katsuta spun out late in the day, allowing Ogier to slip past and claim fourth.

As Sunday dawned, Toyota still had a slim chance of taking home the title. Then, fate handed Toyota a sure win when Tänak spectacularly crashed out in the first stage, propelling Evans into the lead and Ogier into second – it also meant that Hyundai pilot Neuville had just won his first driver's championship. Toyota's one-two podium finish enabled the Gazoo team to come from behind and snatch the manufacturer's title

away from Hyundai by just three points, making it the brand's fourth straight championship. And to do it on home turf couldn't have been sweeter. Meanwhile, Pajari's eighth place overall secured the WRC2 title for him in a Yaris Rally2.

Rd 13 ◄ #17 Ogier. ▲ #18 Katsuta.

▼ The end of an eventful year ...

Rally Japan *Overall results, with 38 finishers*

1st	Elfyn Evans/Scott Martin	Toyota GR Yaris Rally1	3:23:41.0
2nd	Sébastien Ogier/ Vincent Landais	Toyota GR Yaris Rally1	3:25:08.3
3rd	Adrien Fourmaux/Alexandre Corio	Ford Puma Rally1	3:25:36.5
4th	Takamoto Katsuta/Aaron Johnston	Toyota GR Yaris Rally1	3:25:43.6

2024 SUMMARY

The season reviewed in a way that provides a quick reference from a Toyota/Gazoo perspective, with driver performance, round by round (overall position, followed by the scoring Power Stage position in brackets), and year-end positions within the FIA WRC championship.

		Ogier	Evans	Rovanperä	Katsuta
	Rd 01	2nd (2nd)	3rd (4th)	– (–)	7th (3rd)
	Rd 02	– (–)	2nd (2nd)	39th (1st)	45th (5th)
	Rd 03	– (–)	4th (5th)	1st (4th)	2nd (7th)
	Rd 04	1st (3rd)	2nd (5th)	– (–)	5th (4th)
	Rd 05	1st (4th)	6th (8th)	31st (3rd)	29th (5th)
	Rd 06	2nd (6th)	4th (3rd)	– (–)	35th (5th)
	Rd 07	– (–)	2nd (7th)	1st (3rd)	8th (5th)
	Rd 08	2nd (2nd)	5th (5th)	1st (6th)	6th (4th)
	Rd 09	1st (5th)	DNF (–)	DNF (–)	41st (1st)
	Rd 10	16th (51st)	18th (3rd)	– (–)	30th (5th)
	Rd 11	36th (1st)	2nd (5th)	1st (2nd)	– (–)
	Rd 12	DNF (–)	2nd (3rd)	– (–)	4th (1st)
	Rd 13	2nd (1st)	1st (3rd)	– (–)	4th (4th)

Drivers

1st	Thierry Neuville	Hyundai	242
2nd	Elfyn Evans	Toyota	210
3rd	Ott Tänak	Hyundai	200
4th	Sébastien Ogier	Toyota	191
5th	Adrien Fourmaux	Ford	162
6th	Takamoto Katsuta	Toyota	116
7th	Kalle Rovanperä	Toyota	114

Co-drivers

1st	Martijn Wydaeghe	Hyundai	242
2nd	Scott Martin	Toyota	210
3rd	Martin Järveoja	Hyundai	200
4th	Vincent Landais	Toyota	191
5th	Alexandre Corio	Ford	162
6th	Aaron Johnston	Toyota	116
7th	Jonne Halttunen	Toyota	114

Manufacturers

1st	Toyota	Toyota Gazoo Racing WRT	561
2nd	Hyundai	Hyundai Shell Mobis WRT	558
3rd	Ford	M-Sport Ford World Rally Team	295

NB: Points totals include Power Stage bonuses for all categories. Although advertised by the FIA as being available at one point, the 'Team' title was again not awarded.

Index

The Toyota company and Gazoo Racing are mentioned throughout this book, along with the World Rally Championship (WRC).